# ALL THE ROADS

# ALL THE ROADS

## By Raymond

LIBERTY HILL PRESS

Liberty Hill Press
2301 Lucien Way #415
Maitland, FL 32751
407.339.4217
www.libertyhillpublishing.com

Printed in the United States of America.

ISBN-13: 978-1-6305-0678-0

# FOREWORD

A ll the roads that I experienced with Raymond and Belinda started in Germany, continued for 56 years, and had stops along the way in Los Angeles and Phoenix before finally settling in Albuquerque.
Our friendship began in the US Army while we were stationed together in a Mobile Army Surgical Hospital (MASH) in Wurzburg, Germany.

Although neither of us were a "Hawkeye" Pierce nor a "Trapper John" McIntyre, the proximity of us working in our respective specialties of Laboratory and X-Ray in the 32nd Surgical Hospital brought us closer together.

The bonus of working with the "Sarge" came later when I met his wife.

As a young soldier far from Michigan, the invitation into their home away from home was a dream come true. Avoiding the barracks and my fellow "G.I.s" for a short period of time, as well was getting to eat a delicious home cooked meal, was wonderful.

Belinda was lovely, humorous, a great cook and an avid reader like me. Time spent with her and Ray during my tour in Germany was like being home with my family.

We continued to remain in contact after my discharge from the US Army, so that I was able to be a part of their lives through the years.

Please enjoy reading "All the Roads" to follow the lives of Belinda and Raymond, lifelong friends that I was fortunate enough to meet, and learn about the roads they traveled together.

Harry Klenner, BS
Westland, Michigan

# CHAPTER 1

Summer of 1941

H ere is the starting line. I was born in the smallest state of
the Union, in a fairly large hospital. As soon as I started the
first grade, I was enrolled in a large Catholic school (first through
twelfth grade) for the first five grades or so. It was right next to
our church where I remember going to weddings and funerals. I
am sure most of you have heard of the discipline that these types
of schools offered in earlier times. Well, there were a few times
I remember washing my hands with a fair amount of pain, from
where the twelve-inch ruler slammed down on my knuckles, Yes,
I was misbehaving.

"Thank you, Sister."

Oh well, that's Catholic life. To be honest, that's where I
learned about our great country and our flag, and the history of
the Founding Fathers, and the Constitution of these United States,
most of all about Christianity. If it took a twelve-inch ruler to make
sure it all set in, so be it! It set me as a Christian for the rest of my
life (not to mention the important knowledge of Roman numerals).
About the time of the fifth or the sixth grade or so, we moved
around several times, counting Grandma and Uncle Fred's. So, I
attended St. Theresa's School, and about four or five others. It was
always about Dad's job. He even took a job in South Africa once.
Thank God for Grandma and Uncle Fred bringing us under a roof
when needed.

One day in 1954, our father informed us that we would be leaving Rhode Island for good, because he was offered this great job that started in California. We would stay in Rhode Island until the summer started. Well, I had just made some new friends again, and even had a paper route. Plus, I had my grandparents and a whole bunch of young aunts and uncles. My mother was one of nine children.(second oldest). It was sad for me to think I would leave them all behind because they were always good to us growing up, and always enjoyed taking us to the movie theater lots of weekends. We loved going to the movies, especially the Westerns.

Okay, we were about to get on the road, It was decided that I would go with my father in our '49 Packard Clipper." Mom and my older brother, Angelo, would come once the house was sold. You would think Angelo should go on this trip. I'll just say for now, they did not get along so well sometimes! So, here I was, a thirteen-year-old co-pilot in charge of the maps and pouring coffee for him while he drove. He never stopped unless he had to for gas and food. We only stayed one night in a motel, otherwise we slept in the car at those rest stops at night. (much fun)

My father was not a man of patience, so therefore, I must tell you that every time we passed a sign of a popular tourist site, I would scream out, "Hey let's stop here."

The reply I got back was, "We don't have time, I am in a hurry to get to my new job. Just sit back and say your prayers and stay quiet."

"Okay," I said with a little growl.

We certainly had a few unexpected stops, flat tires and broken fan belts, whatever. I remember one time that we were someplace in Oklahoma, and we pulled into the station. The attendant rushed right out, started to clean the windshield, he asked Dad what type of gas and started to fill the tank.

Then he asked Dad, "How is you're earl, sir?"

My dad said, "Whoever he is, he's not here with me."

"Dad," I said, "I think he trying to ask about oil."

"Okay," Dad said, "and why don't you check the water too?"

Now we were back on the famous two-lane highway (Route 66), and he said, "Boy, these people in Oklahoma sure do talk funny!" and I said, "Yeeeaaah, for surrrer."

He was always on this time clock. He just had to get as far away from Rhode Island as fast as the car could take him. Needless to say, it would be many years in the future before I was ever to seen the Grand Canyon, the Painted Desert, and the Petrified Forrest. However, I can tell you, it only took three-and-a-half days to get to Burbank, and I still wonder why he had to be in such a rush.

Well, here we were again, starting a new school in Burbank. Everybody seemed to pick up the Eastern accent rather quickly. It wasn't bad enough that I had the accent, but I also stuttered a little when I got nervous. I certainly hoped there were better days ahead! Well, we stayed with my uncle for a couple of months before my mom and brother arrived.

Now, they were going to buy a car that was strong enough to pull a twenty-eight-foot house trailer. That's right, can you picture a family of four living in an area of approximately 300 square feet? Then my dad told me from this point on, we would be moving about every thirteen months or so. Well, so much for settling down, that sure wasn't going to help anything. Okay, now we were settled in a trailer park in North Hollywood. Hey, let's not complain. I'm talking about a twenty-five-foot swimming pool, a Coke machine, and a ping pong table. Not bad, considering we only had to share with about 250 people! The good news was that the school year had not started yet. That meant that my brother and I could start checking out the neighborhood.

Well, this turned out to be a good day. We had no idea that there was a famous horse stable right next door. So, we walked in the front gate, and guess what we saw? The first stall sign read, Trigger, and the second, Trigger Jr. and the third Silver. Western fans like me and my brother grew up watching all the movies and having all the hats and pistol sets, and the boots that my parents bought for us. Of course, they were all signed by Roy Rogers and Gene Autry, plus the Lone Ranger. I walked over to this big man wearing a big western hat and boots, and I asked of him if I could come back tomorrow. Guess what? He started to giggle, and he asked me where were we from. I told him, and he said, "You sure do talk different." Then he asked where did we live, and I told him right across the street. Well, he said yes to my question, and we could maybe rake up the stalls and such. He said, "Come back tomorrow, and I will give you some instructions."

Well, the next day, we were back at the stables, and guess what the big boss told us? It turned that Mr. Rogers was coming with his big trailer to pick up his horses the next day. We ran home to our little "aluminum hacienda" and informed our mom that we had to get to the store today and get geared up with some western duds and boots. Believe me, it took some time to convince her that this was a serious matter.

Well, my brother and I got there real early and the big boss said that we looked liked two brand new shining pennies. So, he threw a little dirt on us, and rubbed us with a saddle blanket, and said, "That's better."

The next morning came, and the big boss made us keep our distance while Mr. Rogers and his wrangler were loading horses and tack into to the big trailer. We were a good thirty or so yards away from our hero when we noticed that he came walking toward us and I thought I was going to freeze or something! So, Mr. Rogers started talking with the boss of the stables for a while, and then he turned his attention toward my brother and me, and asked, "Who are these guys?" After the intro, he moved toward us and shook our hands and said it was nice to meet us, and of course, we said the same, but I said it with a little stuttering.

Well, needless to say, the rest of the summer vacation was eventful, and for some of you reading this who are wondering who is the man I refer to as the "Boss." If you are into movie trivia or in my age bracket, it was none other than Mr. Glen Randall Sr. Look him up on your computer and read about his phenomenal career. Also, Glen Randall Jr. They could not have not made *Ben Hur* without these guys. Well anyway, you will read more about Roy Rogers in a future chapter.

Not much longer after meeting Roy Rogers, I also had an opportunity to meet Mr. Clayton Moore, "The Lone Ranger." I was putting a wedge of alfalfa into Silver's pen, and I heard this deep voice asking me if that was enough feed for his horse. I turned around, and there he was. He was very nice. We chatted just a little bit, and he said, "I guess you are from the East Coast."

I grinned and said, "Yes, sir."

After he left, I said to myself, "It sure would be nice if we didn't have to move again."

And yes, he will also be in a future chapter.

# CHAPTER 2

I was told we were getting on the road again, we were headed to Arizona, to build another steam plant. We did not have to pull the "aluminum fortress" to Phoenix, Arizona. Dad had sold the twenty-eight-foot one and we were moving up to a rented thirty-foot that was waiting for us when we got there. Either way, it would have been nice to stay in North Hollywood. At least I was starting to make friends in school. So now we were residing at North 27th Ave., in Phoenix. Another school.

We found out that we were living next door to Mr. William "Bill" Shoemaker, a very famous race jockey of the 1950s. (Not that I would have known.) I got to learn more about horses from the times we talked. My brother Angelo enjoyed the scenery at the swimming pool, but I always felt pretty much shy, because I was so skinny, and here I was almost a fifteen-year-old teenager. Sure enough, it was not easy hiding the accent. My classmates treated me worse than the ones in California. It was better for my older brother, because he had a strong body, and he was someone that nobody would mess with. I, on the other hand, was exactly six feet tall, weighing in at about 115 pounds. So, if anybody gave me a hard time, my brother would step in and take care of the situation. After a while, he had quite the reputation. Everybody gave him the nickname "Tony," and by the way, he really did well in the co-ed department. As for myself, not so much!

Things sure got better when my dad's boss brought his horses to the area we lived in. They were stabled just about a block away. Mr. Perkins (Dad's boss) asked my brother and me if we would be interested in learning more about horses, and would give us lessons. Needless to say, I was happy! Mr. Perkins was quite the cowboy and hailed from south Texas. His grandfather was born in a covered wagon and his father had a big cattle ranch back in the 1880s. I asked him once how big was the ranch. He said, "Son, we don't talk about that." Okay by me. In other words, I should mind my own business.

By now, you are probably thinking: What kind of job did my dad have?

My dad worked in the shipyards in World War II. and was probably the best welder in the USA. That's why Mr. Perkins brought us out to California in '54. Now Dad became a "boiler maker" and a Union worker, traveling around the country building steam plants. After all, everybody needed electricity! My dad was about 5-ft.-6", and because of his tough upbringing he was built strong, so when people ask me why I didn't follow his footprints, I would simply reply with, "You can't be a boiler maker weighing 115 pounds."

The summers were so hot in Arizona, most people took cover in their air conditioned homes. I was riding every chance I could get. Let me clarify that: I would ride in the early mornings most of the time. and not for too long. By the way, I forgot to mention that my dad bought a horse for me and my brother. She was a gentle white mare, and her name was Audrey Lee. As far as I was concerned, I was living the "life."

Well, that was the year I decided to take Audrey down the middle of Black Canyon Highway. In those days it was all dirt in the median, and most riders enjoyed the long trail. As it turned out, on this particular day it was cool enough to put Audrey into a nice gallop and I was very pleased for such a smooth ride. Right about that time I was getting ready to rein her in for a stop, that's the time when somebody decided to blow their horns and started screaming. That's when Audrey raised her ears and decided to go into a fast run. The past few years I had been taught by the best, but nothing worked that day. The stop sign was coming up fast, and I knew if she went across the intersection, one or both of us were about to meet our Creator. Well, I figured she was a good jumper. If she did encounter a vehicle, she would stand a good chance. Yup, I bailed off without a parachute. It wasn't pretty at all. My left arm was in the shape of a T-bone. After all of that medical stuff, stitches and bruises, I finally was home, and the story goes that one our neighbors saw Audrey still running at full bore heading north on Grand Canyon Highway. I certainly was napping good from all that medicine, but when I awoke I found out it was a successful rescue. Thank God, she wasn't hurt.

It was a long time before I would be able to ride again, and my brother wasn't that interested in that type of recreation anymore. You remember what I said about him a little earlier in the chapter? Yup, he was involved! Well, it turns out my dad was pretty upset about me being hurt, so he sold Audrey Lee back to the ole cowboy he bought her from. I really was not pleased hearing that, but nobody argued with my dad!

Attending high school that year was tough, because my arm was still in a weird looking cast, and I walked with a cane. Of course, you didn't think that I was able to walk down the hallway without some bullies giving me a hard time? Well, the good news was that my older brother was around to see that I wasn't taken advantage of.

# CHAPTER 3

Well, you guessed it, we would soon be leaving for Connecticut to take on a new steam plant. And whoops! Guess who was going to have a baby? Yes, my mother! I told her that about the time the baby would be born, I would be turning sixteen.

She said, "Don't worry, we will have room enough in the trailer, because your brother joined the Navy."

I guessed my older brother had it with all the compressed living quarters, and the fights he got into protecting me. So I asked Mom if we were renting this mobile home, why couldn't we rent a real home in Connecticut?

She said, "Because we bought this one."

Oh boy! At least Dad's boss, Mr. Perkins, told them they could arrive in Connecticut after Mom had the baby. So, a few months later, Mom delivered a baby boy. I ended up driving Mom to the hospital when she was ready, because Dad was upstate at the time, working on a special job. So, when he came home, I drove him to the hospital. We arrived at the maternity ward, and the nurse stopped my dad from going in.

She said, "Just one at a time. First the husband, then the grandfather."

Wow, I always did look older than my age! I really can't tell you what words came out of my dad's mouth!

Well, we were on the road again, pulling a thirty-foot Spartan house trailer with a new 1957 Super 88 Oldsmobile and a new baby brother, just to make the trip exciting. And yes, I got the experience of driving about a thousand miles myself. I really thought this was just as exciting as horseback riding.

Well, days later we were all settled. Grove Beach Trailer Park, right off Highway 1. What a change from Arizona! If nothing else, it was kind of a nice beach resort town with a lot of nice restaurants. The truth be told, I really did miss the seafood that I was raised on in my state of Rhode Island, while I was out West.

So, I guess my dad knew I was nervous about going to my new high school, and he said I could take the Olds. Wow, very nice. His boss was going to be showing him all around the job area for a couple of days anyway.

So, Monday morning, I drove to the high school, grabbed my transcripts from my last school and reported in to the main office. The secretary told me to sit and she would inform the principal that I was waiting.

This principal was all decked out in a three-piece suit, and raised out of his chair and practically screamed at me, and said, "Who do you think you are, coming to school dressed like that?"

I said, "What?"

He said, "Who do you think you are, John Wayne?"

I said, "Sir, my boots are polished, my Levis are pressed, and so is my shirt!" I quickly informed him that my mother raised us to practice hygiene and neatness. What did I do wrong?

He really didn't answer, he just kept tapping the desk. Well, several minutes later he told me to report to my first class, and tomorrow I would be dressed in neat slacks and shoes and a proper shirt! Oh yes, I know what you are thinking: this time, his accent fits in, but not his attire! It was so hard to change schools this much. (It sure wasn't a confidence builder.) Okay, it wasn't too bad at the cafeteria for lunch break. There were a few guys and gals who were curious where I came from. Would you believe that one girl told me that I had a little southern drawl in my speech? I almost fell down! I guess my accent was starting to round off a little bit, so I decided to practice my pronunciation a little every day!

Okay! I finally got to the weekend, and since the little bother was screaming away, I guessed I would go check the neighborhood. Yes, I had casual slacks and my sweater jacket (fit right in). The beach was only a block from our trailer, so off I went. There were a few people shore fishing, and I finally found some kids who were around my age. They knew I was new to the neighborhood, so they asked all kinds of questions. It was early fall, so they had a nice little fire going, and we talked for quite a while. They told me all about stuff in the neighborhood. After that, I went home and brought my mom up on all the info. Yeah, I kind of helped out with the little screamer. By the way, the name of that town that we lived was Clinton (coastline of Connecticut).

So, off to school on Monday. During gym class, the coach was trying to fit me in a sport activity. Well, according to the school nurse, I weighed about 120 pounds, so I told the coach I was not interested in much of anything.

He said, "Can you run?"

I said yes.

"Okay, you're on the track team."

The next weekend, I walked over to this fancy steak place. Its name was the Cattleman's. It was the only place in Clinton that didn't serve seafood. I ordered a coffee frappe and some fries. The waitress was around my age and we got to talking a little. She was very nice, and very cute! I asked her if they would need any help on the weekends. Wow, she said. they just fired a busboy a couple of days ago. She introduced me to the manager, and he and I got along great. Yes, I would now be working at the Cattleman's as a Busboy six hours on Saturday and six hours on Sunday, from 3pm till closing.

By the way, the waitress (Carol) went to the same school as me. Carol and I became pretty good pals. She enjoyed all my travel stories over the next few months. The hard part of making friends was that I never knew how long before we moved again. Well, anyway, I was excited about my new job. My very first Saturday at the restaurant, I met the stars of Mom's favorite TV Show. Yes, it was Jacky Gleason and Art Carney of *The Honeymooners*. I couldn't wait to tell her.

One Saturday evening, Mr. Gleason called me over to table and asked me if the waitress was paying attention to her job. Well, I asked him which one was he talking about? Hmmm, he pointed to Carol. Ooooh!

I said, "She is working twice as hard, because one waitress didn't show. How may I help you, sir?"

He replied that he would require another piece of apple pie, and a scoop of vanilla.

"Not a problem," I replied. I zipped back in minutes and set it down on the table.

"What is your name, young man?" he asked.

I said, "Ray."

"Can I ask you another question, Ray?"

"I said, "Sure."

He looked me right in the eye and said, "Are you Black Irish?"

I informed him I had no idea what that was. Then he asked me if my mother or father were from Ireland.

I said, "No sir, they're first generation Italian."

He said, "That's nice."

He started to work on the pie, and I quickly ran over and told Carol, that I was her "Sir Lancelot", She gave me a nice tap on the shoulder followed by a nice smile. A little bit later, Carol gave them the check, and as they were walking out, he crooked his finger in a "come here" motion. I met them at the doorway and he handed me a $10 bill, and said that was from him and Art. Nice!

Well, the junior year of high school was almost over when I informed Carol we were moving back to California.

She leaned over to me and said, "This is for my tall black Irishman." Right on the lips. Wow! Then another. Oh yes, it was getting better!

*Here we go again, time to muster up some bravery to face another move.* I kept saying to myself that I was sure this happened to other teenagers beside me, Well, we had a few more weeks together and Carol and I had a good time. Also, there were a few more visits with Jacky and Art, as I was their favorite busboy."

We started getting visits from all my aunts and uncles and cousins from Rhode Island to say goodbye once again as we did previously in the summer of '54. It was not that far a drive from Saybrook to my birthplace in good ole Rhode Island. We did it a few times while we lived in Clinton the past year or so. Sad to say, during our stay in Connecticut, we had to make a trip to

Rhode Island for my grandmother's funeral. She was so good to us kids. Grandma was from Sicily and Grandpa was from the coast of Trieste, very close to Croatia. My uncle who was there during the war told me how beautiful the gulf of Trieste was. It's located between the Adriatic Sea and Slovenia, (Best seafood ever.)That explains why I love saltwater fish and shell food so much. If you have not visited the Northeast coastline, Rhode Island, Maine, Connecticut, etc., and you love lobster, crab and all kinds of shell food, and oh, I almost forgot to mention Calamari, you won't find it any better than there.

To mention the family once more in Rhode Island: such a beautiful clan. I had the greatest uncles, aunts, grandparents and cousins. I would surely miss them, for it turned out that the rest of my life was to be spent elsewhere! Yes, there were a few visits there during my career, just enough to visit the folks and stay up with the family gossip.

At the time of this writing, I only have one uncle and one aunt left from that entire generation. I try to stay in touch as much as possible.

# CHAPTER 4

W ell, there we were in California in a cozy little trailer park, nestled in a bunch of sycamore trees. It felt good because of the beautiful weather, and it was only a few miles away from Glen Randall Stables. Since my senior year had not started yet, we had time to go to the beach and all the other great tourists stops in Southern California. My aunts and uncles were taking us all over. Disneyland was great, but I liked Knots Berry Farm. It was a lot quieter, and not so crowded. My dad always came home super tired, not to mention with welding burns all over, but on some weekends we went to visit my two uncles and family. Our favorite pastime, after eating, was playing bocci ball. I could never beat my uncles, but someday watch out!

The following weekend, my dad's older brother invited us to a big charity picnic in Chatsworth. Uncle was always involved with stuff like that. He said there might be some celebrities there. Well, I was hoping to see John Wayne, but of course he wasn't there, but I did have the pleasure of meeting Jay Silverheels. If you're my age or keep up with all the re-runs, he was known as Tonto, the Lone Ranger's sidekick. Late in the afternoon I caught his attention, and I politely asked him if I could speak with him, and he kindly replied, "Of course." This man was such a kind gentleman, and we conversed for about thirty minutes or so. What I found out was that there was over 220 episodes that ran from 1949 thru 1957, and he played in most of them. Jay was a full-blooded Mohawk Indian, born on the Six Nations Reservation in Ontario, Canada. Yes, I did tell him of my summer at the Glen Randall Stables where I met Clayton Moore. We both chuckled over the story, and he promised me he would tell Clayton whenever he would see him. That made me happy!

The summer was busy, and soon it was time to check in with the new school for my last year. This would be great. I could wear my starched Levis and boots again and get away with it! Birmingham High School was also on Balboa Blvd., so my dad said I could walk the five blocks. *But Dad! Seniors don't walk to school, they drive!* He said that his new boss didn't believe in Ride Share either! Too bad my mother never learned to drive. That would mean we would have an extra car. Well, there I was, walking down the boulevard, looking at all the cool cars and hot rods pulling into the school parking lot.

Well, it was time to meet another principal. I was sure happy he wasn't wearing a three piece suit!

He said, "Take a chair while I go over your papers."

About ten minutes later, he said that the news was not too good. My legs started to shake, and I ask him, "What's wrong?"

He said, "You have been to so many schools in your young life, I don't think you will have enough credits to graduate. You might have to go to summer school."

"What?" I screamed out loud, and told him, "I am a good student, and I never flunked any exams!"

"Calm down, young man, and let me review this and I will call you back in here in a couple of days."

Boy, I was so mad after all this stupid moving and crap in my lifetime, and now I got this! I did not go to my first class. I needed to walk around for a while and try to calm down. I started saying prayers, and asking God. *Why me?* I was walking off campus, and I was stopped by the school cop, and he asked for my pass. I told him very nicely with a just a few stuttered words exactly what happened that morning. Well, he was so empathetic and kind and told me to chat with him until the bell rang, and he would write an excuse to give to the second period teacher. Well, my first day at Birmingham!

After a few weeks went by, the principal called me in and said the news was about the same, but I should just keep up with my studies and be positive. I went back to class and said, "The heck with it, just let the dice roll."

It was about three weeks, into the first semester, when I introduced myself to the girl at the desk right behind me in English class. Her name was Sandra. Later, I found out she was a dancer, and her best friend was Annette Funicello of the Mouseketeers. Back in the day, an awful lot of people watched *The Mickey Mouse Club*. Well, the following week, we were to have Senior Ditch Day, and Sandy (yes, my second girlfriend) was going to take me to the studio to meet Annette and the rest of her friends. Sandy was always going for auditions, trying to get a career started, but so far, not yet! Yes, what a day! I had a studio pass clipped on my shirt and felt like a VIP. When Sandy introduced me to Miss Annette Funicello, she quickly asked me for my last name, and she said, "How pretty," and I said, "Thank you." Well, the rest of the day I met most of the cast and got to watch Sandy and Annette do some dancing. It was great. We did a few more of those trips during that school year.

Sandra finally asked me to show her where I lived. She said, "I know you drive a beautiful car on our dates." Oh boy! She wanted to meet my parents and see my house. *What house?* I put it off as long as I could. Finally on one of our Friday night dates, she insisted! At that time, we were having a burger at Bob's Big Boy, our favorite hang-out. I told her it was just down the boulevard and we were close enough to walk.

She then said, "I know that area. There are some stores and a trailer park. I know you don't live there."

I replied, "Yes, I do!"

Sandy said, "Ray, that's all right, it not that big a deal, you don't have to explain."

Well, what a relief! After I told her the whole story, she figured out that my parents weren't poor!

Well, time passed rather quickly, right up to the time we applied for our graduation rings, and caps and gowns. It was getting exciting. Less than two months before graduation! Yep, guess what? I was called into the principal's office.

He said, "Please sit down, Raymond."

Wait a minute, I knew something was wrong! The dice roll wasn't in my favor. He informed me that it was a question of about one-and-a-half credits, and the School Board would not bend, even though I passed all senior exams in the top one-third of my class! Of course he told me I would get my diploma and ring after summer school. I stood up and raised my voice and I asked him why couldn't I just graduate as normal, and still go to summer school? Couldn't he see, I just wanted to graduate with Sandy, and make my family proud! He did not give in to my request.

I slammed out the exit gate as fast as I could, swearing and stuttering, and almost got run over crossing Balboa Blvd. I was walking down the sidewalk, asking God to forgive me for my cussing and screaming at the principal. It wasn't his fault. It wasn't Dad's or Mom's fault. It was just the way of life! How could I face Sandy? I knew I would never go back to that school ever again. We always stayed in touch with my aunts and uncles. What was I going to tell them, after they told me about how happy they were about my forthcoming graduation?

Just about that time, I remember my boot heel hitting on something. I looked down and it was the base of a swinging metal sign. Yes, it said, "The Army wants you." Well, I walked in to ask some question's, and they gave me a coke, and some dried up popcorn. The next thing that happened, was that I signed up for a three year contract. I told the sergeant that I would not turn eighteen until July. "No problem," he said. "Just have one of your parents sign these papers." He and I talked for a while, he and said after Basic training I would take a GED test, and get my diploma, and by request, the school would send me my diploma and ring. Okay

My mom greeted me at the door, surprised that I was home early. I could tell she was also having a bad day. Here she was in her late thirties, trying to take care of a very over-active child who liked to bite and scream. Poor Mom. (She also suffered with severe migraine headaches since giving birth to the little one.) She really didn't know how to react to my news. I told her that if Dad signed the papers, I would be leaving for the Downtown LA induction center by late morning the next day. My dad signed those papers so fast, and did not ask me any questions. (Well, that was Dad.) I made one call to Sandy and tried to explain the situation. She drove over, and that was the first and last time she met my parents. When we started to leave the trailer, that was the time the little one decided to bite her on the arm.

# CHAPTER 5

Sandy and I said our goodbyes while the sergeant was loading me into an Army brown '57 Chevy, and off to downtown Los Angeles we went.

The sergeant was looking in the mirror when he said, "You look pretty sad, ya gotta get over it now, because you won't have any time for that the next three years!"

I started saying my prayers, asking, how did all this happen? It all happened so fast. Here I was in the US Army, where I was to spend the next three years.

When we arrived at the center, I found myself in the middle of a bunch of guys, and they served us something to eat. We all looked down at our plate, trying to figure out what it was. I did recognize the slices of bread! That afternoon, between all the body poking and shots and samples, I was thinking about how nice it would be to go back home to Mom. That was never to happen again! There were all kinds of quizzes and tests and personal questions that would shock most private citizens, not to mention what I witnessed when they screamed, "Strip down to your underwear and stand in line." Well, that was when I noticed two of the men in line were wearing women's undergarments. I found out later that they were drafted. I don't guess it worked very well, because I saw them on the train with us later. Well, anyway, I finally made it to the last station and met Captain Holt, MD. He started moving all my extremities and asked me who fixed this left arm of mine.

I replied, "Dr. Holt, in Arizona a few years back. Are you related?"

He said he had no idea who that was, "But why couldn't they have drafted him, instead of me?" We both laughed! "Well, Private, you do know that this arm of yours can only extend about 85 percent or less."

I spoke up right away and told him the other Dr. Holt instructed me to drop weights on it several times a week, and I had been doing it ever since, and it got longer each year.

Well, I always wondered if I had an assigned angel that always watched over me. That day, the good Captain Doctor told me he could reject me from active duty, because of my arm, and I was also borderline in the weight department. It would be up to me. He said if I was using the arm that well, I should make it through Boot Camp and get away with it. It was going to be my choice.

"If you do go in, you should take all the food they give to you and try to gain more weight."

*Wow! What do I do?*

He said to me, "Go get the rest of your clothes on and sit down at my desk and start thinking."

I did just that! By the time he finished with the recruit after me, he turned and looked at me, and I said, "Thank you anyway, sir."

He said, "Good luck, Soldier."

I turned and shook his hand. I wondered if all the officers that were in the Army were as nice as him. (I would soon find out.)

Here we were the next day, boarding a train bound for Salinas, California, not too far from Monterey Bay area, to a place called FORT ORD. This place offered a lot more shots in both arms, and a wonderful hairdresser, He even asked me about my Ricky Nelson hair style. I knew what was coming, because as I was marching in, I saw all the bald heads coming out the side door. Oh well, if it happened to Elvis, why not me?

For the next eight weeks, it was pure Hell, all kinds of marching, unbelievable physical training, hand grenades, M-1 grand rifle, bayonet and judo training, flamethrowers, pistol practice, classes, and lots more! Sleeping in those cold, damp nights in a half-shelter tent. Yup, you guessed it: who slept in the other half? The worst for me was all that marching up and down those hills with my steel helmet, full field pack with canteen and shovel, and a nine-pound M-1 rifle and bayonet, and me weighing at about 130+ pounds. There were days were my buddies had to pick me and carry me up to the top of Cardiac Hill. The mean drill instructor only caught us once in that eight week period. Anyway, they did give us a full ten-minute rest every hour. That was when I asked my angel if he enjoyed that free ride on my shoulder coming up the hill. Yes, I did graduate finally, and I thanked the good Lord!

Guess what? After the graduation ceremony, we would get a four-day pass and could go anywhere we wanted. Well, we got paid once per month as Pvt. E-1s, a grand total of $82/month. Recently, I looked up what the pay scale is today, and a recruit gets $1,554/month. Talk about inflation! Guess what? I bet I could buy more with my $82 back in '59 than a private can in 2019 for his monthly pay.

The deal was that when we came back from this four-day pass, we would be told our orders as to what school we would be assigned. Imagine how many schools they had: medic, truck driver, radio and radar, cook, artillery, guided missile, advanced infantry. The list went on and on. (Hundreds) I saw the list.

So, my two buds and I decided to go to Salinas. It just so happened this weekend was the National Rodeo event. Just think, we would be around people dressed in civilian clothes for a whole four days. But we would be in uniform, and if we were to conduct ourselves improperly, there would be military police close by. Not to worry, I was raised better! But they felt like they had to read that to us. As I did find out in the last eight weeks, there were some who would be drinking and fighting, and that gave the military a bad name, sad to say. Well, my two buddies and I had a great time mingling with the civilians, and enjoyed the rodeo and all the Salinas hot spots, and ordered all kinds of junk food that the Army didn't serve.

We were back for bed check on Sunday night at 2200 hours. Two hours to spare before AWOL, which would not be good. The next morning, we were standing outside in company formation, waiting for them to announce our assignment for the next eight weeks. Then the drill sergeant told us that we would fall out in platoon order, and report to the day room and read the bulletin board for our orders.

Well, I said, "Take your time, Ray. No rush to get the news. You've been rushed all your life." So I was the last one to the bulletin board.

One of my friends said, "Ray, you're the only one of us that doesn't have to pack up and leave."

Whaaat? I read next to my name, and you won't believe this! Of all the big strong dudes in this Army, plus the draftees, I was the only one they picked for Advanced Infantry. Yes, eight more weeks of much bigger guns, small artillery and 50 caliber machine guns. Whatever! Who knew what was waiting for this 130-pound warrior? Hah! When I went to the mess hall and grabbed my food tray, I asked for double amounts. Yes, in the Army we could do that, provided we ate it all. Don't let them catch you throwing any food away. With my mess hall sergeant, that was almost a court martial offense. I know what you are thinking. You figure everybody would gain weight in boot camp. Oh no! You can't believe how many calories you burn in a day at boot camp.

# CHAPTER 6

I met the meanest looking drill sergeant I'd ever seen. Actually, I did start giggling inside, because he reminded me of Jack Webb. (Do you remember *Dragnet* on TV?) After introducing himself, he peeled off his uniform shirt, and walked right up to my face, and screamed so loud, "What do you see, soldier?"

I replied with the toughest voice I could muster, "Sir, I see nothing but scars, Sir."

He said very loudly, "Do you think you might ever be this close to the enemy? Don't answer, because I was. We both ran out of ammo at the same time, then we started with our bayonets for a couple of minutes, and he is not around to talk about it!"

Yes, he was a highly decorated warrior from the Korean War. Because of him, and all the other heroes, I certainly don't mind making my monthly contributions to the vets and the wounded warriors of this great country! God bless them all! I am proud to tell you that my youngest son, who served in combat during the Panama War (Operation Just Cause), now volunteers in helping them with their PTSD.

So, in the eight weeks to follow, I paid attention every minute, because if I was ever to be in combat, I would want to remember what this man taught us. I am not going to drag you guys through all the events that happened during that eight-week period. But I will tell you this: The Army had designed these long, thick, wooden poles about or close to six feet long, and on each end was attached big canvas bags filled with sand. That was what we used to practice hand-to-hand combat with. Simulating a M-1 rifle with a bayonet attached, we learned how to move left and right, and thrust the weapon directly at the enemy. Sounds gross, doesn't it? Well, that was why we used these bags to wallop the hell of each other in our training session. So, me being the lightest, I was getting knocked down more than I care to mention. Our hero drill sergeant called me off to the side, and said because of my size, I would have to put my opponent off guard for just a fraction of a second by screaming as loud as I could, before making my frontal attack. *Well, let's put that to use!* My sparring mate was a guy we called Big Joe, and when the whistle blew, he came at me with a big grin on his big face. Right then, I let out a scream so loud, you could hear it in LA. In that split second he hesitated, I hit him hard across his face, and he went down! Yes, I was becoming a lean mean killing machine!

When we were at the graduation ceremony, standing in formation, dressed in our uniforms and proudly wearing our blue infantry scarves and our blue ropes around our shoulders, my hero sergeant walked down the line and shook all of our hands. When he was standing in front of me, he grabbed my hand, and said, "Congratulations, Light-Weight, you made it."

"Thank you, sir."

A lot of my fellow soldiers had their families and friends attending. I was quite alone, knowing that my family was sure not going to be there. Sandy wanted to be here, but she had some kind of audition the day of graduation.

I saw the sergeant walking toward the food table, and I said "Sir, thank you." He turned and informed me that now that boot camp was over, I shouldn't address a sergeant with "sir." I must have dozed off in that class. I still think of him from time to time.

# CHAPTER 7

A t this point of my life, I was no longer thinking of being a teenager anymore. All that stuff I worried about before meant nothing, compared to what was in my future military life. What was going to happen next? There was a little talk going around about this Vietnam thing. I was thinking because of all my training, I would be sent there! *Wow, maybe they will post the orders tomorrow? Well anyway, if they tell me I'm going, I guess I'm going! However, my angel goes with me.*

Well, here was the good news: we would get two weeks leave before we went anywhere. Twenty hours of sleep, that was what we all needed. We graduated, and tomorrow was Saturday, and no more drill sergeants. We were told we were eligible to get a weekend pass, so my new friends of the past eight weeks and I said we might go to Salinas and take in some movies and eat hamburgers or maybe even go bowling. According to the company clerk that we pinned down at lunch, he thought our orders would be in by Monday. We couldn't wait.

Yes, we had a fun weekend and Monday came and we were all out in full formation on the company street, standing at parade rest at 0600, dressed and ready. All of a sudden the company's First Sergeant yelled, "Attention," and we all snapped to. Here was the C.O., getting ready to address us. He started by saying he was proud of our graduation, and every one who started advanced infantry indeed graduated, and that didn't hurt his record either! He said everyone in the other two battalions were going to Vietnam, and this battalion was going (a little drum roll here) to Korea. The C.O. said we would be briefed that afternoon and we should get packed, because we would be leaving at 0800 hours tomorrow. Most of us ran to the telephone booths, and started to call Greyhound. I could be back in Van Nuys, maybe tomorrow night. I called Mom, and then Sandy. Oh yeah! Two weeks of no body pain! And I was not shipping out to Vietnam.

We were free from duty until lunch, so we started to pack our duffle bags. Everybody was talking about what was going on in Korea.

One of the guys said, "Nothing as compared to Vietnam."

*Hey, wait for the briefing.* I wondered how many of us would be stationed together. Well, here we were, all assembled in the large mess hall, getting pics, maps, history and the entire peninsula of South Korea, right up to the 38th Parallel, otherwise known as the DMZ. A narrow margin of land (free zone) separated the North from the free South, and it looked like my company was going to Camp Casey, very close to the DMZ. We would be attached to the 7th Infantry Division.

My buddy said, "Ray, that's a long way from Van Nuys."

I said, "Shut up, soldier."

With all this stuff going on, I almost forgot that I would be turning eighteen the first week I'd be in Korea. Wow, did I feel old. That sixteen weeks felt like two years.

# CHAPTER 8

Well, it was good to be home amongst the civilians again. Mom wasn't in a good mood. It seemed she and Dad were going through another one of their spats, After talking with Mom a while, her feelings were starting to echo mine. She was fed up with the thirty-foot aluminum hacienda and wanted a home. She said Dad said no way that could happen with his job! I said now that the baby was almost two years old, she should go home and visit with her father. He was getting old and sick, and she could help her sisters take care of him.

Right as I got the last word out, Dad walked in, and the air turned cold! He really wasn't interested in hearing about my last sixteen weeks. I walked down to my room and noticed Dad was packing his stuff.

I walked over to him and said, "What's going on?"

He said that I could sleep In my own room while I was home, and he would stay with one of his brothers for that time. Well, you can guess I was not going to get a homecoming party. I went out to the front office area and called Sandy. She said she would pick me up in the front street entrance, and she made it very clear I was to keep my uniform on. I dashed back real quick and told Dad I would probably visit him at the uncle's house tomorrow. Sure, he said. What a homecoming. Hey, I was sure Sandy would be interested! Yes, on my way out the door, my little brother stepped on my shiny black shoes and tried to kick me! But I did turn around and gave Mom a kiss.

Speaking of kisses, it was great to be with someone who was interested in my company. Yes, it was great for all the right reasons.

The next two weeks were filled with talks with Mom and the little one. I did spend some time trying to discipline him. He was so spoiled, because Dad worked all those late hours and Mom suffered with those migraines. So, the young one learned to entertain himself and live by his own rules. I was glad to see the uncles and my cousins and aunts. My uncle let me use his car, that was great, and on to top off all that, my aunts gave a party in my honor. That filled my heart right to the top. Since Mom didn't drive, they took good care of her with the shopping and stuff. Oh yeah! I forgot to tell you, I still got waxed in bocci ball.

I did go back to the studios with Sandy and saw the whole gang. It was fun. Annette was busy out on the movie set, so I only saw her for a couple of minutes. On the way out, Sandy and I bumped into Frankie Avalon. Okay, he said hi to Sandy. That was it. I guess my uniform might have reminded him about the draft board. Ha!

Well, again, that two weeks just flew by. I would have to be reporting to Oakland soon. I did all the goodbyes with uncles and family first. My dad and uncle would be taking me to the Greyhound station the next morning. So, that night I was with Sandy. Little did I know, that would be the last time I ever saw her! Well, up bright and early as usual. Mom was crying a little. We hugged and kissed, she gave me a Saint Christopher medal, and off we went. At the station, my uncle told me how proud he was of me, and he said he loved me. I turned toward my dad, he shook my hand, and said, "Good luck, son."

When I think back, right up until the time my dad died, he could never say the word "Love" to me, or to my brother. His two brothers were just the opposite. Okay, that was my dad, and I loved him, but my brother and I, growing up and moving all over the country, we always had nice clothes, and bikes and all sorts of expensive toys. But we all know a child needs more than that!

# CHAPTER 9

Two of the biggest and fattest airplane I ever saw, the Lockheed C-130s, were taking off with the entire company, with some Jeeps and equipment. What was a young man to do with all this excitement? While this monster was trying to take off, we were wondering if we would be flying to Korea, or driving. By the time we got to moderate elevation, we were halfway to Hawaii. *Yes, I am exaggerating just a little bit*. So, we made a stop in Hawaii, and another in Wake Island. That was great. After landing and putting the brakes on, by the time we came to a stop we were almost touching the ocean. Look at your map and see how big Wake Island is.

We were getting close to the coast of Japan, and they informed us of a hurricane in that vicinity. Yeah, I started getting nervous thinking about that. Minutes later this big monster started shaking and bouncing up and down, and the airman started passing out those little brown bags. I sure took one. This was the day I decided I did not like to fly! We bounced our way into the Yokohama area, and when we came to a stop (oh thank God), they said to keep seated while they attached a rope from the cargo door to the building. The wind was blowing something fierce. If it wasn't for that rope, we might not have gotten into the building.

So, we would be guests there until the weather cleared. I sure did like the Air Force food, and I wasn't in a hurry to get back on that plane. Two days later, we are flying to Kimpo Airbase in South Korea. Great, no storms, and when we landed and deplaned, we all looked at each other and wondered what was that peculiar smell. As we found out from talking with the resident troops, it was called kimchi. At that time, the South Koreans were living pretty much in poverty, only about five years after the almost complete annihilation of their communities. So, they did a lot of cooking in pots over hot coals in the ground for lack of kitchens. The kimchi was a lot of vegetables, onions and whatever other greens and rice they were growing. I did sample it at a later date.

I must say at the time of this writing, I'm glad to have the pleasure of seeing what a booming economy South Korea has become. When I lived there for my thirteen-month tour, there were no paved roads or sidewalks unless you traveled south to Seoul or Inchon and the like.

Well, back to the fun. They brought a whole bunch of two-and-a-half trucks and loaded us all up, and away we went to Camp Casey, home of the 7th Infantry Division. We arrived just a little dusty, because we had the luxury of riding in these huge convertibles. The weather was so hot, therefor, the canvas was rolled up.

So, we de-trucked and fell out in formation, and then were told to stand at rest while the top sergeant gave us a welcome speech and such.

He said, "As I call out your names, report into building one and get your company assignments, and when you get there, you will be issued weapons and proper clothing and such."

Naturally, he started off with the A's, so my two pals and I were getting excited, hoping we would be assigned the same company. By the time it got to the G's (my last name), next thing you know, he was already into H's and beyond. Stupid me, I raised my hand, and the next thing I heard was "Put your hand down, soldier, and remain in position."

Well, there I was, just standing in my spot, quietly. The top sergeant walked into the building, leaving me standing there.

Then I saw a 1st lieutenant, dressed sharp with his blue scarf, and infantry rope, etc., and I noticed his CIB badge right off. He then told me to follow him as he walked to the headquarters building. Inside, he told me to drop my duffle bag and grab a chair. My head was still spinning with curiosity.

"Well, Private, did you have a nice trip over the Pacific Ocean?"

"Not really, sir," I replied. Then it just came out go my mouth so fast! "Sir, am I in trouble?"

"Why do you think that?"

I said, "Well, sir, I'm sitting in this nice office and all my buddies are gone."

He said, "Don't worry about that, you will see them later."

*Yes,* I said to myself. *My angel did make the trip with me.*

Oh yeah! If you had been there, you would have been looking at the new company clerk, with the keys to a brown '57 Chevy four-door sedan and a private room with a real bed and running water. That night I knelt.

The next day I met the supply sergeant and was issued summer dress khaki, dress winter, and the standard green work uniforms, and an M-1 rifle. I might add here that this weapon still is considered today as the ideal rifle for competitive target shooting. During my sixteen weeks of training, I always qualified as Expert. I was also issued a 1911 .45 caliber ACP pistol with belt and holster, and two clips of ammo, plus several more infantry blue scarves and ropes. The lieutenant found me and we both went to his office. Would you believe I still had not met the top sergeant yet? By the way, the 1st lieutenant's last name was more Italian than mine. He inquired if I was ever in trouble before or had a police record of any kind.

I proudly answered, "No, sir."

I was not really going to be a clerk. They had a very nice looking Korean civilian for that. He said by tomorrow I would get my first stripe (Private 1st class, that was me! I would start training in a military defensive driving course, plus some military protocol. Wow. He informed me that he had already initiated a background check, and once that came through, I would have some level of a security clearance. After that was all done, I would become the headquarters division driver and would be assigned to the 7th Infantry Division. Whoever needed to go somewhere, I would be the man! He said there would be other duties as well, that would come a little later. I was so excited with all these current events, I almost forgot to tell these people about my GED problem. When the lieutenant asked me what grade I completed, I told him the story. He informed me that he would send away for the test, and I should find time to study, and in a few weeks I just should take the test. About three weeks later or so, I took it, and passed it!

Well, anyway, my mail finally caught up with me after three weeks. The first letter I opened was Sandy's. She said that she finally met someone who was able to get her career a kick start. I said that would be great. A couple of days later, I wrote her a letter and told her of my exciting news, Then a letter off to Mom.

So, the other duties were a little more complex. Well, I should not complain, because I wasn't out there digging foxholes with my buddies. The other duty I was to get involved with was the KSC(Korean Service Corps.) These guys were local Korean civilians who were contracted to work for the U.S. Army, everything from bricks to highways, they did it all. In my case, I was to select the workers for updating the 7th Division parade field, and build a tall cement marker with our 7th. Division symbol, which was a red and black hourglass with a bayonet. The good news was that I employed a KSC manager to supervise the construction. I would pick them up in the early morning hours with a two-and-a-half-ton truck every day, and then, around 5pm take them back to the local village. This lasted for several weeks. I doubt the marker would be still there, but if it is, you will find my initials on the lower back side of the stone. I am pretty sure the base looks a lot more modern than it did over sixty years ago!

If I was busy driving officers around during those hours, I would get a soldier to replace me. Yes, two months into the program, and they promoted me to Corporal (E-4)

One late afternoon, on a cold and snowy day, I got a visit from one of my buddies from boot camp. He informed me that he was scheduled for the midnight guard shift, and he asked if I could replace him. After all, he insisted I owe him something for the fact that I was not in the infantry with him. He referred to me as the Golden Boy. Well, I asked my top sergeant, and he said this one time would be okay. The duty rooster showed no driving for the next morning. I had to go off and draw my weapon and bayonet.

I really should take this time to explain that in the late '50s South Korea was in serious poverty (through no fault of their own).

It seemed that some of the civilians made a living stealing off the Army camps. Right down the road from my headquarters was the Turkish Army camp, and I have seen with my own eyes what they did to these people once they were caught. Believe me, you don't want the details!

So, there I was, walking guard duty on the coldest night that I could ever remember. I was dressed in all my arctic gear, but still shivering. I had my rifle positioned across my chest, and I almost couldn't feel my fingers. I was just getting to the corner of my post. I stopped to make my turn, and at that very moment I heard a noise like a twig snapping. I spun around so fast I almost slipped in the snow, and there he was! He was just a big black shadow, but I knew he was coming at me. Without any hesitation, I let out the loudest scream, and thrusted toward him with my bayonet. In a split second, he dropped something on the ground, turned and ran down the road. I guess he was thinking of getting shot or stabbed. Right there in that spot, I looked up and said, Thank You" to God, and my beautiful drill sergeant at Fort Ord. Yes I did bend down and pick up what looked like a handmade billy club." That morning at breakfast, I knew my angel was also on guard duty.

Oops, I forgot to tell you: after four months into my tour, Sandy informed me that the guy who was going to kickstart her career was now her boyfriend. Well, why should I compete with Hollywood? I knew in the future, the Good Lord was going to find me a mate someday. Those days I was much too busy to worry about it. Back in the day, living with my grandmother, I remember the wall plaque in her bedroom. I think a whole bunch of you already know it: *God, grant me the serenity to accept the things I cannot change, courage to change the things I can, and wisdom to know the difference.* Maybe someday I might get married, and I would put that in our house.

Yes, I did get my security clearance about seven weeks after my arrival, and I did get a high score on my defensive driving test. There were a lot of exciting events during the rest of my tour involving some visits to the DMZ with officers and such, and even some rifle fire coming from the North side aimed at the front two tires on my Jeep. The colonel quickly said to get going as fast as this Jeep would go. (That was not the exact language he used.) Once we started down the little hill, the Jeep was wobbling all over the place. Yup, both front tires shot out! When we got to the guard gate, the military police helped us out with a new tire. I already had one spare of my own.

This was the most intense and exciting thirteen months of my young life, and I thank God for all those angels He sent in my direction. I did get time during my tour to visit my infantry buddies now and then. We had a few beers and some great chats and shared a lot with each other. Do you remember the Korean secretary I told you about? Well, because of her and her wonderful family she got me active with the local orphanage, and on a lot of weekends I would hit the local PX store, stock up with candy and games, and a whole bunch of American comic books, and we would spend a half day with these kids. They were basically between about six to nine years old (post-Korean war), and half-Korean and half American, Turkish, Canadian, Greek, French and the list goes on and on. A lot of these great kids did get adopted to all these different countries, (mostly America). I am praying they are all living good lives! Certain people always mention collateral damage after wars. Just look at all these homeless children.

When I told them I was going back to the U.S., they all jumped up and said, "Ray, please take me with you." That was tough, but I would like to inform you all about all the different churches from all denominations that were involved with them, and I am glad to say that still goes on today!

Would you believe that I finally became friends with the top sergeant of the company? He rotated back to the States about a month before I did. My friend, the lieutenant, got promoted to captain and got stationed to Fort Bragg as a company commander. He fought in the Korean War, and I was proud to have known him.

Well, I got my orders right before my nineteenth birthday, and I was going to be assigned to White Sands Missile Range in Southern New Mexico. I asked the colonel if there was any Army Infantry there.

He said, "I don't think so."

What in the heck would I be doing there?

I said goodbye to all my friends in Korea, and I can tell you after this tour I had just finished, I felt a lot older than nineteen! Well, I was on my way back to Kimpo Air Base, and yes, my old friend the monster C-130. *Dear God, please, give us good weather. You know how much I like to fly.*

Thankfully, we had a good flight back to Oakland. Back to Greyhound again — and guess what? I would not be headed to Van Nuys and the trailer park. During the past thirteen months, there were a lot of changes with Mom and Dad. It seems that Dad went into the restaurant business with his two brothers. He told Mom with no certain promises that he would try it and see what happened. Yes, they were living in a real home! (Unbelievable.) My little brother was now around four years old, still a big handful, I noticed, and Mom was still suffering with her migraines. I was always glad she had my two aunts there to help her out. Just think, I was on a thirty-day leave, and I guess I wouldn't be spending time with Sandy, that was for sure. Besides, someday I might see her in a TV show, or a movie.

# CHAPTER 10

I was back to being a busboy again, but now working in the family restaurant. I used all my energy to convince my two uncles and Dad that I would work there for free for the remainder of my leave, if they would all chip in for a down payment, and co-sign, so I could buy my very first car. Boy, they all chuckled out loud and said to me, "Do you think we were going to pay you that much for about three weeks of work?"

"No, but you should chip in the rest, because you are talking to a United States Army soldier who is protecting this very piece of land that this restaurant is sitting on!"

Yup, more chuckling. Even I was laughing! Uncle Frank, who was also a World II veteran, gave me a lot of support, and told his two brothers to shut up and kick in their one-third! Back in those days, I was able to buy a beautiful 1958 Chevrolet Impala, one owner, excellent condition, for a $350 down payment. You can't do that today. Oh, by the way, my payments were $60/month. It was going to be very tight on a corporal's paycheck. The next three weeks were mostly work, but my cousin John and I challenged the two uncles to three games of bocci ball one time, and beat them three out of three. Yes, finally. Another round of family goodbyes, and as usual I get love and hugs from everyone, and there was Dad, last in line, grabbing my hand and saying, "Good luck, son." That was Dad!

Let's take a drive from Burbank, California, to the southwest desert of New Mexico. Well, here I was, dressed in civilian clothes, driving a beautiful yellow Impala sport coupe with all green leather seats, feeling good!

And I might add, listening to dual speakers, almost like stereo! All this luxury, but no air conditioning. *Oh boy, I hope it's not too hot in southern New Mexico!*

Well, I got through Phoenix and Tucson okay, By the time I got to Lordsburg, New Mexico, the man on the radio said it was 102 degrees. I guessed I would have to get used to that. Once I left Lordsburg, I decided to open this car up, and see what she could do. After all, it was all open country. Yes, there were two things that said I was doing 100 mph. One was the speedometer, and the other was the ticket I received from the officer who stopped me.

The officer said I was to follow him to the town courthouse and pay my fine. Oh boy, I was down on my funds. Well, there I was standing in front of the man who could have put me in jail, if he so desired.

He asked me, "What do you have to say for yourself?"

I showed him my military ID, and informed him of my assignment at the White Sands Missile Range. I told him I had just bought my very first car after serving a tour in Korea, and I certainly did something stupid by putting my vehicle at that speed, even though the road was wide open and free from traffic. I should have known better, because I was raised better. I also had a few stuttered words that were thrown in, and I think I had him at that point! (I learned this from my uncles, I guess.) He quickly told me he had a nephew in the Army, and he knew we got paid at the end of the month. I was to send $30 at payday. He gave me the paperwork and a self-addressed envelope. He then reminded me of the fact that if I failed my obligation, he would know where to find me! Once again, I got off pretty light. My plan was to make it to this town called Las Cruces, and rest for the night, then the next morning trek out to White Sands Missile Range.

Morning came, and I was hesitant to leave the nice cool motel. So, I got info on the directions and off I went. The man said that I would be going over this mountain, and once I started down the other side, I was to look out for the entrance road that led out to the base. Boy, I thought I was on another planet!

I finally got to the entry guard gate, and I was pulled over by the military police for due process: checking my orders, inspecting my vehicle and license, registration and such (all routine). I gazed forward while all this was going on, and there was this impressive array of all different types of rockets and missiles. Quite impressive! So, I was thinking this was going to be a whole new chapter in my life, as usual. Well, I had approximately eighteen months before my enlistment was up. With all the changes that had been taking place in my life, this would be another experience. The military police were now giving me instructions to find where I was to report, and I was on my way, with butterflies and knots in my stomach.

# CHAPTER 11

I reported into the building, and met the sergeant 1st class who was in charge. The usual, "Drop your gear and have a seat, Corporal." He proceeded to open my orders and started reading. Every few seconds, he would hmmmmmmm, and then more hmmmmmm's, again.

I jumped in and said, "Is there something wrong, Sergeant?"

He replied that he did not know why they sent me there to a medical company.

I said, "This is a medical company!" Here we were again!

He proceeded to ask me tons of questions about my tour in Korea, and by that time, he said to me, Why don't you go upstairs, and find yourself a bed and locker? Take a shower and get some rest and report back to me in the morning."

Well, when I got upstairs I started meeting the guys and they gave me all of the company gossip they thought I should know. Okay! We got to talking about my last tour, and they said, 'If you are not a medic, what are you doing here?"

At that time, I was thinking and wondering: Did my assigned angel make a wrong turn somewhere? "Hey, guys, I am very hungry. Where is the Mess Hall?" The food wasn't bad at all.

I was starting to think about my first car payment that would be coming up near payday, and I was sure I would be eating in the mess hall a lot! (Sorry, on this base, it was called the base cafeteria; a lot more civilians than military.) Coming back from eating, I stopped to check my car, and that was when one of the guys screamed out and said, "That's yours?" I found out that a car in White Sands was gold! It is a distance of forty-five miles to the city of Las Cruces, so naturally the soldiers would spend a lot of time in town mingling with the local civilians. So, from that point on, I would not have a problem with gas money and restaurants and such. I was the main chauffeur, and my price was fair.

I reported to the sergeant at 0800 hours. He was busy and I waited for a while. Finally he called me in and informed me that I was going be to assigned to the base hospital. Off I went and I parked my Chevy in the parking lot and walked in and asked where and who I would report to. The next thing I knew, I was sitting down talking to the sergeant in his office.

He said to me, "You seem nervous."

I said, "Really?"

He said, "Yeah, do you stutter often?"

I replied, "Only when I am nervous."

We both chuckled!

There I was, sitting there, and thinking, "Lord, is there a reason You sent me here? Okay, Maybe You will tell me later."

The sergeant asked me if I had any questions. Oh yes!

"What am I going to be doing here since I am not a medic?"

Right about that time, a very tall and very attractive nurse walked into the office, and introduced herself to me. I stood to attention very quickly and said, "Yes, Ma'am, my pleasure."

Wow. I wondered if a corporal could date a major, or was that a court martial offense?

Well, back to the major. She informed me that they were looking for someone who had a security clearance and my records showed that I was a good driver and was trained in Korea. So, I asked her what type of driving were we talking about? She informed me that it was the 1958 Cadillac Metropolitan ambulance that was parked in the rear of the dispensary. She then proceeded to explain that since this was a missile range, it only stood to reason that during the test flights, there was an ambulance standing by on the site.

My first remark was, "Ma'am, I am not a trained medic."

She replied, "That's okay, Corporal, there will always be a nurse with you."

Yes, and if a nurse wasn't available, there would be a skilled Army medic. Oh!

The subject got more interesting. I was also going to be the medical driver for officers who required rides to and from the William Beaumont Army Hospital in El Paso, Texas, plus driving for the colonel every once in a while. She said during the inactive hours, I was expected to hang inside the hospital during the business hours. She invited me to go outside and check out the ambulance, and she gave me the operating manual that showed me where all the bells and whistles were. I had some studying to do.

We went back inside, at which time she walked me back to the ward area and introduced me to the whole medical staff. There were three nurses, another major and a captain, all women Army career officers. I found out later two of them served in a MASH during the Korean War! There was two army physicians, and one Navy physician. There were about ten to fifteen medical corpsmen, some of whom lived in my barracks.

Well, I was sure glad the weekend was there. I was so behind in my laundry, I needed a haircut, and I sure wanted to get all the bugs and dirt off my car. What was good about staying on the base that weekend was I only had to spend money for my haircut. Actually, that was about seventy-five cents. The base laundry would clean all military uniforms for free and a small fee for civilian attire. FYI, if a soldier was content living on base, it would cost nothing to exist. There were some guys and gals who did that to save all their money for future needs or to support their families. As for myself, I was quite the opposite.

Monday morning came about rather quickly. I ate a large breakfast, then I reported to the base hospital, and the sergeant informed me there were no firings scheduled for the day. However, I was to draw a vehicle from the motor pool and drive one of our doctors to the Air Force base in Alamogordo, New Mexico. A nice ride there. I got to make some acquaintance with a few of the Air Force personnel.

By the way, another '57 army brown Chevy. I think the US Army must have bought all of the '57 Chevrolets!

We were back about 1500 hours. I dropped off the captain, turned the vehicle back in, made the walk back to the hospital, and decided to go to the break room and get a cup of coffee.

# CHAPTER 12

W ell, I do remember asking the Lord, "Where are all these roads leading?" I was sitting there relaxing, and I heard something that sounded like a woman's high heels clicking on the tile floor. When she walked into the room, my jaw just dropped on my lap!. My little angel said, "See, leading right here!" Wow, what a beautiful face. Big, beautiful dark eyes, and her hair was cut kind of short, very black with a little bang curled over her forehead. When she turned, I got a glimpse of her ID badge, as she was walking out with her coffee. Her name was Belinda. I was hoping to get a peek at her left hand, looking for a ring. *That's okay, I will find out for sure!*

I had not even heard one word come from her lips, and I didn't know one thing about her whatsoever. I could tell you that she was just beautiful. When I was home just recently before arriving here, one of my aunts took me and Mom to see the movie, *Gigi*, and this Belinda reminded me a little of Leslie Caron, but much more beautiful! (Sorry, Leslie) I had never given any thought in my life to marrying young, but this Belinda sure got me thinking!

After my heart rate slowed a bit, I went down to the ward to inquire all about this Belinda. The Red Cross lady was sitting at the counter at the ward entrance, and asked if she could help with anything. I quickly told her that I was the new guy assigned to the hospital, and yes, I was stuttering just a little as I asked if she knew Belinda.

She replied, "Oh yes, she is one of the medical transcribers."

So I said, "Then she works here in this building."

"Oh yes, she and Carla work in the office next to the pharmacy, and if you need to speak to her, you better hurry because she will be leaving about now."

"That's okay," I said. "Will I see you tomorrow?"

She said, "Yup! And I am bringing doughnuts in the morning."

And I said, "That's a date. Good night."

As much as I loved doughnuts, I just could not get my mind off of Belinda. I sure was hoping that she would walk down to the ward for a doughnut tomorrow morning. (I would be there early.) I hoped I didn't have an early assignment.

The next morning, I was having coffee and doughnuts with the gang in the nurses' break room, and of course, asking a few subtle questions about Belinda. It seemed that everybody agreed that they all liked her, and she did her job well, and they said she was a student at New Mexico State University. I did learn she was not married, Yes! I had better get moving. My assignment for the day said I was to get our ambulance down to the motor pool for service. I sure was liking this job and this base a lot more, now that I knew Belinda worked there.

As soon as I got back, I reported to the sergeant. He informed me that I was going to William Beaumont Army Hospital, and I was taking the pharmacist with me to pick up some kind of meds our hospital needed. Naturally I was taking a '57 Chevy. It turned out my new friend was a pretty nice guy, and yes, during the drive to El Paso and back I gained a lot of info on Belinda. My new friend, Corporal Virgil Clemente, was drafted into the Army while he was in college studying to be a pharmacist. He was from San Bernardino. He did know Belinda a little because she spent time on her breaks meeting with the civilian pharmacist. Yes, it was a sad fact for me to find out she was dating this civilian. That was okay, because I was not going to back off. I remember while I was driving from California while listening to the radio, there was Elvis or somebody singing, "Only fools rush in." Well, call me a fool, because I was going to rush in.

So, we got to the supply dock, and this civilian who worked there said, "Si. can I help you?"

Right away, my new travel companion started speaking Spanish with him. Next thing I knew, he took off, then came back with a large package. My buddy signed the paperwork, and off we went, back to White Sands. Important note here: the road that we would take between White Sands and Ft. Bliss, Texas, was called the "war" road. It was a direct road between those points. You would have a much longer drive if you had to go through the cities of Las Cruces and El Paso.

During the drive back, I said to Virgil that I did not know he spoke Spanish.

He said to me, "Can you guess who else is bilingual?"

"I give up," I said.

"That pretty girl Belinda you have been asking about." Then he proceeded to tell me she came from a large family that resided in Mesilla. It was just on the outskirts of Las Cruces.

"How does a married man know so much about Belinda?"

"Did you forget where I work?"

"Oooh!" I said. "That's right, she is dating your boss."

He explained to me that might not be the case. He did not think it was that serious. *Here's hoping.*

Well, there it was, coming on the end of the month, and I had to send $30 to the fair city of Lordsburg, That was when I decided that I would start charging my barrack friends for rides into Las Cruces. After all, I wanted to learn more about the town, and its neighboring township of Mesilla!

Las Cruces is home to New Mexico State University (Go Aggies), farming and ranching families, military, engineers and science personnel who all worked out at the base. I found out later from driving the area that just next to the outskirts of Mesilla was one of the largest pecan growers in the world, the Stahmanns pecan farm starts in the Mesilla Valley and borders the Rio Grande River. I was told it was around 4.000 acres.

Well, my job really got busy for about a run of six to seven weeks. I didn't have time to pursue my relationship with Belinda, that was for sure! But every night I would ask the good Lord for His help.

One day at work, I decided to talk with Clemente at lunch time and he said, with a grin, that the civilian pharmacist was leaving his job, and moving back to New York. Yes! Then he told me that just about everyone in the hospital (including Belinda) knew of my intentions.

He said, "Get up, and please don't stutter, because I am taking you to her office right now and introduce you formally!"

# CHAPTER 13

A fter the official intro., Belinda and and the other Medical transcriber, (Carla ),were just smiling. Somebody had to say something, darn it!

So, I said with just a little stuttering, "It is nice to meet both of you."

At that time, Belinda said, "Please sit down."

Just a few seconds later, Carla started to leave, saying, "You two people talk a little, I am going on a break."

So, I started to speak by saying something stupid like, "Belinda do you like working here?"

That sure as heck didn't come from Cupid! We chatted about the traveling distance she had to make to the base. She told me that most days she rode with friends, and her younger sister who also worked on the Range. There were also days of taking the bus.

Then I said, "You must stay pretty busy with college and this job. Do you find time for any hobbies or such?"

Her answer was quick. "I love to read every chance I get!"

That night, I barely made it through my prayers, but I did for sure add at the end, "Thy will be done," and for the first time in a long while, I would sleep good! The next day, and all the rest that followed, we started to talk to each other, and learn about how different our backgrounds were. Pretty much opposite, that was for sure. I started to realize right about that time how sincere she was, no bells and whistles, no false exterior, just a good honest country gal, and I was looking forward to meeting her family in the future. So now, I knew why I felt this way the moment I first saw her! I started to recall my past life, including all the chaos and all the arguments that bounced around, sometimes watching my older brother trying to win a point with my dad, that never turned out good for him. You remember, I told you my dad was not a man of patience!

So, now I was becoming friends with a beautiful, cool and calm book reader. What more would I need? It was like being in a sand-storm in the middle of the desert, then the wind stopped, and you were suddenly surrounded by all this beauty and calmness. That was where I was that day! Now I knew why I had to be on all those different roads. They finally led me here!

I guess by now the entire staff knew of our relationship, and that brings me to a very important point. I started getting invites to sit and chat with all the docs and nurses. By this time I knew them pretty well. So, what was the reason for all these little chats? I am proud to tell how much they valued this woman (for all the right reasons), and they are concerned about my intentions, considering I only had about another year to go for my discharge. So I guess they didn't know what my career path was to be. Heck, neither did I at that point!

There was no doubt how much they liked her, and there was also no doubt how much thinking I would be doing. I had better slow down a little.

Well, once again the holidays were approaching, and I knew Belinda and her large family would be busy. Right about that time, I was getting letters from Mom about the usual "spats" between her and Dad. You know, I wondered what it would be like if things were different in my family (meaning better). Suppose it was better! That meant I would have not joined the Army, graduated from high school, gone to college, whatever, But, see how Fate gets involved in our lives. Suppose I did have a somewhat "normal" life? That means I would not have met Belinda!

During the pre-season holiday time, Belinda and I had lunch together a lot and we drove around the base and looked around, just having fun and learning more about each other. By this time, Belinda knew most of my personal life. Except one more little item she needed to know!

"Belinda, how old do you think I am?"

She replied, "Yes, I know as a matter of fact! Who do you think printed up your assignment papers when you arrived at the hospital? Yes, I did think you were older."

By the way, those two months were filled with some intense moments involving my ambulance. The first being a major chemical burn at a missile site. The second was a very complicated pregnancy. The good news was that I had the two top nurses on board.

# CHAPTER 14

The new year was filled with all kinds of good things! Yes, we were officially dating. Nothing fancy on my military budget. Belinda was getting me introduced to the local Spanish foods, but as much as I loved the entrees, I was not big on the local green or the red chilis as of yet. It was a slow process, but years later, I am hooked.

I finally met her family. What a pleasant afternoon. The very first one I met walking in the door was Mom. Now I knew where Belinda got her good looks. What a pleasant and warm lady this was. She greeted me with a big smile and hug, and I just felt so welcomed. Then, I met Dad. He too displayed the same type of warmth and kindness. I had to look up a bit, because this man was "tall." Later that evening, I found out that he was a star basketball player on his high school team. They showed me some of the newspaper clippings the family had saved.

Well, of course I met most (not all) of her brothers and sisters that same day. Let's see, there was Fina, a younger sister; then Jane, a much younger, and all very pretty." Then her brothers: Guy, Ricky, Jeppy and Firpo. Interesting stories behind those nicknames. A very handsome family indeed. The complete family made me very welcomed. If you were there, you could smell homemade cooking aromas all over the house, and everybody getting along so well. Wow, this was what a home should feel like. I knew someday soon, I would ask Belinda to marry me, and if she turned me down, I would certainly ask her mom to convince her otherwise. Well, for sure, my assigned angel was working overtime!

Things were starting to change at the base. The hospital staff x-ray tech was Sgt. Converse, a super nice guy. I had got to know him fairly well over the last several months. He had been on base for over two years as the only technician, on call 24/7, and was married with three children. So, it was impossible to get off base, plus it had been over eighteen months since his last vacation. My favorite nurse, Major Jarma called me into her office, and explained to me that Sgt. Converse was no longer able to draw any techs from William Beaumont Army hospital for help, due to the fact the Army was suffering from a shortage of techs.

I asked the major, "How does this affect me?"

She informed me that the chief medical officer suggested that I could be trained by Sgt. Converse just enough to be able to take call on the weekends, to get him and his family some personal time away. If the case was complicated, they would take the patient to William Beaumont by ambulance. She then informed me that the colonel would like to see me tomorrow morning.

I think by now you have enough of knowledge of this family-sized hospital that everyone knew of my relationship with Belinda. However, I did not know if the colonel was up to speed. Well, he sure was, and I sat there and listened to him right to the point where my heart had dropped to the floor. Yes, I was on orders to go to Vietnam under my previous MOS 111.20 (infantry).

The colonel put his hand on my shoulder and said, "Listen to me, Corporal, I didn't tell this to the major, but I can help you here, are you listening?"

I said, "Yes," with my head hanging toward the floor. "Sir," I said, "I only have about thirteen months left! I can get you assigned to work in x-ray, then in a couple of months, take an early discharge and re-up for x-ray school in San Antonio, and the Army will benefit from your training. If you re-up for six years, I will promote you to E-5, and after that, maybe a three-year tour someplace in Europe. Just think, Corporal, you will only be about twenty-six or so when you get discharged. And by that time, you will already have your AA degree as a Registered Technologist, and a GI Bill to get to college. And yes, Belinda will have no doubt that she married the right guy. If you are okay with all this, you will report to Sgt. Converse and listen and study hard under his guidance. I will make sure to get you all the right books, you okay with this?"

"Thank you, sir, very much."

"Okay, get your butt out of my office!"

That afternoon I went to Belinda's office and told her the news from the colonel. She was so happy for me.

I said to her, "Before I sign any papers with the United States Army, you have to say you would not mind being married to a RT."

"What's that?" she said.

I said, "If I pass all these classes, I will be a RT in about two more years."

By day's end, everybody knew the news. Starting tomorrow morning, Sgt. Converse and I would become teacher and student. Yes, no more driving or infantry, just in case you're keeping count, This was the second time I did not hit the shores of Vietnam.

My assigned angel reminded me to pray!

I forgot to mention that Belinda's sister, Fina, and her husband, Sal, also worked on base. Fina worked right down the road in Bldg. 1524 (Administration). There was a time or two that Belinda and I would meet her and Sal for lunch at the base cafeteria. A lot of times they would bus to the base together. Sal was stationed there while he was in the Air Force. It seemed that his job was very critical, and after his discharge he applied for the same position as a civilian. He stayed there until he retired.

The next morning, our favorite Red Cross gal brought fresh doughnuts to X-Ray, and wished me luck on my new career.

I said. "You give me doughnuts, I give you hug."

The sergeant said, "Before I get you into the x-ray machines and other stuff, you need to learn anatomy and physiology as fast as you can. Here are the books. You can return them to me when the colonel gets yours."

Well, I had lived all those years by looking at the outside of me, So now was the time to learn the inside.

Whether I was eating or doing my chores, or spending time with Belinda, I always had these books with me. Bang! That was when I learned that this little country gal who spent all her spare time reading books was, in my opinion, super smart. I can't begin to tell you how much she helped me with my studies. But, oh how much she helped me with *me*! Everything about my study habits, my confidence, my so-called nervous persona and sometimes stuttering. Many years later, Belinda found out that I was always searching for something that might have been out of my reach, and she would listen to my moaning. and groaning.

She said, "Raymond, if wishes were horses, beggars would ride!" Well, in the subject of Belinda, I was riding!

# CHAPTER 15

About seven weeks or so, I had been training with the Sarge, and believe me it was tough. But Sgt. Converse said I was ready! (I hoped he didn't just say that to get off base.) That weekend the Converse family took off, and I was sure they had Fun. My studies continued to a point where I was learning the harder procedures, hoping the sergeant's family could take a real vacation.

Well, finally came the weekend I had been waiting for. Sgt. Converse was taking call, and I was on my way to Belinda's mom and dad to ask for her hand in marriage! If you have been paying attention to the previous paragraphs, you know they said yes. Now, since this was a family that ran on tradition and Christian values, that meant the next step was to meet the priest and post banns of matrimony. We had set the date to be June 24,1961.

That evening I called my parents to give them the good news, and instead of excitement, all I got was a bunch a questions and negative comments. Oh well, at this point, it was going to be obvious that her family would end up doing all of the necessary planning and such. But, as you probably have guessed, they were quite happy doing it all for Belinda. After church that Sunday morning, I was introduced to the pastor, Father Potzer. He was from Spain, and as soon as he heard my last name he started talking Italian to me. Oh boy.

I said to him, "Non parlo Italiano, Father."

He said loudly, "You don't capice Italiano? Mama mia." Then he started speaking Spanish. Oh boy, I was in trouble again.

So I said to him, "No hablo Espanol, Father."

At that point, the good Father turned to Belinda's mom, and said in his broken accent, "Whya you wanna leta Belinda marry thisa boy?"

Then he started to laugh and messed up my Ricky Nelson hairdo! Then we all laughed. I can remember after being married a while, every time he saw me he would say to me, "Hey, Ramon, arra uuaa being a gooda boy witta Belinda?"

It sure would have been nice if i could have replied in Italian or Spanish!

So, after that I asked Belinda, "How would I answer in Spanish?" A week or so later, sure enough he asked again, and I said proudly, "Desde luego, Padre." I would get a big smile back.

Well, back to work at the hospital and still studying every night. It looked like the good Sgt. Converse would be able to spend some prime time with his family, because at this point I was capable of doing routine exams. Once I got to school, I would be learning all about x-ray physics and radiation production and all kinds of science that dealt with Wilhelm Roentgen's discovery in 1895.

During our engagement, I would spend a lot of time with Belinda's family in Mesilla, We always had fun visiting with the whole family on the weekends. If I wasn't on call, that is. That was the time when the sergeant and I would alternate days and weekends.

Belinda's whole family was busy planning the wedding, and every time I would ask if I could help, Mom would say, "No mieto, you just sit there and relax."

Later in the day, Belinda would say to me, "Don't expect me to spoil you like that once we are married."

Ahhh, Belinda! Some of those weekends we got in the car and Belinda would show me around and tell me what it was like growing up on a farm, doing chores and picking cotton and helping her mom around the house. A lot of hard work, but she and her brothers and sisters all pulled their share together. Her dad had told them there would be no staying with friends and trips away from the family. If their friends wanted to come visit, that would be okay! He was the shepherd, and they were his flock. I can tell you, they all grew up with family bonds, and to this day, most of them still live close by to each other on the family property that their father left them.

Belinda and I got to talking about the differences in our backgrounds. She would say to me, "Yes, Raymond, I did have the pleasure of being raised in a stable situation right from elementary school right up to college, and if it wasn't for your bouncing around life, we would have not met." (Time for a hug.)

So, we were getting close to the month of our big wedding, and I was still trying to convince my parents that it would be nice to have them there. Otherwise, I would be the only one representing my family! They said they didn't know why I would marry someone they didn't even know, and also they didn't want to have to get a travel visa. They thought my Belinda was from Mexico, and that was where the wedding would be, Well, I was sure Mom's migraines were getting worse and such. They insisted that we go there for our honeymoon so they could have a reception for us, and they could meet my bride!

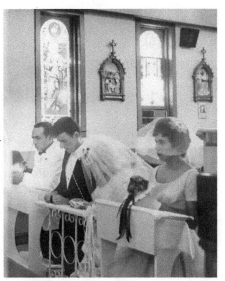

# CHAPTER 16

June 24, 1961
This was the day!

 If Belinda's family wasn't big enough here in Mesilla, it sure grew larger when all the aunts and uncles and cousins arrived from surrounding states. It was wonderful meeting all these folks, very kind and gracious. This wedding would have not been possible without Belinda's mom and dad, and even though I gave my warmest thanks to them back on that day, I would like to say on this day of this writing, looking up to Heaven, "Thanks, Mom and Dad, for being so supportive and full of love."

We all were at Saint Albinos Church in Mesilla and the weather was about 100 degrees, but who cared! That day I got to marry the one person who would change my life by teaching me all the things I missed before I met her. I thanked God for all those crooked roads that led me to her front door! The wedding Mass was very traditional and beautiful. We knelt at the altar together while the priest wrapped a very large rosary around both of our heads, then he handed me a box of thirteen silver dimes that I was to present to my bride as a promise that she would always have security. Today,

I still have that box in safekeeping to attest that we were never without money! And, if you are curious to know why the number thirteen: Jesus is one, and His twelve apostles.

Years ago, back in our Army years, at the end of the month when our funds were really low, I would make Belinda laugh by asking her, "Honey, can you open that box and loan me a dollar?" Ya! Sure, Raymond! The good old days. (I always loved making her laugh.)

It was indeed a great day. I had fun talking and visiting with her relatives who came to the wedding, to see who was this "alien" that Belinda married!

Well, now on the day of our wedding, we said our goodbyes and got in our Impala, and west we went.

Belinda said, "Everything will be just fine, Honey. You know I've got to meet your parents sooner or later."

As we drove through Lordsburg, I made a little wave at the good old courthouse.

Belinda said, "Would you like to tell me why you did that?"

Yes, I told her everything, and she said, "Boy, I did not know I married a race car driver!"

Our first stopover was Phoenix. Boy, was it hot!

Well, I said to my bride, "Before we check into a hotel, let's find a nice restaurant and have a nice dinner."

So, we finally got settled in this restaurant, and the waiter came over. "How are you two young people doing this evening?"

I said, "Just fine. We are on our honeymoon."

He said, "Wow, that's just great, please allow us to offer you guys a cocktail on the house."

I looked over to my new bride and noticed a negative look, so I said, "Thanks, why don't we just have a glass of champagne?"

He said, "Great, do you mind if I ask for an ID?"

My heart was beating so loud, and I was about to be embarrassed on my honeymoon, and I said, with a little deeper voice, "Me, sir?"

"Oh no, would the lady mind?"

Belinda opened her purse, and was snickering at me when she handed over her ID. The waiter informed us he would be right back with the drinks and the menu. That left us with a little time to laugh.

We stayed in Phoenix for two nights, then got to my parents' house about 4 PM, the day before the reception. I planned that arrival time on purpose, because God forbid If I showed up too early or too late! So, the next day was the reception, and my uncles, aunts and cousins all showed up, plus my brother Angelo, whom I had not seen for quite a while. He was accompanied by his fiancée (surprise!). Her name was Sally, and she was very tall and pretty. I personally think everybody there was duly impressed with Belinda's beauty and quiet demeanor, as compared to my side of the family. We had a good time, and I was glad to find Mother without any migraines. So, the next couple days I took my bride all over the place, even showed her Birmingham HS.

Everybody asked me about the Army life, and there were all the usual questions about, why was I staying in so long. I tried to explain to them, it was all about my education and how much I liked radiology, but after a few minutes of that, I really wanted to change the subject.

I could easily tell that my bride was not used to this fast pace and excitable atmosphere. So, I announced that we had to get back and secure an apartment in Las Cruces. Meanwhile, back at the base, they were trying to get us military housing, because I would be splitting the call with the sergeant.

So, after about five days in LA, it was time to get back to the desert. Yes, I was getting used to it, and I started to like all the fresh air and no smog!

Wow, you would not believe this little apartment that we got on Willoughby Street on the north end of town. It was so small, if I sat down in our living room and wanted to turn on the TV, all I would have to do was just lean forward a little bit and turn it on! Well, we were excited, it was furnished, and at that time, it was fairly new, and as far as the necessities went, we were blessed by the generous nature of her entire family. We had all the dishes, plates, silverware and whatever we needed. That had to have been planned with excellent communication, because we did not ever get two of the same.

# CHAPTER 17

Well, just like the colonel said, all the paperwork was correct, as soon as I took the oath of serving my Country again (yes, six years). There were the orders that showed approval for attending x-ray school in San Antonio, Texas. Next, there were the papers that said I was now a Specialist E-5. The colonel said the orders for x-ray school would be delayed for a while, because he needed me here in x-ray. That was okay with me and Belinda. Yes, Belinda did attend the brief ceremony that day, and she told me she was proud.

Well, we finally got our house on base. It was a cute little duplex, and I actually remember the address. I never forget all the addresses that I lived on. This one was 300 Loki Street. I just looked it up on Google Maps, and it is still there. Fond memories. I remember that we had the old-fashioned clothesline poles in our yard there.

Well, now Belinda was driving my '58 Impala, and naturally I had to remind her of the fact that it was my "baby," and I only had one little scratch on it, and she was over three years old.

"Yes, Raymond, I know how you are with that car, but I am a good driver!"

So, that afternoon I decided to watch *Bonanza* on TV (black and white of course), while she was going to make her very first trip to the base commissary and stock up on some needed food items. Now, please remember what I told you about the clothesline poles in the yard.

So, I said as she was leaving, "Honey, don't forget to park in between the poles when you come back."

She replied, "Gotcha."

I don't remember how long she was gone, but I was up getting a glass of water, and I was looking out the kitchen window, and I saw her approaching the yard. She wasn't coming at a 90-degree angle, she was more like 45 degrees or so, and then I heard this loud metal scratching noise while she proceeded to park between the two metal poles, Both poles just flattened the side panel chrome strips all the way down on both sides of the car! These chrome strips were very thick and shaped in a half-moon fashion.

I ran out so fast and said, "Honey, what did you do?"

She said, "What was that funny noise, Honey?"

I opened the door to let her out, and walked her all around the car, and said, "Sweetheart, thank God you managed not to damage the body or paint, but you flattened both strips so evenly on both sides."

Then my lovely new bride said, "They should have made them much thinner." I didn't know whether I should laugh or cry! Then she said, "Now help me get these bags inside."

To this very day, her brother Ricks always brings that up, and we laugh for a long time. Now, for sure you know how calm she really is! It was not too long into our marriage that her brothers and sisters started to tell me about her driving. They didn't give her a passing grade! The next payday we drove to the Chevrolet dealer and put the chrome strips on order. Back in the day, that did not cost much. Can you imagine what that would cost today!

One morning, we were driving to work, and Belinda said she was feeling kind of dizzy with an upset stomach. I told her that was the advantage of working in a small hospital, she would be seeing a doctor in ten minutes. Well, naturally, our favorite doctor took her in right away. After a few minutes of examining, he said I should wait outside for a little while. About ten minutes later, I found out that my bride was pregnant!

No doubt everybody was happy with the news all around the hospital. When I called her mom, wow, she said, "Thank You, Lord!"

What the heck, I thought I'd just go outside to the payphone and call my mom, and give the news that this would be her first grandchild. My call woke her up, and to say the least, she wasn't thrilled that I called so early. Oh well!

Knowing that I was B-pos, and Belinda was o-neg. the doctor said it was not going to be easy for her up until the time of delivery. Well, the next few months, we made sure she took it easy. Sometimes the doc would just walk over to her office and check her out, How was that for VIP treatment?

Meanwhile my studies carried on, because I wanted to have a little advantage, once I got to school.

Belinda was doing fair, she was holding her own pretty good. The staff at the hospital put on a really nice Christmas party. Belinda's mom made me a beautiful dark blue corduroy vest that matched the maternity dress she made for Belinda. I sure think we were a cute couple.

Belinda said, "Honey, I will just sit here with our friends, you go and dance." She knew how much I loved to dance.

It was great dancing with the nurses. We all had become very good friends, during the past year!

The Christmas season was good. We spent it with Belinda's family. We certainly prayed to celebrate the Lord's birthday, as well as praying that Belinda would do good for the remainder of her pregnancy.

# CHAPTER 18

It was also a good New Year. Belinda had a few bad days, but otherwise she was not complaining. This was about the time that I started to realize that my wife was not the type to complain, and she did have a high pain tolerance. Well, guess what the colonel told me? My orders for San Antonio came through. My class would start the middle of April. Doing the math involving Belinda's pregnancy, I would not be a bit surprised if the good colonel didn't have all this planned.

Our poor Belinda was in labor for about eleven hours. Thank the good Lord we had a great doctor. He actually knew her way before I met her. I was so glad to hear that we now had a baby boy. We named him Phillip, and he was a healthy baby.

It looked like we were going to be busy, with a new child, and me going away for five months to San Antonio, The good news was that I didn't have to worry about them, because I had this wonderful family to look after them while I was gone.

Just think, If I had not met Belinda, I would have been discharged from the Army last month. The roads that we travel are paved by the good Lord. I am so thankful. Boy, that was an eventful three years.

Well, here I was leaving, my beautiful wife and a brand new baby behind, and once again, another road!

Here was a twenty-year-old E-5 reporting to school headquarters to find out that they had selected me to be the class leader because of my rank. The top sergeant informed me that I would be responsible for waking these guys up in the morning and marching them in military order to class every day, and back in the evening. Plus making bed check at 2400 hours every night! *Are you serious?*

He said to me, "What are you complaining about? They all have to sleep in the barracks, and you get a private room!"

I said, "Okay!"

Sure enough, by Sunday evening just about everybody was checked into the barracks. I now was in possession of the roster. The orders strictly stated that you must be checked in by 2200. If you did not make it by that time, the only thing that was going to save you would be a life-or-death situation!

Well, I was missing one person at 2200. Just as I was walking out of the barracks to make my report, here came a guy walking upstairs, dropping stuff all over the place, and he almost slipped down the stairs. I quickly helped him out and asked his name. Thank goodness, I now could go to bed. I was glad I made a dry run to the classroom that afternoon, Now I knew where to march my gang tomorrow morning.

We were sitting in the classroom, meeting two civilians and two military staff instructors. They said, "Please pay attention. It's a tough course, you will have lots of quizzes and exams, and you have to study at night, in order to pass the morning quizzes." Then they passed out the complete course. It looked very tough to me.

That night, I called Belinda and told her, "Maybe I don't belong here."

Belinda said, "Raymond, you listen to me, we will get you through this, and you are going to do fine. You know how much I read, and I will get the proper books and start reading every chance I get. We will get you there, working together."

My wife was not only pretty, and very smart, but look at the support she gave me. She then told me that I should double up on my prayers every night to ensure my assigned angel stayed with me. You bet!

She said the baby was doing fine. She met the neighbors and they were nice and supportive. Her friends at the hospital and her family were looking after her, so I didn't have to worry about her/ I sure did miss her a bunch!

It turned out there were a couple of classmates that offered me gas and lunch, if I would take them downtown San Antonio. We always got a weekend pass, that was great. But the best part was that Sullivan was great in algebra and physics, Garcia was king of the slide rule, and Williams was an electrician in his civilian life. I was great with anatomy and physiology. So, we formed a weekend study group to help each other, and it really paid off. Not to mention the help I was getting from Belinda. I used a lot of quarters in that phone booth!

They forgot to mention one more item when I arrived. By reading the bulletin board (mandatory reading every AM), I found out that I was pulling CQ duty next Sunday. What was that? I went over to headquarters and simply asked. They informed me that all E-5s and above had to pull "Charge of Quarters." That meant during off-duty hours, I was in charge of the phones, bed check and signing passes. I told the sergeant about our Monday morning quizzes.

He said, "No worry, bring all your study materials to the building with you."

Well, here it was Sunday morning, and I had to relieve the CQ at 0800. I made it with one eye open. In between phone calls and whatever, I tried to get in as much studying as possible.

Here it was, getting close to my student bed check, and all of sudden I heard sirens and saw flashing lights all over the place. I guessed the MPs were chasing somebody or who knows. Right about then, I was going to unlock the door and do rounds, when all of a sudden, *crash*! I was lying on the floor with this broken door on top of me. Then I felt an arm around my neck and was being dragged. Everything was a blur, then I realized I was sitting in the chair at my desk, with this big arm choking me something fierce, and his other hand was holding this big switchblade at my chest. Then I saw two MPs with their billy clubs drawn and screaming at him.

The next thing I knew, I was lying on the floor, watching this monster throwing these MPs all around like they weighed nothing. Then, two more MPs ran in. Next thing I saw, they finally got the knife away from him and he was completely knocked out and handcuffed. One MP was bleeding really bad, and another one was standing there with his top uniform almost ripped off, He was the one that picked me up from the floor and called the ambulance. I think all but one was taken to the hospital, including me. They thought I might have had a minor concussion and a few cuts. I was released the next morning and driven back to headquarters. I walked into the office, and there was the sergeant screaming about the broken doors, windows, furniture, even the typewriter was shot! He turned and saw me in my soiled uniform and bandages all over my face.

He said, "My God, are you all right?"

I said I was okay, and inquired as to who marched the students to class.

He said, "I did, you don't worry and go to your room and rest!"

I said, "Before I go, what did we find out about this monster?"

He told me that he was a draftee who was strung out on cocaine and all kinds of different drugs, according to his blood tests.

The one MP who was hurt badly was stabbed in the shoulder and required major surgery, plus the other two required major stitches. As for this writer, I talked to my assigned angel and then went to my room and personally thanked God!

The next morning, when everybody was seated, I was greeted by the teaching staff and they all expressed that they were glad I was okay. I was able to take my Monday morning quiz during lunch, and I did pass!

One week led into another, and before I knew it, we were preparing for our final exams. I really couldn't believe I would be home soon.

# CHAPTER 19

I never told Belinda anything about the "monster incident " until I graduated. Well, sure enough, every week at that school was filled with all kinds of knowledge. I could not have asked for better teachers, and my three amigos who were in my study group. But, most of all, I must thank my beautiful wife for her extensive reading and studying, and lifting me up to feel good enough about myself and my abilities. Out of the thirty-five who started the class, we graduated twenty-nine.

Just great being home. I thought I would slip into the back door, and try to surprise her. She was bending over and putting something in the oven.

I said, "Is your husband around, lady?"

She turned and looked at me and did a quick little scream. The reason being, for almost all of the thirteen weekends of our school, we would spend about an hour of soaking in the sun while we studied. One of the classmates mixed up some type of iodine and baby lotion together, and believe me, we were dark. For sure, my baby son had not a clue as to who I was! (Sun tan or not.) It was so great being together again, and I found that the thing she was putting in the oven was a pork roast with sweet potatoes, and served with corn on the cob. She knew what I liked!

Now I told her everything that happened for the past several months. When I got to the part about the "monster," she responded, "Ooooh Raymond."

Then she told me who was dying to see me back at the base. Of course, poor Sgt. Converse. I then informed her that for the next six weeks I was assigned to William Beaumont Army Hospital in El Paso.

Monday morning, I was heading down the good ole "war" road in my Impala, hoping to find that working in a large radiology department was going to be not too hard. Nobody told me if they were going to issue my medical whites or not, so I grabbed a pair from the base. Halfway down the road, I remembered that there was no Specialist E-5 chevron on them!

I finally found who I was to report to with my papers, and he was a rather pleasant sergeant, but his news wasn't "pleasant."

He said, "Have you been to surgery yet?" and I said, "I beg your pardon?"

"No, what I meant to say is that I am sending you to surgery with the portable x-ray machine."

"Excuse me, Sarge, we were told that we would learn more about portable exams during O.J.T."

He loudly said, "Dammit, I am shorthanded today, can you do it or not?

"Okay, Sarge, show me the way to surgery, show me where your portable is, show me where you keep your lead aprons, show me your technic chart for the machine, and I will do my best."

When I entered the non-sterile doorway pushing this heavy machine, the nurse said, "Stop right there, I will drape your machine, and you get in that room and get in sterile greens, cap and shoe covers, and come right back here."

I was so thankful that we saw all this at Brooks Army Hospital, but I was scared to death I would do something wrong.

She then said, "Are you new here?"

I said, "Yes, ma'am."

"Follow me, I will show what you need to know."

There was my angel again.

In the six weeks that I was there, I did about ten surgical cases, fluoroscopy and everything else. I learned a lot about "Special Procedures." That would help me in the future. And yes, Sarge and I did get to the NCO club for a couple of lunches together.

He said to me, "If they cut orders for you to come and work here, I would be glad to have you!"

"Thanks," I said, "I think I am on my way to Europe."

I must tell you, those were long days, plus driving round trip every day, but, there was this beautiful woman waiting for me with a delicious meal every night, and she always said, "Tell me everything that happened today, and did you get in any trouble?"

By this time Belinda was no longer working because of the baby, so we spent a lot of time playing with him.

I guess it was right about this time, I started to wonder why every room was starting to look a little smaller. Oh yes, it was the books. Everywhere I looked, there were books.

One day, I said, "Honey, if I were to ask you about how many books could you read, let's say, in a week?"

"Well, let's say all the time you were in school, and then working in El Paso, I probably went through four to five books a week."

"Wow. Are you one of those so-called speed readers?"

"Well, sort of, because I know all my authors pretty well, and I kind of know what will be in the next page." Raymond," she said, "you have to know that ever since I was able to read, I always had a book in my hand. When I was in the first grade or so, I remember when teachers would put you in that little room under the staircase, if you didn't behave in class. The room had a whole bunch of books, plus a light, so when the class got boring, I would get in trouble on purpose!"

I told her that they were school books.

"Raymond, I just know one thing, I love to read, period." She told me that, as a child, whatever money she got from doing odd jobs or selling bottles, whatever, she'd been a member of the Book of the Month Club for as long as she could remember.

So, I asked, "Where did all these books come from?"

Her dad's house was rather small. That was a lot of paperbacks.

"Belinda, could you say that I might just be married to a smart ___ "

She said, "You betcha, Raymond!"

That indeed called for a kiss!

# CHAPTER 20

I very seldom get the chance to talk with the sergeant major (E–9), but one day he came down to our x-Ray department and saw that we weren't that busy, and invited me to his office. The moment I sat down, he slid a thick envelope toward me, and said, "Sprechen sie deutsch?" The man just told me I should learn a new language. The orders read I would depart for the Fort Dix transit division in New Jersey by the middle of November.

He said, "Take all that home with you tonight. Let Belinda read it."

"You know how she loves to read."

"Really."

I walked in the house that evening, and Belinda was sitting on the couch holding our son on her lap with her left arm, and a paperback novel in her right. Why wasn't I surprised? So, I said hello with a big kiss for the both of them, then I asked her.

"Belinda, sprechen sie deutsch? Honey, we're going to Germany," I said. "Yeah, you betcha, Belinda."

So, as soon as she got the baby down with a bottle, we started to read everything.

My orders actually said that I was going to report to the 32nd. MASH hospital in Wurzburg, Germany, but it also read that they only set up these field hospitals during training alerts. It stated that once they returned from the field, I would be working at the Wurzburg Army Hospital under a board certified radiologist, so I could complete my RT program.

Saturday morning, we packed up the baby and headed to Mesilla, to give the family all the news. There were a whole bunch of questions from everybody, but I did not have a lot of answers, because I had a lot more people to see next before next week. So, I told them to stay tuned until we came back the following weekend.

Monday morning I was getting my orientation in detail about my assignment. I would report to Germany next month, and I had to give up my military housing and move Belinda and the baby to an apartment. Then they told me that since the government paid for the complete move, including my vehicle, it was not recommended to bring my Impala; too big for the European roadways. Wow, me without my Impala. That was like Roy Rogers without Trigger!

Well, that following weekend that we spent in Mesilla was also a good time to take my yellow chariot down to the Chevrolet dealer and ask about this little sport car that Belinda's brothers told me about, called the Monza. They loved my mint Impala, got a good trade and doable car payments on the Monza. I ended up getting the upgraded Spider edition. So, we now owned a correct-size two-door coupe with rear engine drive, and I got me a four-speed manual stick shift on the floor, yeah! For you car buffs out there, you can look up the 1962 Monza Spider. It was unique, but it never became famous. You will hear about that in the following chapters.

Yes, time flew by, and thanks to her sister, Fina and her husband, Sal, we got Belinda in an apartment close enough to the family, they all could keep watch on her and the little one and I felt good with all that. Once again, Belinda and I would be separated, but hopefully not more than two months.

Boy, it was so tough saying goodbye that time, knowing I would be a whole ocean away, and I would worry about everything.

Belinda said, "Raymond, I got my whole family here with me, it's you I will worry about. You always find adventure, so be careful, you."

There were the three of us, just crying away. The whole family wished me well. What a great family. Belinda's mom made the sign of the crucifix on my forehead and prayed a prayer for the traveler. What a beautiful woman. I would miss her and the rest of the family a bunch.

We got to go for a two thousand-mile ride. Really, I was tired already just thinking about it! Everything was going smoothly until I got to Ohio. Then I started to get chills. I had a fever and shaking all over. How I got my car to the New York pier, I don't hardly remember.

I was sitting and dying on this bus and it finally stopped. The driver spoke loudly: "Any of you guys that are going overseas, please report to building number (whatever)."

I crept in there, and I was in line, with my duffle bag and a suit-case, just about ready to pass out, but I made it to the desk, This sergeant started talking to me, and I was answering him while I was dripping water off my head, and my teeth were chattering. The sergeant picked up the phone and called for an ambulance. That was the last thing I remembered.

When I awoke several hours later, I find myself in bed at this hospital, getting a shot in my arm, and I look up at the nurse, and I asked her, "What's going on?" She informed me I was admitted with an acute case of bronchitis and running a very high fever. Okay, I fell back to sleep. Every day they would take a portable chest x-ray on me, and all kinds of pills and shots. Five days later I was discharged and feeling oh so good! I grabbed my gear and found my way back to that sergeant, and I gave him a big hand-shake and said, "Thank you!"

So, now he told me I missed my ship to Germany!

I said, "What happens now?"

He stated that I would be in Germany long before that ship got there, because he got me switched to a TWA flight that would leave in two days from La Guardia, directly to Frankfurt, Germany. "Here are the keys to a single room in the barracks across the street, and get lots of rest. You don't want to get a relapse."

So by now, you civilian readers are starting to realize where your tax dollars go!

Oh! My God, when was the last time I talked to Belinda? Well, we didn't have a phone in the apartment, so I called Sister Fina and told her to have Belinda there at her home, and I would call that evening.

"Honey, I was worried there for few days, not hearing from you, just praying and praying."

"Sweetheart, I am fine now, and so sorry to have worried you."

"There's nothing routine about my Raymond."

I said, "Let's just keep thanking God, for His loving care. Now, I am going to find out where the mess hall is and just eat! Maybe it's those pills they gave me, sweetheart. I will call you from the airport right before I get on the plane."

She said, "Honey, I know you don't like to fly, get one of those pills at the airport."

"I love you and the baby very much!"

"Honey, we are both fine, and I love you very much!"

Great, that left me a day to get my uniform pressed, and whatever else I needed to do. Oh yeah, go to the PX and find those pills.

I did contact my Belinda on my last night and told her I found the air sick pills, and I said all kinds of mushy things, and she replied with all kinds of "you know."

# CHAPTER 21

T hank You, Lord, it was a great ride over the big pond. The guy
    sitting next to me said that I slept most of the way, which was
just great! I am not a person who sleeps a lot usually!

Yes, a lot of people speaking a strange language. (Reality
check.) I guess I was in Germany. That was the good thing about
wearing a uniform. You always knew who to bother and ask questions. Well, this fellow soldier told me that if I was headed for
Wurzburg, I had to go to the Bahnhof (train station). He told me to
find the military information desk right in the airport, and I would
get a ride to the train station. That was easy! I got to the desk, they
asked for my travel orders and confirmed my destination, and off
to the Bahnhof I went, courtesy ride on a military bus.

Once I arrived there, I already had my instructions as to what I
had to do. It was in the early hours. and I didn't think I was going
to like this weather (cold and damp). I got off the train in Wurzburg.
I found the military desk. They called up the MASH hospital to
arrange my ride. They said I was to go outside and stand by this
big sign that said, US military pick-up. I was freezing, hoping it
would not be long. I heard this horn blowing, and I saw this large
two-and-a-half ton truck pull up, and the driver said, "Are you
G_____," and I said yes. "Okay, jump up."

A few minutes later we arrived at this big steel gate: US Army
Hindenburg Kaserne. I found out later it was originally built around
1934, named in honor of Paul Von Hindenburg. He served in World
War I as a field marshal. Later, he was elected as president of the
German Reich.

Following World War II, the Kaserne was occupied by the US Army (good guys) from 1945 until its closure in 1993.

The only person in the office was the CQ, Staff Sergeant Wilkins. He shook my hand and said, "Welcome. It will be another hour before first formation."

"Good," I said. "Can you get me the overseas operator? I need to call my wife and tell her I arrived safe."

He made a good suggestion about waiting until the evening hours. I completely forgot about the time change. Then I met the company clerk. He said the colonel (MD) was expecting me, but not this early. I explained about missing my ship and all that stuff, He had a good chuckle! He was super nice. His name was Corporal Van Zandt. He took care of getting me winter gear, boots and a big fluffy parka for the cold weather.

He said all the enlisted men lived on the second and third floors. He assigned me to a nice single room downstairs. He also informed me that I was now the new section chief of PLX. He explained that the MASH hospitals were simply large tents of different sizes that housed surgery, pre-op, recovery beds, pharmacy, lab, and x-ray, blood banks and supply, and several mobile generators and mobile heating units, and of course, the motor pool.

All of the previously mentioned was completely mobile. Everything got moved in two-and-a-half ton trucks. He also stated that other E-5 x-ray tech had put in for a medical discharge, due to back injuries. So, pharmacy, lab and x-ray were all in one big tent.

He said he would be the one who would be working on the paperwork that involved getting Belinda and baby processed for their trip to Germany. I asked him if he could get her on a plane, rather than a ship. She would be traveling with a baby. No problem, as long as she was carrying an infant, she would fly. And of course, I mentioned the overseas phone call. Yes, he said, come to the office about 1600 hours (4PM), and, "I might be able to get you about five minutes."

"That's it?"

"Sorry, that's all the government's going to pay for!"

I sure got to liking this Van Zandt. He and the motor pool guys were the only ones who were not Medics.

In walked Colonel Lopez, and Van Zandt introduced me.

"Grab a chair, now we are going to get into details." He told me that he was a career soldier. He was born in Puerto Rico, his family moved to the States in the '30s. In college, he took pre-med, then joined the Army to enroll in medical school. He said that was better than his parents trying to pay for It.

I said, "Sir, I was wondering, where are all the surgeons and nurses?"

"Good question. They're all at the same hospital where you will be, when you are not here. As a matter of fact, I've got business there this afternoon. If you like, you can go with me, and I will introduce you to your radiologist, Dr. Donald Hebert. He's a captain, because he has only been in the Army a year or two. (draftee) He will be the one that will get you to complete your degree program."

The hospital was a fair size, not too big. The chief tech was Billy Joe Tucker, staff sergeant E-6 (yes, he was Alabama). There was one German civilian tech (Frau Bicke) and one other military. The X-Ray Department was only two exposure rooms, and they did not do any special vascular exams. They would send them to the big hospital in Frankfurt. Dr, Hebert was indeed a board certified radiologist, and that was all I cared about.

Driving back with the colonel, I did ask more questions as to why did I got stuck with this Section Chief position?

Well, the story went that this other E-5 was spending most of his time on sick call, complaining about his back pain. He said that his plan was to keep him on light duty.

"Sir, he has more time in grade by far than me."

The Colonel replied, "We will have to see where this medical problem is taking him, meanwhile you're it! And during the field alerts, we will see what happens."

# CHAPTER 22

It was a very cold American Thanksgiving holiday here in Germany, but as I told Belinda in a letter, our motor pool sergeant was kind enough to invite me to his home and family. His house was very interesting. He did not live in the military housing, he had rented this old German farmhouse that had survived the war in the outskirts of Würzburg. This was something I should have taken a picture of. The entire barn structure was converted to a two-level home, with these old-fashioned wood burning stoves, and a large fireplace that heated the entire home. The original owner's nephew worked at a wood mill, so he purchased scrap wood at a great price. Here is a bit of news: In 1963, the American military survived very nicely because the currency rate was four marks to an American dollar. That was why the Germans called us "three times over." You ready? Over-paid, oversexed, and over here. (I only fit into the first and the last.)

Yes, about two-and-a-half weeks in this cold and damp motor pool, going through every box of inventory, which included x-ray equipment, lab and pharmacy. I did have Gifford showing me everything that I had to learn. Once I was completely trained on set-up procedure, and one two-and-a-half-ton truck that I had to sign for, I told the first sergeant that I needed to speak to the CO. The sergeant accompanied me into the colonel's office and confirmed my unit was ready for the next alert. The good doctor told me to get my butt over to the hospital and report to Dr. Hebert. Yes!

Every night, after going to the NCO Club and trying all those delicious German meals, I would write all the details to Belinda, so when she arrived, she would know as much as I did. Oh by the way. The previous weekend, one of my guys gave me a ride up to Bremerhaven sea port to get my car. It felt good driving my own car, learning my way around. Now I could show Belinda were everything was.

Speaking of cars, my new Monza Spider was already spitting out some oil from the bottom of the so-called "pancake engine." The reason I found out was because everybody in the barracks were so excited to look at the rear engine. Well, so much for the warranty. I couldn't drive it over to the local dealer. Here was the good news. My new friend (motor pool sergeant) said not to worry, he would open up the garage that weekend and put it on the lift and take a look at it.

That weekend, I wrote all this news to Belinda about the car and the hospital. So, after lunch I walked down to the motor pool, just in time to see Bill bringing the car off the lift. He told me to get in and start her up, and keep it revved up for a few minutes.

"Okay, shut her down." So, there he was, looking under the motor, and he kept saying, "Aaa-huh, Aaa-huh, better than new."

I said, "What are these parts on the floor?"

He said, "Those were the problem. They are spring-activated vents that are designed to release all the heat from the motor, but they don't work!" What he showed me was that he removed the springs and hinges that operated the vents, and now he had them locked in an 80 percent open position. For the remainder of my tour in Germany, never had that problem again.

This Bill was a genius. I couldn't wait for Belinda to meet him and his family. I really did miss her and the baby. I realized that I would not be with them for Christmas. According to Van Zandt, he was thinking around early February. Well, that was more than the two months!

My first alert! It was about 0400 hours when the building buzzers went off. It was a weird sound, but let's not forget who owned the building before us. "Jawohl."

Yes, it was so cold when we got down to the motor pool. Thanks for the parka I was wearing. So, here's how this worked. Every one one of those trucks that belonged to us were always in standby mode, fully loaded, and ready to go. Everything needed to erect a canvas hospital and operate such, was in those trucks

So all the big bay doors were open, everybody had their truck running and just waiting for the word. In my truck, I had Gifford. I heard others call him Gif and the lab tech. My pharmacy guy would be riding in one of the surgery trucks. Other than the offi-cers, I was the only other one that carried a .45 sidearm, because in my truck I had three chests of narcotics, and other potent stuff! This was all new to me. I was getting excited about driving out to the boondocks of the German forest. Then it dawned on me there were no heaters in these trucks. I would probably have frostbite before the day was over!

Then, my bud Bill, who ran the motor pool, started to load all the docs, nurses and medics on board. They got to ride in three-quarter-ton trucks that had heaters. Those guys all got phone calls about the same time we got up. They also had to make sure if they lived off base, that they had their gear and field clothing ready at all times.

While we were just sitting there and wasting gas, I ask Gif, "Who in the heck helps us to put up our large tent, there is only three of us?"

He answered, "All the motor pool staff are trained for this, you won't believe how fast those tents go up!"

That was also one more question I had. "How do you get them down if the weather is below freezing?" Good question

"You have not seen them yet, but the Herman Nelson heaters are set outside of the tent, and the hot air that is blown in via the large ducts usually takes care of that, but if necessary, once the tent is completely empty, they just leave the heaters on."

"So, how cold does it get in this famous Black Forrest?"

The lab tech replied, "Last year in December it averaged around twenty degrees in the early morning hours, and the dampness goes right through your bones!"

Well, at least I did spend one week in the hospital, and most likely, we would probably be in the field all this week for sure. Boy, I got so much to tell Belinda about all this MASH.

Everybody was hoping it would not last too long, because it would be Christmas soon. So, I imagine everybody wanted to be home for the holidays. I knew I wouldn't be!

Okay, we were on our way. By the time we got the whole convoy of trucks on the city streets, we had a large amount of our military police, and the German police paving the way for us. That was exciting, because most of the German citizens were on their way to work, and most of them all pulled over and waved. My lab guy was not married, and he was waving and talking to all the Frauleins. But we told him, "Roll that window up now!"

Now we were on the country roads, and it was cold. When the windows got frosty, all you did was lean forward and loosen the latch and push at the bottom and it opened up to about twenty degrees. Then, you got all that nice "fresh" air.

Some of you might be wondering: how did Ray learn how to drive this big truck? Well, let's go back to Korea, that was my first training on the two-and-a-half-ton, On my arrival here, Bill took me out on the back roads and we practiced skidding and turning maneuvers, and that was fun!

About the middle of the day, they led the convoy off road and we all jumped out to find the mess hall truck, and we had hot coffee, sandwiches and doughnuts. Who says the Army doesn't take care of their own? That hot coffee saved my life, and took some of the chill away. About 1700 hours, the MPs led us off road for about five or six miles. When we came to a stop, my eyes popped open, The entire horizon was lit up with all these trucks and tents and big vans with radar antennas spinning around, all kinds of tanks and artillery. What a sight. I realized we were not near any forest, but in this huge grassy plain. Now, we gathered around the mess hall trucks and we had a nice hot meal, Yes, they did warm up the sandwiches for us, and not just coffee, but hot chocolate.

Then the colonel called for a section chiefs briefing. Hey, that was me. I got to the front of the convoy. I found where the colonel had this what I would describe as a Class C motor home on a two-and-a-half-ton truck. Nice. There were about twelve or so of us sitting in this warm trailer, drinking hot chocolate, and were informed by the colonel that we were now camped in a classified NATO exercise with our allies, and when we got home, it was not to be spoken about.

Well, what I can tell is that it was very good to learn that we were in good hands! With all this and God on our side, you can sleep well!

So, of course all this was well planned in advance, according to the colonel. The English and French anticipated our late arrival, so they set up a very large tent with folding cots and we were to use our own Herman Nelson heaters. Then, in the morning we would set up our hospital. By the way, that was the night I finally met the chief nurse of our MASH unit. She didn't look a bit like Margaret (Hot Lips) Houlihan. Oh well!

The next morning, our mess hall staff already had things popping about breakfast. (What time did these guys get up?) Their tent was nice and warm, and the food smelled good. By the way again, I did tell Belinda that since the last time she had seen me, I had gained about fifteen pounds. When she wrote back, I really had to laugh.

She said, "Honey, that's great, now the Army has clothes that fit you." God, did I miss her and my son. I would write her as soon as this big field adventure was over.

There we were, listening to the first sergeant screaming out as to who would pick what different size poles and tents, and rope, heavy mallets and such. I was amazed that we had about six large tents set up before lunch on that cold, but sunny, day. After lunch, the sergeant loaned me four extra men to unload the heavy x-ray equipment. I noticed Gifford was starting to get involved quite seriously in the set-up. I walked over to him and asked him if he was all right.

"I will stop when the pain returns," he said.

Later in the day, I saw him take out some pills and sit down on one of the boxes. The rest of us kept working, and the lab tech made a negative remark. I quickly informed him that from what I could see, Gif was no "sandbagger." I think he really had a serious problem with his back!

We are just about set up around 1700 hours, and here came the chief nurse, asking me when would I be ready to receive a patient.

I said, "You mean a mock up?"

That was when she said, "Since we are out here to support these war games for the next five days, you will be working with real casualties." She said that she had a possible broken wrist on a British soldier waiting.

Gif said to me, "Ray, while you are checking the generator and transformer, I will get the Polaroid film ready."

Hey, thanks Gif. I was starting to like this guy! Meanwhile, I was told that my lab and pharmacy were ready.

About thirty minutes later, here came a corpsman with my patient. I greeted him, and sat him down next to the x-ray table.

He yells out, "Morning, mate."

Then I called Gif over and asked him about the Polaroid exposure. This Polaroid stuff was new to me. Gif was very helpful. We made the exposure and told the corpsman to take the patient back to the holding tent. A few minutes later, I brought the film over to the doctor.

"Yes sir," he said, "this soldier does indeed have a fractured radius bone."

The next several days were not boring. I think all these allied NATO troopers must have been paid to test out our hospital. The good news was that nobody needed surgery, but we sure treated lots of fractures, cuts and abrasions. Gif and I took turns doing the exams. He was a good radiology tech. One night when things were kind of quiet, we got to know each other rather well. He was about five years older than me, and had four years in rank as an E-5. I asked him if he was a RT, and yes he was, He had attended x-ray school in his home town area of Dayton.

I started to tell him about the program that I re-enlisted for. He said he already knew all the details, and he would be spending his time at the Kaserne, while I would put my time in at Wurzburg Army Hospital.

We would be back in Würzburg for Christmas. Thank the Lord that the NATO guys worked out all their war strategy. It was quite an experience meeting all the docs and nurses and all the different troops I met from other countries. Other than the cold weather, it was not too bad. Now when we got back I could start writing Belinda with more news (but not the NATO stuff), and I would be looking forward to working indoors again. But, I had better go check my car!

By Friday, we had everything cleaned and put back in their steel crates and started an inventory, and then started ordering new supplies. Gif told me, now that all the heavy moving was done, he would take care of the paperwork and whatever. That same afternoon we had a section chief and top sergeant meeting in the colonel's office. The colonel ask me about Gif, and I told him that he pulled his duty very well, and I thought he had a real serious back problem. Then he said that he might send Gif up to the big hospital for re-evaluation.

Just think, back in those days, there was no such thing as MRI, CT, ultrasound or other fancy technologies that Gifford could have benefited from. I can remember back at that time they did spinal myelograms, at the risk of puncturing the spinal cord.

Christmas was Tuesday, and that day was Friday and the colonel wished us all a merry Christmas, and "Don't come back to work until Thursday." He mentioned that all passes off base would be approved by each section chief.

I walked down to Van Zandt's office, begged, pleaded and offered to drive him anywhere he had be that weekend. All I wanted was five-minute call to my sweetheart before the Christmas load on the overseas operators.

Then he said, "You know dang well that I have my car parked outside next to yours, but I will take cash! Be here in my office at 2100 hours sharp."

If it was ten years later, I would have said, "Thanks, Radar." Just as I was leaving, he screamed out and told me I am getting a new lab tech in about middle January.

"The one you have is being sent back to the States."

"Okay, see ya tonight."

I took a ride down to our bay area and informed everybody about the holiday schedule. I walked up to Gif and shook his hand and wished him and his family a very merry Christmas. I found out that he and his family lived up at the Skyview Apartments right near the hospital. That was where we would live, hopefully once Belinda and Phillip got there. (I couldn't wait.) I walked into the motor pool office, and there was Bill trying to get things done, so he could get home.

"Oh! Ray, am I glad to see you."

"Okay, Bill, what's up?"

"With all this NATO excitement, I forgot to tell you that we will be expecting you Christmas day. And come early, we will all go to church together."

I grabbed his hand and said, "Thank you, Bill."

Now, back to the barracks and get all my clothes ready for laundry. And why not wind up my alarm clock, lie down and start my prayers, and tell our Lord thanks for a safe field trip. The alarm would go off ten minutes before my call. "Good night."

Dang, that was no alarm going off. It sounded to me like someone was trying to kick the door down.

"Ray, if you want the good news, you got to get down to my office."

Well, I was already dressed. I practically beat him to the door!

"Ray, I've been so busy since that field exercise, I just got around to the mail. Here it is."

Lord, thank You, thank You, Belinda and child are flying from El Paso to La Guardia via Pan Am, and then jumping on a MATS airline (military air transport system) to Frankfurt Main Airport, arriving on Feb. 2, 1963. That was a Friday. (Also my brother's birthday.) What a Christmas present! Van said he would contact the housing officer and submit the paperwork ASAP!

Van and I left in my car to go to the NCO Club for a nice schnitzel dinner to celebrate at only a dollar per plate. (Yup)

Van said, "You want more news?"

"Okay, if it's good."

Van had this folded paper in his pocket, handed it to me, and said to read it. Then he went across the room to visit a buddy. Well, to sum it up, it looked like the Army made some kind of mistake, starting back in the Vietnam War, by overloading too many x-ray techs. So now, since there were too many E-5s that normally would get promoted after three or four years in grade, the plan was to take a pro efficiency exam, and if we passed, we would get P-1 pay, which equaled to E-6 pay grade, and then it graduated from there, way too many details. Once Van gave it to our colonel doctor, I was sure I would find out. What a great day so far. Thank You Lord!

Now, to the phone. As soon as I said, "Hi Honey," she yelled out, "Guess who is going to Europe?"

"Sweetheart, I am so excited, that's only about five weeks away."

Then she informed me of all the things that needed to be done, including shots and medical records and such. Knowing her mom, I bet she would sew something up for Belinda and baby.

She said little Phillip was doing great. By the time we got him settled there, he would be turning one year old. Wow! I told her I only got a month to find us living quarters, and to wish me luck. Then, the last two minutes or so, I was saying Merry Christmas to the family. I did tell Belinda that this would be the first and last Christmas that we would ever be separated from one of another. Van explained to me that even though he was going to file for military housing, I should get my butt in gear and look for a civilian apartment to rent, because at this point, we did not know how long the waiting list was. The good news was that the Army would pay my rent. (By the way, just to be sure everybody knows that the Army life for sure is not easy, but I will say this: If the Army had more Van Zandts, it sure would make it easier. Thank you, Van.)

Christmas Eve, I drove in more snow, but I had to get to the main PX to get some presents for Bill and his family. There was no usual good spirit, knowing that I wasn't shopping for my family.

December 25, Christmas Day 1962. The good news was that my wife was home with her whole family, so she wouldn't have time to be too sad, I hoped, but I was missing my son's first Christmas. Thanks to Bill and his lovely family, it was a great day. We all went to this beautiful cathedral in Würzburg for services. It was beautiful, and all spoken in German of course. Once back at his farmhouse, we sang carols and then sat down to a beautiful turkey and ham dinner. "God is good."

# CHAPTER 23

Working at the hospital was just great. I got along with every-body pretty nice, and I was getting free German lessons every day from Frau Bicke. Better than that, she knew a lady who had an apartment in the town of Randensacker, right off the Tauber River. She was going to take me there that weekend, and introduce me.

This hopefully would work out, because Van said the list for military housing was long! It might take up until June!

Dr. Hebert was a super nice guy. I met his wife and two children while I was visiting the bowling alley one night. It was cute seeing their six-year-old trying to get that ball to go in the right direction.

I should mention something about this winter weather here. I barely made it up the hill going to the bowling lanes that night. If you live there, you should become a defensive driver ASAP. The guys drove rough in that country, and then all the snow. The local population there had a big surprise coming soon. My Belinda drove rather fast, and she never turned her head left or right. She just plowed straight away. Before I left, I had to teach her about the four-speed floor shift. I told her it was designed to work without that metal grinding sound.

She replied. "Sweetie, I was driving a tracker on the farm before you got your driver's permit."

I said, "Okay, Honey, love conquers all."

"Jawohl Meine Damen und Herren."

I met my new landlord, Frau Brummer, who happened to be a Grundig stereo and electronics dealer. The building was brand new, the entire bottom level was the showroom, and the top was two separate apartments on both sides of the stairwell. Her English was not that good, but I had Frau Bicke (not to worry). It was very small, one bedroom, one small living room, with one sleep couch, and one small kitchen. And the hallway bathroom was to be shared by her and us. She said that I could park my car under a shelter in the back. Wow, this was not that much bigger than our first apartment on Willoughby St. in Las Cruces. So, I asked Frau Bicke to ask her about the cost. She came back with 325 marks. I showed her the guidebook that the Army gave me. (Remember, after the war was over there were all kinds of agreements that both countries signed, once we became occupants.) I also informed her that one of the military officers would have to come here to check everything. I found out from Frau Bicke at the hospital, when I went to get the snow off my window, that Frau Brummer said to her, "Man, the American military sure takes care of their own."

After a couple of days, Van called me at the hospital and it was approved, and my rent would be 280 marks. ($70 American) Okay, Belinda and child, we don't have to sleep in the car! Speaking of cars, I really had to get Belinda to concede to the fact that she would need lessons to learn about driving in the snow.

That night, I went straight back to the Kaserne, and headed for bed. Just as I was ready to shut off the light, somebody was knocking on the door.

He introduced himself by saying, "Sarge, my name is Harry, and I got the room right next door, and I am your new lab tech."

"Well, that's great, I am new here myself, and you don't call me Sarge."

He told me the top sergeant informed him that the PLX section was all E-5s now since they just promoted the pharmacy tech to E-5, and I was the section chief. He would just call me Sarge."

"Please, call me Ray," I said.

He replied, "Okay, Sarge."

We hit it off really good, and here is where I will tell you now, that Harry has been a lifetime friend to me and Belinda ever since, and right up to the time of this writing. We will talk about him later.

One day at the hospital, Billy Joe asked me if I had been to the museum yet, and I asked him which one.

He said, "Didn't anybody ever tell you that Würzburg was the home of Wilhelm Roentgen's laboratory? It was in 1895 when he discovered the principles of x-ray, and right downtown is the famous museum."

"Billy, guess what I will be doing this weekend?"

That would keep my mind busy for a while. I was just so eager to see my wife and child. It wouldn't be long now.

I went to the museum on Saturday. It was very interesting seeing all the gadgets, wires and tubes that he was playing with. It's interesting information, if you wish to Google it.

Late that afternoon, I went over to visit Frau Brummer and signed the paperwork that I had to return to my housing officer. She was in a good mood, and offered me a glass of white wine. I told her it was very good. She then told me that I would be living right across the street from the famous Randensacker Winery. Okay

You might want to Google that. It's a beautiful place.

Putting all the days in at the hospital had been great. So far this month, no field alerts. Who's complaining? Well, I got back to the barracks just in time to see Harry, our new lab tech.

He said, "Turn around, I got something to show you."

Yes, Harry bought a new Volkswagen Bug. Imagine how much money he saved compared to buying it at home. His plan was to travel to all the interesting cities on the weekends. So we went for a nice ride that included having dinner at a nice riverboat restaurant on the river. I realized that before I picked up Belinda and Phillip, I had to get a camera. So many beautiful places here!

# CHAPTER 24

Well, finally the week I had been praying for had arrived. My sweetheart and child would be flying in. Van Zandt had already given me the paperwork that I would need. The butterflies in my stomach sure were buzzing!

Dr. Hebert gave me Thursday and Friday off, and I picked up Belinda and Phillip Wednesday. I spent Sunday afternoon at the apartment getting it all ready. Frau Brummer said that she would leave flowers on my front door. I told her that was very nice of her.

She said, "Oh, Yah, it is your second honeymoon."

I replied, "Yah."

Working at the hospital Monday and Tuesday didn't go by fast at all!

You would have to guess that my drive up to Frankfurt would have to be on a snowy day, that's why I left kind of early. I had no intention of driving fast and furious in this kind of weather. This was no time to have a fender bender on the day I picked up my wife. I was so excited, it was almost like meeting Belinda for the first time all over again.

There she was, walking down the stairway coming off the airplane, holding the baby in her arms. As I watched through the glass window, I said to myself, "Wow, that beautiful woman is my wife. Yes, I am blessed!" We could wave at each other while she and the baby were in line being processed, and I felt like I should just jump over the rope and grab her, but that would not have ended well.

Finally she was walking toward me and we grabbed each other with the baby in the middle, and just kept squeezing and crying with happiness. Thank You, God, for bringing them safely to me!

I realized how tired she was, so I suggested going to the airport restaurant and let her and Phillip get their breaths. I told her that it would not be wise to stay here too long, because driving in the dark with all this snow coming down would not be fun. Later, while we were driving home, she told me how hectic it was flying all that distance with a baby. About twenty minutes into the trip, she and the baby were fast asleep. That was when I just remembered how my wife could fall asleep before her head hit the pillow. This woman got all the benefits of patience, calmness, easygoing attitude. I certainly hoped that this would rub off on me in the future years. (Not to mention of her memory retention of any book she read.)

"Wake up, lady." I knew she was groggy, so I said, "Well, Honey, here you are in a new country and a new apartment, and we've got to get you upstairs and get you and the baby to bed."

Yes, tomorrow we would start another chapter in our lives, and this soldier did not have to sleep in the barracks anymore!

No, she didn't notice the flowers that night, so I put them in a glass on top of the table. There she was with Phillip in her arms walking from window to window, then she started to wave. When she sat down, I asked her who was she waving to, she said it was a large boat with a bunch of people waving at her. I explained about the cargo boats that carried supplies up and down the river that had families living on them. Then I warned her that Frau Brummer did not have a curtain in the full-length window in our bathroom.

That weekend we walked all around the town, and visited all the little shops, and I showed her all the quaint little Gaststattes (local taverns and restaurants). Then I drove her to the Hindenburg Kaserne, and explained that this was the place where I lived, and it was where the MASH hospital was. I told her we would do this several times, so she would be able to drive me to work and learn all the roadways.

She said, "Raymond, this is all so different from our country, so overwhelming."

I told her we would get used to it together, and that would make it easier. (It was hard holding hands while trying to shift four gears at the same time.)

We did invite the Frau to our apartment for coffee, for her to get acquainted with Belinda and Phillip. She told Belinda that she had a beautiful baby, and she would teach her some German, and Belinda could teach her some English. (All is well in the Fatherland) In church that same day, I prayed to the Lord and thanked Him again for the safe arrival of my family. I also asked Him to watch over us while we are living in a new country, and keep us safe. Amen!

After a while, when we were pretty much settled, Belinda finally told me that our apartment was way too small, and she having some doubts about our landlady. I quickly agreed, and I told Belinda that I would stop by the military housing office and see where we were on the list. The next day at work at the hospital, I asked Frau Bicke if she was close friends with Frau Brummer. She said, "Not close, my husband used to work with her husband before he died. Is there something wrong?

I said, "Oh no, I was just curious."

During the lunch hour, I hitched a ride with Billy Joe down to the housing officer. The news was that maybe in about a month and a half or so.

Belinda picked me up at work that night, and I told her of my visit with housing and all. I asked her, what was it that bothered her the most about our landlady. She told me that she asked way too many personal questions.

"Like what?" I asked.

"Well she was trying to find out about our family tree sort of, like who comes from what countries in our family, First, I thought she was just curious, then it sounded more like an investigation."

"Well, maybe she is just lonely since her husband has died " Then I changed the subject and ask Belinda how she and the baby were getting along. She said she did a little shopping in the local town, because it was so cheap, considering the power of the American dollar. She was delighted when I told her that the Army was going to let me take the test for P-1 pay next week. I gave her all the details over dinner.

Since I had been working at the hospital lately, I had not seen my buddy, Bill. I gave him a call and told him that Belinda and I would like to have his family over, but the place was way too small.

He said, "Ray, you bring her and the baby over for Saturday."

I told him that was only going to happen if I brought over the steaks. He agreed!

We had a great time. Belinda and his wife, Nancy did all the cooking, while Bill and I played with the children. After dinner, it was fun keeping those large fireplaces filled with wood. While we were bringing the wood in, I found myself engaged in a snowball fight with Bill's kids. A great day.

I am sorry that I never kept in touch with him after he and his family went back to the States in '64

That Monday morning, I got a phone call from Van Zandt about the P-1 test. I was to take it Wednesday morning in the colonel's office. I informed Dr. Hebert, and he was excited for me and gave me the time off.

Belinda said to me, "Are you prepared for this test, Raymond? I have not seen you with any books in your hands these past evenings."

"Okay, Belinda, I will study tonight and tomorrow night, you do know it's been less than a year since I graduated!"

"Go Raymond.now!" As soon as she turned around, I grabbed the kitchen towel and snapped her posterior lightly. "Oooh, Raymond, you're going to get It!"

I said, "Just tell me the time."

Yes, I did some studying and took the test, and Colonel Lopez sent it to some place in Munich. He did tell me it would take a while. I sure could have used the extra money, because it was coming on to March 13, and that was Belinda's birthday. And Phillip's was on March 17. Yes, I could use the extra dollars. Especially once I turned them into Marks.

During lunch break, I decided to take a walk down to the lab. Sure enough, I found Harry working away. And guess what he said?

"Hello, Sarge."

I said, "Stop that, Harry. Let's go to lunch."

We chatted about our good old MASH unit. Harry and I were both lucky that we were getting this TDY at the hospital. Harry told me that there was a rumor around that there would be a field exercise coming up. Well, I told him it was about that time, they usually did two in the winter and about the same in the summer. I found out that Harry had been putting a lot of miles on his new Bug, visiting all the towns in Bavaria. I told him as soon as Belinda and I got our military housing, we were going to start to travel also on the weekends. Harry was eager to meet Belinda, so I invited him over for Friday night for her famous soft tacos. He said he could not wait.

As usual, Belinda's taco dinner was a hit. It seemed like Harry and my wife got along just great. They both enjoyed reading as much as possible.

Some good news: the weather was starting to break. When we waved at the river boats, they were usually covered with snow. I guess these were really not boats, but rather barges. These things were huge. I do know one thing: I covered my six-foot-high window!

Well, guess what? The bugle went off for my second field exercise first thing Monday morning, It was a good thing Harry lived in the barracks. He was the one who banged on my door at about 5:30AM. I told Belinda to be real careful with the baby and driving around, and if anything seemed wrong at all, just jump in the car and look up Van Zandt. Yes, big kiss. grabbed my field gear, gave our son a hug and a kiss.

By the time we arrived at the Kaserne, Gif had already pulled the truck out of the bay. I went to the arms room and drew out my sidearm. My pharmacist was ready. Gif said he would ride with Bill and the nurses, Oh yeah! Heated trucks! The weather was nowhere as cold as the last NATO exercise. Thank God for that.

This time we did land in the middle of the Black Forrest somewhere in Southwest Germany, near Baden. What a beautiful site. I was told later that this area was a place you wanted to visit during fall when the leaves changed colors. Okay, now we were all parked and doing hot chocolate and coffee. The colonel doctor called a meeting. We were to set up in this meadow area, and to be extremely cautious with the land. We could actually see some roof tops of the local farms. FYI: the Army had already signed papers with the German Government in advance of this exercise, and if we were to damage any property, we would certainly pay for it! Okay, here came about eight hours of agony. Time to set up. My friend Bill was standing by with his crew to help unload the x-ray equipment. By 1800 hours we had the PL and X tent up, and ready for business. I made sure Gif did not lift any heavy stuff. As a matter of fact, he said he had an appointment next week at the hospital in Munich.

It was amazing how much heat those Herman Nelson heaters threw out. I decided to put my sleeping bag on top of my x-ray table, and slept pretty good. The next morning, I was walking back from the mess tent and noticed a bunch of soldiers unloading from trucks. I found out from talking with our nurses that they were to be our triage patients for the duration of the exercise. That explained the extra tent we put up yesterday.

I started to realize why Gif's pain could worsen, because this was my third time of being involved with taking my x-ray stuff off that truck, and setting it up inside the tent, and my back was starting to hurt. I decided to go in the post-op tent and request some APCs (aspirin, phenacetin, caffeine). Back in the day, that was the Army cure for just about everything! The nurse not only gave me the aspirin, but also issued me a large Ace bandage and advised wearing it every time we did break-down or set-up. (No, it wasn't Margaret Houlihan.)

Well, for the next several days, Gif and I took turns with our patient load. These patients were mock-up. They had a little blood on them and splints or whatever. We would read the doctor's request, and would perform the exact procedure as if they were real patients. Then, we would pin a note on their clothing that would include the exact views that we took. The only thing different was that we didn't take an actual exposure. Of course, we did take occasional live patients who managed to hurt themselves in the set-up or whatever. I have to tell you something hard to believe, but our mess sergeant was quite the opposite of the one you probably saw on the *M*A*S*H* TV show. The food was really good, and yes, Ray was starting to gain a little more weight!

Van Zandt made a Jeep run out to our site to bring mail or stuff for the colonel. He was kind enough to stop by my tent to visit. Then, I just remembered what I told Belinda to do if there was a problem.

I said to him, "Did you hear from my wife?"

He said, "No, was I supposed to?"

"Nope. No news Is good news." (I'll sleep better tonight.)

It all came down Friday morning, and everybody was happy to be going home. This time, I also was going home!

Oh yes, I had my Ace bandage strapped really tight for the work. We arrived at the Kaserne late that evening, and the top sergeant said to put all the vehicles in the bay, and lock them up. We would all meet there tomorrow morning for cleanup and re-check the inventory. Gif was kind enough to drop me off at my place.

I rang the doorbell, and Belinda said, "Who is it?" and I replied, "It is I, Casanova."

"Oh Raymond, you!"

The good news was that everything was well with Belinda and little Phillip (almost a year old). I told her that I had to work at the Kaserne, but I would take her and Phillip with me. She said, "How early are you leaving?" I told her I had to be there by 0800. She informed me that was okay, she would be driving down to meet me later. I certainly knew that my wife had two books on the nightstand she was working on. So, the next morning, big kisses all around and off I went to the bus stop. It just so happened that bus went right by my Kaserne. I found out that morning that I had several civilian neighbors who worked in the Kaserne PX and cafes.

Right close to noon, Harry said, "Hey Sarge, look who is walking this way."

My heart just swelled up, looking at this young lady dressed in tight ski pants and boots and waist jacket, waving to me as she got closer and then put little Phillip down, and he was already walking. There I was again, thanking the good Lord and my little angel for putting me on the path that led me to her! I didn't know if all married men were as happy as I was!

Oh yes, there was a bunch of whistling going on, so I walked over to the top sergeant and asked him if he didn't mind, and called the men to attention so I could introduce my wife.

He quickly screamed out, "Attention, stand at rest."

I then proudly told my fellow soldiers that this was my wife Belinda and son Phillip. Belinda let off a little wave, and about that time somebody in the group said, "You lucky dog!"

Sergeant Dockery just yelled, " Everybody back to work."

I then walked her and my son to the cafe, where she said, "I sure was so embarrassed!" and I said, "I never been more proud."

"Oooh Raymond, I do love you."

I walked back to the bay area with some lipstick on me, but who cares? Later that afternoon when we were at home, Belinda told me that our landlady kept asking more questions. I said I was getting concerned also, but other than just being curious about Americans, what did we know? I once again told Belinda that the Frau was getting old and very lonely.

Back to work at the hospital Monday morning, and Billy was all curious about what went on in a MASH hospital. I brought him and Dr. Hebert up to date. Then, the good doctor said he got a call from Colonel Lopez, concerning my test. Amen, I passed it! Then I turned to Billy and asked him, and he said he could not take the exam, because he was accepted to OCS.

"What?" I said.

Then he informed me that he decided to make the Army his career, and why not become an officer? All the rest of us wished him all the luck. So, the Army is losing an x-ray tech and getting a new infantry officer. He would leave in two weeks. Anyway, I could not wait to tell Belinda about my pay raise. Later down the road, I heard it referred to as ghost staff sergeant. I did not care about the title, only the money!

Belinda picked me up with Phillip strapped in the back seat, and I told her to drive straight to the NCO Club to celebrate.

She said, "Celebrate what?" I brought her up to date. She was happy to hear about the pay raise, and Billy Joe. I did tell her that in two years I would be eligible to take the P-2 test. We had a delicious schnitzel and bratkauttoflen dinner. Lin and I tried for years to find the same here in the US, but not even close. That same week, I took Belinda for her birthday down to the famous Riverboat restaurant on the river in Wurzburg. There we had a beautiful view of the Marienburg Fortress, up on the hill, and also the famous St. Killian bridge. Our friend Harry went back to Germany back in the '90s and said it was as beautiful as ever.

# CHAPTER 25

T he weeks in the hospital were going by rather quickly, and it
was getting close to us moving into the Sky view Apartments.
We were getting excited, because we had been there several times
before, and we knew how much space they had, not to mention
all top grade wood furniture. (I know I keep surprising all you
taxpayers.)

Well, I got home one evening to find that we had company.
Belinda gave me a quick kiss and then introduced me to Barbara
and Irving. Belinda was shopping at the main PX when she witnessed this seven-month pregnant woman faint right there in the
store. Well, Belinda attended to her for a while, only to find out
she was totally hungry and she was without funds. My dear wife
bought her lunch and then drove her to where her husband was
working. It turned out that her husband was a PFC draftee (E-3 pay
grade) working at the Signal Corp division right at the Hindenburg
barracks where the MASH hospital was. The story goes that she
had paid for her own transportation to Germany to join her husband, and they were paying rent in downtown Würzburg, which
they could not afford. Well, here they were in my apartment and
we were all discussing the problem.

The good news was that her mother and father back in Florida
were going to pay her way home. There was no way they could
afford to have the baby born in a civilian hospital in Germany.
Irving did not have those privileges, because in those days the
Army only gave that to E-5 and above! (I am pretty sure that they
now have those benefits.) Okay, I asked Irving if he had married

friends in his company who lived in either Sky view or anywhere else. His answer was yes.

I said, "Let's get in the car and go talk to these friends, because you only need a seven-day favor." I certainly would have had them stay with us, but our apartment was way too small, not to mention that the Frau would say no anyway!

Well, we were back in two hours with the problem solved. They said that their rent was due tomorrow.

I said, "Let's drive there first and tell them you're moving out tonight." That part was rough, because their landlord said they should have given prior notice. I quickly told this lady that I would gladly post her vacancy with the military, and it would rent quickly. That worked! Now we packed their clothes in my car and off we went to their friends' place. I sure liked these guys a lot, and I told them I would pick them up Saturday and we would squeeze in tightly and have a home cooked meal.

I finally got home, and Belinda hugged me and said that I was a kindhearted person. I told her that this all started with her being at the PX at the right time. Either way, we were taught way back as to be good to other people in need.

Here it was Saturday night, and I was walking up the stairs with Barbara and Irving, and out comes Frau Brummer. I introduced them and told her that we were having dinner. Well, she surprised me by making an offer to have some wine together in her apartment first. Wow, how nice. By that time Belinda had been standing on top. I quickly told her to bring Phillip down for the occasion. We were being served with a delicious Riesling wine that she said came from the vineyard across the street. Belinda mentioned that she had a roast in the oven, and we should be getting upstairs. Right about that time I bent down to pick up a fallen wine coaster and my dog tags slipped out of my shirt. The Frau noticed my Christian medal that I wore. Right away she expressed how nice it was, and she said to Irving, "Do you have one also?"

Irving unbuttoned his shirt and pulled out the Star of David. What happened next was beyond belief. Frau Brummer let out a scream so loud, and said, "You people get out of my house now!" And she spoke in good English. She stood up so fast that she hit the table and all the wine glasses hit the floor. We all stood there in complete shock, then she was cussing in German and screaming.

Finally I said to Belinda, "Go upstairs and shut off the oven and lock the door and come right back down." By that time, I had Phillip in my arms, and I told Barbara and Irving to get in my car quickly. At that point I was concerned about what Irving might do. (If I didn't do it first.) Thank God, Belinda was down in a flash and we left very quickly. Belinda with tears in her eyes asked what was I going to do. I told her I knew where the German police station was. We all piled inside the station.

I walked up to the desk and said, "Guten Abend, Spricht zen English?"

The officer replied, "Yah moment bita." He then pushed a button on the top of his desk and out came a tall officer who said to me, "How can I help you?" I told him it would be better if we could all sit in one room and explain. He agreed, and then said to Belinda, "Do you need any help with the young one?"

She replied, "No thank you."

We gave him all the details of the horror, and I informed him that I had a military responsibility to report this to my company ASAP! He agreed. He proceeded with his most profound apology. He was at the point of shaking while he was writing all this down. He said this by no means reflected on all the good German citizens, and he assured me that in moments they would contact the US Provost Marshal and begin his next move. Barbara walked up to the desk and informed him that she appreciated his understanding and his rush to justice! He picked up the phone and spoke in German and asked us all to wait until the military police showed up before we tried to go back to the apartment. He proceeded to get info from Barbara and Irving.

The little one was getting tired, and a female police officer brought in a folding cart for him. I told her that it was very kind of her, in English. She probably didn't understand, but gave me a big smile.

That was the time I looked over to Belinda and said, "Well, sweetie, we now know what we need to know about Frau Brummer." I noticed she and Barbara were holding hands.

Now the action started. The US Army police were working with the German police, asking us all kinds of questions. Finally they figured out that Barbara and Irving didn't have their own vehicle and told them they would give them a ride home. The US officer told me to stay with my family and we would not go home until our landlady was brought into the station. At such time, we would be allowed to go back to our apartment, because they would have a guard on the building most likely. We said goodbye to Barbara and Irving, and that was the last time we ever saw them. Years later, when I was living in LA, I looked up his last name, and sure enough I found him and Barbara living a good life in Miami. When I told him I went to his company to look for him and found out he wasn't there, and they said they could not discuss the reasons why. He informed me that most likely both governments must have had discussions, and Irving got a compassionate type discharge and they also paid Barbara's fare home. He said he owed it all to me for inviting them over for dinner! Wow.

Ten years ago prior to this writing, I received a call from Irving, informing us that Barbara was laid to rest after a serious bout with cancer. Before he hung up, he told me how many times she talked about Belinda.

It was only three days after the incident that they moved my family to the Skyview Apartments. The Provost Marshal called up my colonel and informed him they needed me a little longer for questions or whatever, so I was given a week off of any duties. I had to sign all these papers as to the confidentiality of the horror. When I finally got back to the hospital, everybody was popping questions left and right. Later that week, I finally got Frau Bicke off to the side and she could not wait to tell me that according to her sources, Frau Brummer was not known by that name in the war, and she was thought to be an informant for the Hitler police. Whatever! She told me that she drove by her place and found it all boarded up and all the showroom was completely empty. She asked me, "What did happen actually?" I told her it was not open for discussion until 2013. She put both hands over her face and said, "Auch de Lieben," and walked away.

That night at home, Belinda and I talked about all this abnormal activity in our lives that had been going on. She turned and said to me, "Raymond, all the things you told me about growing up and all, I think you should write a book about it."

I said, "I can't put this last part in it unless we live to be pretty old." She asked why. I had to remind her of the confidentiality thing.

I would like to end this chapter by telling you that I stand proud to have been in the presence of all the fine German people who Belinda and I had the pleasure of knowing. I would like to think that all free countries would have acted so swiftly against an injustice as our military and the good citizens of Randersacker did. If you think you might be going to Germany on a vacation, be sure to include Würzburg and Randersacker areas, and don't forget to try the local wines.

# CHAPTER 26

Things were running so calm lately, it was time to put in for a two-week vacation (in the military, you get thirty days per year.) We packed up the Monza and decided we would first go to Salzburg, Austria and just go from there. We really had a wonderful time in Salzburg, so many beautiful places to visit. Belinda said she would like to go back there once more before returning to the States so the four of us could all see it.

About a half a kilometer later, I slammed on the brakes and said, "What did you mean about the 'four' of us?"

"Oooh! Raymond, I am pregnant."

I said, "When?"

She said right around Christmas. Wow!

I took out the map and decided to head toward Berchtesgaden, Germany. We arrived late in the day, because we stopped and took pictures everywhere. Anyway, I found a nice hostel (hotel) for a good price. When we awoke in the morning and looked out the window, we could see Hitler's nest on top of a snow-covered peak. What a sight! I told Belinda that we could stay another night so we could take the tours. Sure glad we did, but I told Belinda that I wasn't going to take in the "nest" part, and she agreed. He was no friend of mine. That's my little country girl!

I looked at the map and told Belinda we could go south a little and end up back in Innsbruck, Austria. She agreed, and we were sure glad to see how beautiful it was. If you ever get there, take in the tour of St. James Cathedral.

Even though the money exchange was good, we decided to head back to Würzburg before we ran out of funds. This way, we could lounge around, and catch up with letter writing. I also needed to get on my car for some detailing. When I saw Bill, I would tell him that the engine was doing fine. That week we did take Belinda in for some tests. Because of o-neg and my B-pos, they told her she would have some problems, about the same as the way it went with Phillip.

We were in the commissary shopping, as I recall, when up in my face walks a brand new 2nd lieutenant with a big smile on his face. Yup, it was Billy J. Tucker, and his beautiful wife. We pulled the carts over to a table and started talking. I was so glad to hear that he got stationed here in Germany in an infantry company. I was worried they would have sent him over to Vietnam. Second Lieutenants made excellent military advisors in Vietnam. The place was full of them, because our job was to teach the South Vietnamese military tactics, and at that time we were not involved in their war.

Then, like a big ball fell out of the ceiling, he informed Belinda that every graduate had to leave one name that they would recommend for a candidate. Yes, he sure enough gave my name. He must have thought I was happy with the news. Well, Belinda was thrilled to death, that was for sure! It took me five minutes to explain to Billy that my plans didn't go in that direction at all, but I thanked him dearly for his thoughts. Billy said not to worry, he would have the name scratched.

He then said, "It sure sounded good to me, Lieutenant Ray J. G_____."

Yes Billy Joe, but this Ray Joe wasn't an Army career person. The Army had done a lot for me, that was why I was giving them eight-and-a-half years. I looked over to Belinda, and I noticed a frown, and I believe it was the first one I ever saw on her pretty face!

Yes, that was our first marital spat. It lasted right up until we went to bed.

"Belinda," I said, "I know this happens in marriage, God only knows I know too well. watching my Mom and Dad always in constant disagreement. I grew up with different problems, I guess. But, listen to me, I love you more than anything. First of all, I am only a candidate, and there would be an entrance exam and whatever. Honey, why do you want me to do this?"

She told me I would be a great officer, and by the time I retired at fifty-five or sixty years old, I would probably be a colonel or maybe a general, and we would be set for a nice retirement.

"Honey, thank you for having that faith in me. I can tell you this for sure. The way you support me, teach me, guide me and all, I have no doubt that I could do all that. But, I am planning to be married to you for a lifetime, and will never let any argument last past bedtime. Okay, Belinda?"

"Yes Raymond."

"Good," I said. "We will talk about this in the morning, and we can discuss this over a nice breakfast."

"Are you cooking, Raymond?"

"Well, since I am on vacation, you can teach me."

That's when she grabbed my hand.

My pancakes did not come out that good, but I sure ate them anyway.

She said, "Raymond."

I jumped in real quick and said, "Would you like to replace Raymond with the word Honey?"

She said, "Honey, is this Vietnam thing really that bad?"

"Honey, I hear every day that there are so many of our boys coming home in boxes with the American flag draped over the top. The major newspapers are just starting to mentioned it. I want you to read the *Star and Stripes* every day like I do, and you can see where this is going! We have been there for over two years already."

"Honey, you really like Radiology."

"Sweetheart, I really do."

"You're very good at it, huh?"

"Yes, I really am."

"Did Colonel Lopez tell you your score?"

"Yes, it was 91 percent."

"Ooooh Raymond, let's not talk about OCS anymore."

"Hey, Sweetheart, why don't you dress up Phillip and yourself, and we will go to the Bahnoff station where we found that great Pizza place."

"This early, Honey?"

"No," I said. "A little later."

"Oooh," she said.

During the summer months, we did travel to most of the cities in Bavaria, and there were times when we got together with our friend Harry. Wow, by that time he had been all over to Belgium, France, all over Europe. He did not waste his weekends, unless he was on duty.

Belinda was starting to have some rough days with her pregnancy. So, I made her slow down some. One thing about Harry, he could not go too long without Belinda's cooking. He would always bring my favorite Würzburg Hofbrau beer, and after dinner we would get on the floor and play with Phillip and his toys, then play cards. Harry always was pleasant company.

We did have a big field problem that summer. It lasted for eight days, another NATO exercise named Summer Lion. There were again live casualties to keep me busy. Gif was evaluated in Munich, then sent back to the States pending a medical discharge. We all missed him, but his pain was getting worse. He wrote us and told us they moved to El Paso.

I would now have to spend a couple of days each month working with the equipment at the MASH.

I managed to put in a lot time working at the hospital. Every once in a while, Dr. Hebert would throw a quiz at me. He was preparing me for my exam next year. I did keep up with my studies. It was easy when Belinda read her books and went off to another planet. After my study time I took Phillip out for walks. He enjoyed that.

Belinda was doing pretty good, although she suffered with a lot of dizziness. If she laid down, it got better. She wished it was December already. I wished I could do more for her. I really missed that big smile of hers. I was praying for a healthy baby, and a healthy wife!

# CHAPTER 27

Yes, if the phone was ringing 4 am, it was going to be another field exercise. I guessed they wanted it all done before Thanksgiving.

"Hello,"

"Raymond, it's Van Zandt, is your wife up to date on the evacuation drill."

"Yes, Van, but why do you want to know all this at this hour?"

"Raymond, President Kennedy was shot dead yesterday afternoon, and we are now on full alert."

"Whaaat!"

"Listen, is your gas tank full?"

"Yes."

"I'm sending Harry up to pick you up, Ray. He will be there soon. Make sure you get your wife and son over to the bowling alley parking lot to make sure she is in the right convoy. You will see Lieutenant Johnson wearing a yellow band around his helmet. He will give Belinda and the rest of the wives that live in your building maps and instructions, and be sure to check her gas tank!"

"Oh my God. Belinda, sweetheart, please wake up. I know you love to sleep, but this is an emergency!"

"Honey, what do you mean?" She finally started to wake up.

By that time, I looked out the window, and all the buildings were lit up like it was broad daylight, and there was Harry knocking at the door. I let him in, and he quickly started dressing little Phillip, while I was explaining everything to my Belinda. My heart was racing so fast! The one most important regulation was to fill up your gas tank after each trip). Here was my wife, a little over a month away from having a baby, and she had to go through all this.

"Sweetheart, are you going to be okay?"

"Raymond, I am worried about you."

"I will be fine. From the last meeting I attended, I think I will be seeing France before you do."

"Honey, please be careful."

"We don't know anything yet, we will pray." I finished getting my field winter clothes and grabbed Belinda's emergency evacuation kit (canned food and water, flashlight and whatever) out of the closet, and off we went to the bowling alley. I followed the lights and verbal instructions from the military police, and put my car in the proper convoy, then talked to the lieutenant. Now it was time to say goodbye to my wife and child, not knowing what the future held. I walked over to her open window to say goodbye to her and Phillip, and we were both crying, and here is what she said:

"Don't forget to put this event in your book!"

"I know the way you drive, Belinda."

"Do you also know how much I love you, Raymond?"

They started to pull out to the road while I kept waving!

Harry yelled out, "Belinda, don't worry, I'll take good care of the Sarge."

Oh God, I pray!

As soon as we arrived at the Kaserne, I saw Sgt. Dockery sporting a .30 caliber carbine over his shoulder. He had his guys pull my truck out of the bay. All the nurses and docs were already in the half-tons. Here came Van Zandt, all decked out for the very first time in field clothes, carrying my .45 over his shoulder. He handed me the weapon.

"Guess what? I don't stay behind this time."

Harry yelled out, "Where is our pharmacist?"

I realized I did not know this new guy much at all, but Harry told me he had been doing real well at the Kaserne while I had been working at the hospital. Needless to say, this was the first time I saw the complete company wearing steel helmets. I remembered how they gave me headaches in boot camp. Sgt. Dockery came over to me and asked if Belinda and child got off okay, and I asked about his wife also. It turned out that since he lived in a different row of buildings than we did, his wife would not be in the same group as Belinda, but at least in the same convoy.

"Sergeant Dockery, you been in this Army a long time, what do you think is happening?"

He said, "Well, if this assassination is related to a country, and not a person, we will probably be at war soon. Our families are going to be fine, Ray. Are you okay?"

"Thanks, Sarge." Then I ran over to Bill's motor pool and asked about his family. He said that she would have been assigned to the same area as Belinda, but probably not in the same convoy.

Right about that time, the whistle went off, and there we were driving to an unknown spot. It was pretty light outside, and I couldn't help but notice all the flowers and USA flags displayed in all the German residential areas and sidewalks. It was mind blowing, I could hear them yelling, "God Bless JFK" as they waved at our trucks. It was also noticeable that the entire German Army was out in full force.

All my thoughts and prayers were with JFK and his family, and all that time of driving that cold truck, I was thinking of my dear Belinda. Knowing her like I did, she was not shaking like me. She was way too logical, and she was always ready to accept whatever happened. Remember: *God grant me the serenity to accept the things I cannot change, the courage to change the things I can, and wisdom to know the difference.* Yes, at the time of this writing, we have one in our house, just like my grandma's. There were many times when I used to express my woes to Belinda, and she would just walk me down the hallway and point her finger right to the plaque.

Harry was very supportive, and tried to keep me talking and such.

I turned to him, and said, "We will pray for all our families back home."

He said, "They are just as anxious as we are to find out what the hell is going on."

Then it dawned on me. "Harry, where is our pharmacist? He sure isn't here with us."

Harry, replied, "Since he was the last one to fall out of the barracks, while you were talking with Sgt. Dockery, I put him with the nurses and the docs."

"You also are a bachelor, why didn't you jump in their truck?"

"And what did I promise Belinda?"

We were talking about our Colonel Lopez, and we wondered If he knew where we were going. One time we had to come to a stop on this curved road, and we noticed there was another group of vehicles ahead of his van. Harry knew his way around from all his weekend capers, and according to him we are headed toward Belgium.

Harry said, "Hey we might catch up with Belinda, because by tonight, we could be in France."

That would be great, but he no sooner spoke those words and the military police turned us into a gravel country road.

I told Harry, "I don't think we are going to France."

We finally come to a stop. We were told to get out and stretch the ole legs. All of a sudden, we heard this loudspeaker telling us to walk up to the front of the convoy. Here was our Colonel Lopez with this big grin on his face, telling us that it was over.

He said, "If you believe like I do, this would be a good time to remain quiet for just thirty seconds, or say your prayers of thanks!"

Harry and I just hugged each other, and started our prayers for sure! Then the colonel told us the details of the shooting in Dallas, and said that he would have the mess tent put up, and then have coffee and sandwiches, and turn around and drive home. Then, he called a section chiefs meeting in his van.

As soon as I got back, Harry asked, "What's up?"

"Well, the colonel is on the radio with somebody in this Army, trying to find some fuel trucks to gas us up this afternoon so we can make it home. However, if they don't make it here now, his plan is to set up one large tent and two heaters, and everybody will have a co-ed sleepover."

Harry started jumping up and down with delight and told me which nurse he was going to share doughnuts and hot chocolate with. One half hour later, they were refueling our trucks, and Harry said, "Dang it!"

All I had on my mind for the entire ride home was Belinda and her pregnancy and Phillip. I certainly was still thanking the good Lord for our news. I had no idea where she and Phillip would be. Perhaps they beat us back to Wurzburg. Harry told me that as soon as we got the truck filled up with gas, and back in the bay, he would drive me home. Several hours later, we pulled in front of my building. There it was, my little Monza, so dirty, I could not tell what color it was. But who cares? I ran upstairs, tripping over my gear, and she already had the door opened. Man, what a scene. Phillip was giggling, Belinda and I were crying, and just kept hugging and kissing. Belinda finally said it was getting very cold, and perhaps we should shut the door!

Yes, we talked about her condition on the trip. Thankfully she said there was no time to be pregnant during this ordeal. Harry was right, they were only two miles from the French border when they got turned around. Belinda said she finally met all our neighbors in our building. It seems that they all made a pact, that every Friday night we would rotate apartments and sample their traditional foods. She said a lot of our neighbors' wives were from all different countries. I could hardly wait. Yup, we talked most of the night, and Phillip fell asleep in our bed. Life could not be better than this!

Monday morning, I was back at the hospital, and Dr Hebert filled me in on all of the details. It seemed that they had an entire infantry company guarding the entire hospital while patient care went on as usual. Other than the fact they certainly missed having the nurses and docs that were with us. After all that, everybody was pinned to the TV news every chance they got. A lot of the local German population shut their businesses down while they mourned President Kennedy's death. They fell in love with him when he came to Berlin in June to give a most powerful anti-communist speech, quoting, "Ich bin ein Berliner."

We all read about it in our *Stars and Stripes* newspaper. If JFK would have moved to Germany, they would have built him a castle for sure!

Well, it was the best Thanksgiving we would ever have. We had so much to be thankful for. We had Sgt. Dockery and wife, Harry,

Bill and Nancy, Van Zandt and my pharmacist, John, and one more medic from the barracks. Everybody knew of Belinda's condition of course, so all we did was cook the turkey and everybody else brought a side dish. Here it is, years gone by, and I can still taste the food. But, as my wife always said, *Raymond never forgets anything*. I kind of agree!

Well, it did not stay routine for long. Belinda made several trips to the hospital with a lot of pain and discomfort. It was not a normal Christmas for us, Belinda was not feeling good at all. The doctors gave her what medicine they could, but it did not help. We prayed.

December 27, 1963. Yes, a baby boy named Gregory Ray, and it was a five-hour ordeal for him and his mom. Gregory was in the blue light incubator for almost five days before his jaundice disappeared. Otherwise the doctors told us he was a healthy newborn, and once again, prayers. I sure was thankful for my P-1 pay. It was going to come in handy for a family of four.

What a year! It was hard to believe all this activity happened in just thirteen months after my arrival here in Germany.

It was a pretty quiet New Year's. Belinda needed all the rest she could get. Frau Bicke, as you know, was an x-ray technologist, RT, and it so happened her sister Lora was a nurse, RN. She told me that her sister would visit Belinda once every day until she got her strength back. I couldn't believe how kind that was of her. I was very happy for Belinda, because her mail came in once per week, and it was mostly books. Now, she could get back to it. *Belinda without books, would be like a full grown bird without feathers.*

I must tell you, I did get letters from Mom, and her headaches were still there. Dad and Uncle Angelo were now running the restaurant without Uncle Frank. It seems that he got a nice job working for Pathe Film labs down at one of the movie studios. Way to go, Uncle Frank!

I finally invited Frau Bicke over to meet Belinda, since her sister Lora had already met her. She told Belinda she had two beautiful sons. She said that was because they looked like her. Then I told her that I was going to buy her lunch today!

"Ooh Ya! Raymond, just making a little joke."

# CHAPTER 28

L ora came every day for an hour or so to check on Belinda, and even did some laundry. So, about the middle of the month, Belinda was doing much better, and I told Lora she was welcome to come over for coffee and cake, but she need not make her daily lunch hour calls anymore. I tried to pay her, but she said she didn't mind helping Belinda out a little. She said she would not take a penny. We were good friends right up to the time we left Germany.

Belinda got her monthly mail from her mom, and this time we got some homemade tortillas and chili peppers. Belinda perked right up. I think it had something to do with the endorphins in the peppers. Well, in the letter we found out that Belinda's older sister, Ramona, who was also married to an Army soldier, happened to be stationed in Munich. She was looking forward to a visit with her sister. I called her up and asked if they would like to drive over. Ramona quickly explained that she had a weekend job at the local NCO Club. I informed her that once Belinda was a little stronger, we would make a visit to Munich. Belinda said we could stop by there, on our way to Salzburg in April.

I said to Belinda, "You certainly mean to keep your word from last year, don't you?"

She replied, "I told you that all of us would go back to Salzburg."

It was hard to believe, Belinda and Phillip were having their birthdays already. Phillip would be two that March.

Here we were on a little vacation, and we were definitely bound for Salzburg. We did go to Munich to visit her sister, Ramona and her husband, Jim. Ramona was happy to see the children. We stayed the night, and saw some of the sights of Munich. The people of Munich liked their beer fest, and it was going on at the time of our visit.

Now we were in Salzburg again, and this time I told Belinda that we were staying for at least three days and enjoy all the great food and scenery.(Oooh, you have to try the pastry here.) The highlight of this beautiful city was the Salzburg Castle, and all its rich history. Just Google Salzburg, and you will tempted to jump on a plane!

I did tell Belinda when we were driving in that there was a bunch of trucks all over the sides of the beautiful mountains. When we drove out three days later, I couldn't believe how many more. I pulled over to the side and asked Belinda for the binoculars, then I told her that this was a movie production. Once she looked through the binoculars herself, she quite agreed. We both agreed with that much equipment, that was a very big production.

Allow me to just jump ahead about twenty months into to the future. We were living in San Francisco, and it was the talk of the town, must-see movie. Yes, it was *The Sound of Music*. I did Google it to find out the production started in April 1964. We were there.

The rest of the year was filled with some great car trips and having total enjoyment going to different apartments on Friday evenings, trying out these culinary delights from Italy. France, Germany, Japan, China, and Puerto Rico, just to name a few! Belinda learned a lot of recipes, and I personally can tell you, all of them couldn't wait for our turn, when Belinda cooked the famous dishes her mother taught her.

Then came the time we had to say goodbye to Bill and his lovely family. They were going to be stationed at Fort Hood, Texas.

I said to Bill, "What am I going to do if this Monza breaks down?"

"You really want me to tell you, just get a Volkswagen." Hah.

That summer was kind of warm, and everybody told us to check out the local schwimmbads (outdoor pools). It was great fun with the kids and all. I told Belinda how nice they did with all the flowers and gardens inside the pool area.

"Raymond, you come here because most of the frauliens don't wear any tops."

"Belinda, you're kidding, I never noticed."

*Bam,* right on the back of my head! We found out after that, our friend Harry became a good swimmer while stationed in Germany!

I knew I was a fast runner, but could I actually play soccer? It turned out that Frau Bicke's family were all avid soccer players, and they were actually the league team of Randensacker. It seemed that Frau Bicke's husband was the team goalkeeper, and he told his wife that they would challenge the Americans to a match.

I informed Harry, and he said he would find nine good men from our MASH unit. He managed to have Sgt. Dockery inform the colonel to see if we could make this a big deal. Later, I told Harry that these guys were professional, and we didn't even qualify as amateurs

Sgt. Dockery told Harry that the colonel was all excited about this. The colonel knew the recreation Officer in our division to get us what we needed; shoes and whatever else. Wow, this was going to be embarrassing when we got slaughtered.

So, at work I ask the Frau, how many points would they spot us, since we were amateurs? She came back the next day and said ten. *That's it!* I asked the Frau what was the average age of these guys. She said they were about her husband's age, around forty-five. (I said to myself, "These guys are old!").

Harry said, "We'll kill them."

"Harry, we don't even know how to play."

"Don't worry, Sarge, I found out we got a couple of guys that can teach us."

So, we all met at the NCO club and hashed all this out, and we figured we would set a date for late August, or early September. I said we should forget about it.

"Hey, Ray, where's your spirit?"

I said, "I never played sports my entire life."

"Whaaat!"

Back at the hospital, Dr, Hebert told me that we were all crazy. I said this was not my idea. He said he was glad it didn't involve his hospital. I agreed, but we got almost a couple of months to get ready.

"Speaking of getting ready, do you know I am sending out for your Registry Exam in December?"

"Wow, that's up already?"

He informed me that counting my school time, and my OJT, thats it! I did tell him that I would start studying up on the books again.

It was a beautiful day in late August, and at the soccer field in Randensacker. I can't tell you how shocked they looked with our impressive outfits. We certainly looked more like a soccer team than they did. Not to mention our 6'2" goalkeeper. Yes, I finally met Frau Bicke's husband, Hans, their star goalkeeper. He was very polite. He gathered his whole team together and made sure everybody was properly introduced. You wouldn't believe how many people came with us. There was the colonel, his wife, Dr. Hebert and wife, a bunch of nurses from the hospital, Sgt. Dockery and wife, and about the entire group from our MASH hospital, and the most important of course, Belinda and the boys.

There was one gesture that really impressed me: Fraulien Lora (Hans's sister-in-law) came and sat on our side with Belinda and they had a blanket and snacks. I sure was thinking I would rather have been with them! We only practiced for about four weekends and a few evenings, not to mention we had another six-day field alert in between, which wore us all out. I was to be a center back defender (CB). Do you have any idea how hard I was praying for a flood?

Well, if you looked at the score board, you would see that 32nd MASH already had ten points, and the game hadn't even started yet.

Harry said to me, "Ray, these guys, are old. Piece of cake."

Sure, Harry!

It wasn't more than thirty minutes or so after the whistle blew, the score board read 10–10 . We had several injuries on our side, of which I was one. I would be singing female opera for a long time. They called another break (they felt so sorry for us). Someone from the crowd screamed out and said, "Look at Hans the goalie, he is lying down taking a nap!"

Well, I guess that woke him up, and he walked over to our team captain, and called the game over at a tie score! 10–10. Would you believe it? I told Harry, "Your so-called old men scored ten goals in a half hour. Piece of cake." I was lying on the ground with an ice-pack, and Belinda came over and said, "Honey, you guys played good." The only time in my whole life that I played sports, and I couldn't get up off the ground! Just think, come Monday morning how much ribbing I was going to get from Frau Bicke and probably Dr. Hebert!

It was pre-arranged that after the game we would be going to this huge Hoff Brau Restaurant in Randensacker. There must have been forty or fifty in attendance. Hans and his fellow teammates got on a microphone and told everybody in the restaurant that this was the toughest game they ever played! You could not believe how loud the whistling and applause got. Hans called up our goalkeeper and presented him with a team beer mug that had all the names of their soccer team on it. How nice was that! They were the greatest bunch of people you would have ever met. Then Hans yelled out my name, and said his wife stopped over to their house to pick up a present for me. So, I limped up to the stage and Frau Bicke presented to me this beautiful ice bag. There went the whistling and applause again!

Fraulein Lora was kind enough to take our boys into a private room where there were a whole bunch of kids playing games and eating ice cream. Lora stayed with little Gregory and kept an eye on him. She was so nice. Well, the fun started, it seemed while I was visiting the kids' room. That was when Hans challenged Belinda to some kind of a game called Einundzwanzig (twenty-one). It seems that his wife had told him that she was a farmer's daughter. It turned out that all that info was exchanged over their coffee and cake get-togethers.

Anyway, it was obvious that Hans was already running on high octane. So, I asked Frau Bicke what this was all about. She explained that one man would deal Blackjack to Hans and Belinda, and for each hand played, the loser had to drink a shot glass of schnapps. The game ended after twenty-one deals. I told Hans that my wife did not drink, and I also told him that just because Belinda was born pretty, didn't mean she was not tough. Belinda assured me that if she got too many losing hands, she would just quit. I was glad I taught her all those card games when we got married.

The truth was, she always beat me, and as far as her stomach went, she's eaten the hottest chili I've ever seen.

Get this. Everybody in this joint was standing around their table, and Belinda said, "Hey Hans, if I beat you at your game, what's in it for me?"

The whole crowd turned so quiet. Hans said, "Frau Belinda, I doubt that you can, but if you do, your name will go up on the wall, and I will buy you the next five meals you eat in this place." I leaned over and told Belinda that he was just about gone, and he might pass out quickly. She looked at me and gave me a wink and a smile.

I really can't remember how it went exactly, but Belinda only lost six of those twenty-one deals, and Hans's head dropped on the table right at the twenty-first deal. The whole soccer team started to scream, " a, Belinda hat Haas geschlagen," over and over again. Translated: *Yes, Belinda has beat Hans.* Her name was put up on the wall, Hans was still in Dreamland, and I was married to a celebrity! I highly doubt that six shots of schnapps would affect her iron-clad stomach! That was the first and last time she ever drank straight alcohol. Oh yes, we still went there a lot, and sure enough, somebody always recognized her when we walked in.

# CHAPTER 29

The months just went past, and we were getting ready for the holidays. It was great this year, because all the nurses and docs that joined us on our field alerts threw a big Christmas party and they invited the entire MASH hospital. We all gathered in the headquarters gym. You would not believe how many tables of food there were. Turkey, duck, goose, elk and deer. I tried them all. We had a band and sang Christmas carols and we and the kids had a great time. I got my share of dancing in.

Yes, I took the big exam the week before, and it was sent off to the ARRT from Dr. Hebert with his address. He told me at the party, "Ray, just think, when they send it back to you, you will know if you passed, because the envelope would say Spec.5 Raymond G _____, RT." I told him he would be the first one to tell me. (I knew it was going to be there. Belinda would put the whip on me if I slowed my studies down.)

That test was over 300 questions. That was a big difference, compared to today, which I believe is about half, due to the fact that today, it is all digital. Back in my day I had to know: Chemical content for developer, fixer, cassettes, illuminating screens, fluoroscopy, tomography, film processors, algebra, the Inverse Square Law, and slide rules to figure out the exposure time and amount of radiation, hand-selected collimating cones, and the list goes on and on. All the previously mentioned items are all selected by a computer today. Just think, if there were no computers, there wouldn't be MRI, CT, Nuclear, Ultrasound. Yes, today is much better.

Happy New Year, 1965

Dr. Hebert asked us if we could work for an extra hour come Friday evening. It was something to do with education whatever. So, we all planned for it. Just think, this would be my last winter in Germany. I didn't know where my next assignment would be, but I was hoping for less snow! (The next would be my last in this Army; my discharge date was May 1967.) The colonel back in White Sands was correct. I would turn twenty-six two months after my discharge. When I think back to White Sands, that was the turning point of my life and career. They all cared so much for Belinda, and that meant they started to care for me. It was like a family. They gave me great counsel and career advice. They even threw in a promotion that allowed my wife a free trip to Europe. My wife and I always remember those times in White Sands, wich brought me a beautiful wife and a new career, and friends I will never forget.

It was not that long ago when Belinda said, "Hey, Honey, maybe they will send us back to White Sands when we leave Germany."

I told her, one never knows!

Here it was Friday, and now we would all know what was going on. Right outside of Radiology, was a big and wide hallway with couches and chairs. The good Dr. Hebert led us all out there to sit and get comfortable for the meeting. I was sitting next to Frau Bicke, and she was just giggling and rubbing her hands together like something good was going to happen.

I said to her, "Was hast du vor Frau?"

She said, "Oh Ya, you will see."

Right about that time, I heard all this noise coming up the hallway, There was Belinda and Phillip and Greg with Fraulien Lora, Colonel Lopez and wife, Sgt. Dockery and wife, and of course Harry, and behind him was Van Zandt pulling a big cart behind him. Dr. Hebert told everybody to please sit down. Then, he handed Belinda a big manilla envelope.

He said, "Ray, I think your wife has some mail for you. Belinda, please read who it is addressed to."

She walked over to me, and said, "I have a letter addressed to Specialist Raymond G_____ R.T."

Well, my legs just crumbled and I fell back in the chair. Belinda jumped on my lap and said, "Now, are you going to buy me a real wedding ring, Raymond?"

It was just great. Dr. Hebert was one of the best.

That noisy table Van Zandt was pulling was full of beverages and a beautiful cake, and guess what it said on top: *My Raymond, the RT, xoxo*.

"Honey, thank you for supporting me, loving me and just being you."

"If you want to catch up with me, Raymond, you got to get your name on a restaurant wall first."

"Belinda, I thought I married a country girl, not a celebrity."

I went around to everyone there and thanked them so much. It was great way to end the year. Belinda and the children were all healthy and I certainly thank our Lord for watching over us. The following Monday, I arrived a little early, hoping to catch Dr. Hebert before he got busy. Sure enough, he jumped out his chair wearing his red goggles.

"Oh, good Ray, you're here. Get your goggles on, we got an early fluro case."

That worked out great. I would talk with him later. This week that room was assigned to Frau Bicke,she did come to work on time, so when the case was over, she got me a doughnut. (FYI: Once a person got their RT, they now could work anywhere in the fifty states, because, the registry is on a national qualification, same as an RN.)

Later that day, I finally caught up with the doc, and we talked about me completing my RT. Now, the question was: Will Colonel Lopez let me stay?

He said, "Let's call!"

Luckily, he got him on the line, and they started gabbing. He finally got around to asking the question. There was Dr. Hebert saying, "Hmmmm, Hmmmmm, I see. Okay, catch you later, thank You." He hung up. "Ray, here it is." He proceeded to tell me that the 32nd was going to have a IG inspection at the end of January, and he needed me back. I said I understood.

Dr. Hebert and I became good friends the last two years, and I certainly thanked him for teaching me so much.

He said, "Ray, keep your whites here in the locker, and as soon as you can come back, I'll be happy to have you." Then he said one more thing. "Ray, I love the way you make most of our patients laugh. I am going to miss that!"

Okay, see ya!

There is a big difference between wearing whites in a nice heated hospital, as compared to me being back in the cold motor pool dressed in all this heavy gear. Well, I sure as heck wouldn't complain. The Army had been good for me so far!

Oh, no, I got hit with more news. Harry's enlistment was up, and next week he was going home. I knew he told me this a while back, but I forgot because of all that studying. So here we were, standing around the bay area, and Harry proceeded to tell me that he wass irreplaceable.

"Look, Sarge, do you want me to re-up so I can stay and help you?"

So I said yeah, Harry, I do!"

He replied, "Look, you know I like you very much, but not that much."

Then he took off running.

I screamed out, "You better come back here with hot coffee and warm doughnuts."

He did. Like I told you earlier, we are still best friends and we always talk on the phone in between his visits. (It's been fifty-five years already.)

Well, the next day was the IG (they didn't get bigger than this one) and I got a new lab tech that had only been there one week. Yes, for this inspection everything we had was laid out in the bay area, all the trucks were outside. All the generators were hooked up, even the Herman Nelson heaters, and my section was ready to make an actual exposure if they asked me to. Just in case, I had some Polaroid packs warming up near the wall heater. Try to imagine looking at an entire surgical hospital completely all set in a giant size parking lot, with all the doctors and nurses, techs, and the mess tent actually cooking a meal. It's an awesome sight.

There were about four high-ranking nurses, five or six high-ranking doctors, and engineers, and since PL and X were in the first bay, they started with me. All kinds of questions about the mobility of my x-ray equipment and my experience. This full bird Army nurse asked me: How do I know if I am getting the right exposure after set-up? I told her that we had KVP and Ma readings on the panel just like the fixed units that are in a hospital, and I actually had a few phantoms in my inventory. She was impressed with that so much, she asked me if I would do an actual procedure right there and then. I can't tell you the look that was on Colonel Lopez's face at that time. I walked over and started the generator. I whipped out a plastic phantom of a pelvis, centered it on the table, inserted my Polaroid cassette and moved over to my panel and set the proper technic, told her to step behind the lead barrier with me, and had the rest of the lookers stand back at a safe distance. Then I said to my patient to hold his breath and made my exposure. Everybody walked back into the bay, and then I handed the cassette over to the nurse and told her how to open and peel the top cover. There she was, holding up a perfect view of the pelvis. She was just tickled and showed it to the other docs.

Then I closed in for the kill, when I said, "Colonel, you may keep that as a memento of your trip to our field hospital." She was thrilled and shook my hand and said that she was impressed! And there was my Colonel Lopez smiling ear to ear. They moved over to the lab and pharmacy and asked my guys a few questions, then moved over to the surgery area. Colonel Lopez walked up to me and said, "Tell your wife we will all be dining at the Officer's Club Saturday night."

"Yes, sir."

Then, my two techs told me thanks for taking the pressure off them. I told my new lab tech that I was glad, because I did not know if one week was enough time. He said thanks, and he would be ready very soon! That night at home with my family was so relaxing. I told my Belinda that it would hopefully be the last one of those for me. Yes, I got a big kiss from all three of them.

# CHAPTER 30

A bout the end of February, I was called into the colonel's office, and he presented me with a letter of accommodation that came from the IG's Office in Washington. He said that he was very proud of the way I handled the IG that day, and he noticed that I had not stuttered one time. I informed him that Belinda and I still did those verbal exercises. He said that my wife was a peach, and they enjoyed talking Spanish with her at the Officers Club. Then I said I was glad, but I had no idea what they were talking About. He just laughed.

The snow was not too bad there, which would be our last winter in good ole Bavaria. It was a quiet March. Belinda got a lot of reading in. This month we had two birthdays (Belinda and Phillip). Phillip was already three years old. Belinda and I realized that most of all our military friends had left Germany. We still went to Belinda's favorite Gaststatte in Randensacker. Just about every other Sunday, we met up with Frau Bicke and Hans, and Frauline Lora. She loved the Children. Hans and Belinda played Blackjack (no alcohol). Hans was still trying to beat her score. (Best out of twenty-one dealt.)

I had been working two straight months at the Kaserne. We had so many new people around, it felt strange. Colonel Lopez and family shipped out right after Belinda's birthday. It was a great farewell party, and guess who showed up wearing his uniform with his new rank of major? Yup, it was now Major Donald Hebert, MD. He had decided to go for a military career. Belinda and I wished him and his wife all the luck. He certainly holds a special place in my life. That was the night that he also told us they were shipping out in April. Well, all these roads in my life had definitely crossed for a reason, and I always thank God for His grace. It's nice knowing that I have had the best military doctors involved in my career, and I am thankful for their kindness and support.

It wasn't that long ago that I stormed out Birmingham High School, feeling pretty bad and confused, and yet that day, I felt just the opposite! It was great knowing I had an angel in my pocket. It was even greater knowing I had a fantastic wife who was always helping me. I still think that I disappointed her in not pursuing the OCS application. Yes, she did bring it up every few years or so.

Here we were, celebrating Mayday already. It was the season in Germany that was considered the end of the cold weather. Well, I would not put any money on that, because we were still cold. If I remember correctly, they even opened up the local swimming pools on Mayday. Belinda said if we want to take the kids swimming, we could go to the base swimming pool. (I wondered why she didn't want to go to the schwimmbads. I think that was in Chapter 28.)

I went home just a little early, and caught her in some type of mood I could not figure out. I even tried a joke, and caught nothing back. I said, "Belinda, I know I came home early, but did that upset you?" I put both of my hands on her shoulders, and looked her right in the eye. "Okay, what gives Belinda?"

She said, "Don't you ever get homesick?"

"Oh sweetie, that's the problem? Well, I can just imagine you miss your family very much." Then I told her that we were going downhill and only got about five-and-a-half months to go.

She said, "Okay, honey, but I miss everything else too. I wanna go back to my country."

"Yes, I feel the same way as you do, and if it wasn't for you being here with me, I would have suffered, but we're together, me and you and the kids, right?"

Phillip also said, "I want to go with Mommy."

We laughed. We both agreed that this was a great country to see, but we had been there long enough!

That Monday I went to the Kaserne for roll call, and there was our new company commander standing out in front of our formation introducing himself. I really can't recall his name, but he was a major, and he was a career orthopedic physician. Right before dismissal, he called for a section chiefs meeting. I looked around the room, and I realized there were only two of us old guys left. Since he arrived after Colonel Lopez had already gone, our good colonel left him a long letter as to what went on in a MASH hospital. When he turned to me, he said that he had read my 201 file, and mentioned my letter of accommodation, and he also said he was not up to date as to what this P-1 pay was all about. The company clerk spoke up and told the major he gladly would explain it to him later. He then told me there would be another tech showing up soon.

I said, "Great."

Then he said, "I noticed you were TDY at the Wurzburg hospital. What was that all about?"

Well, after I told him everything, he seemed content. I can tell you that he couldn't hold a match to Colonel Lopez, and maybe this was why I can't remember his name!

The middle of June was upon us, and the new company clerk wanted to see me. So, I checked in. We greeted each other, I took a seat, and said, "What's up?"

He said, "I don't know if anybody told you, but your replacement is here, Specialist 4, Jerry Langley."

Whaat!

"Wait," he said, "it gets better. You and your family are going home five months early. It seems that the casualty rate is high in Vietnam and they need x-ray techs."

"What? I'am going to Nam?"

"No. no." he said, "I told you it gets better! You are being sent to one of the main hospitals. You are going to Letterman General Hospital at the Presidio in San Francisco."

"When are we leaving Germany?"

He told me, right around the middle of July. He also told me I had better get my car up to the Bremenhaven sea port. Wow, all my friends with cars were all gone. The clerk told me if I could not find a ride back, I could take the train back.

"As a matter of fact, you and your whole family can ride the train back to Wurzburg."

"Where is this guy Jerry?"

The clerk said, "I think he's upstairs getting settled, let me go get him."

I started thinking that I could not wait to get home, and tell Belinda the great news! I even told my angel, "What a slick operator you are." Okay, I met Jerry. Seemed like a nice character. He informed me that he also was a graduate of Brooks Medical Center. He was very confused as to why he got sent there. I told him the reason I got to work in both places was due to the re-enlistment contract that both parties signed. Of course, he wanted to know what were his chances to get TDY at the Army hospital. For sure he was aware that he needed to complete the whole twenty-four months to take the National Registry. Then, he told me the good news. He had already worked one year at Valley Forge.

I told him, most likely they were going to make my E-5 lab tech the section chief. "It's up to you to learn your job very well, and maybe let you get in some TDY." I also promised him if he did do well in the next two weeks of learning set-up and break-down, I would try to convince the new major that it would increase his skills to have him in the hospital in between field exercises. We did a few hours of orientation with him that day, and I introduced him to the new motor pool sergeant to set up his driving school for the two-and-a-half-ton truck. And now it was time I went home and gave some good news to Frau Belinda!

Belinda was so excited, she started to cry. I had to tell the kids that Mommy was happy. I didn't need three people all crying at once. The first thing we had to do was to get our car to Bremenhaven for the next ship to New York.

"I'll get the company clerk to cut the orders tomorrow, Belinda, and we will all leave here Saturday morning. Is everybody happy? Yeah!"

Then we had dinner and started to discuss what was waiting for us in San Francisco. One thing was for sure, I hoped I could get approved for P-2 pay. There were no four marks to a dollar in San Francisco. I told Belinda that I would have over forty days of leave coming. I thought tomorrow morning I would drive to the hospital early and talk with my Army nurse friends and see what they could tell me about the Presidio.

I found two of the old gang. Boy, everybody including me had or was about to leave Germany. Okay, Nurse Sally had a nurse buddy stationed at Letterman, and she would send an overseas wire and get the information I needed.

Well, I would spend the whole day asking the "new" top sergeant for help pulling out all those heavy steel crates and teach Jerry all he had to know! Next week he would be driving my old truck. The only way I could ever fall in love with that truck was to have a heater in it. Seriously, that old GMC two-and-a-half-ton truck never ever had a problem. You can't believe what the standards of vehicle maintenance are in the military. My friend Bill taught me a lot,

He said, "There is no such thing as a vehicle not being ready. In case of war, everything has to be ready!"

I got my shipping papers on my car, but I found out that the hotel and the train ride were going to be out of our budget. Belinda said not to worry, She would get Fraulien Lora (she had a cute little Bug) and they would have fun going swimming or whatever. I said I would miss them on this trip, a 500-mile trek. I told my Frau that I would be back late Sunday evening if everything went well.

Belinda woke up early with me on Saturday, and prepared enough of food and coffee for the ride. Always tough saying, goodbye to my gal.

She said to me, "Don't forget your prayers, and is your angel with you?"

I said, "Yup, indeed, Just one more kiss."

"Ooh Raymond, how many is that already?" Then she pushed me out the door! By the time I got down the stairwell, I would bet you she already had a book in her hand!

I was so thankful I was not making this trip in the winter months. The weather was beautiful. As for this car of mine, I hope it had another three thousand miles left in it. I needed to get us to San Francisco, and then I would trade it in. I also realized that it was going to be tough without a vehicle while I still had over three weeks to go. (I sure wished Harry and Gif were still there.)

The ride up was beautiful. It was too late for me to drop off my car. I asked the guard at the gate if he knew where I could park safely, and go to sleep. He said there was a campsite about five miles away. He drew me a little map, and off I went. That was a very interesting evening, all the European campers asking me all kinds of questions. That was okay, because it only cost me twenty-five marks, and I had an indoor bathroom and shower, and of course it was definitely co-ed. (Totally normal in Europe, when on the highways.)

Well, I said goodbye to my Monza, and told it not to get rusty crossing the ocean. I grabbed my bag and a taxi, and off to the train station. We sure made a lot of stops in the major burgs, but we pulled into to Wurzburg about 2200 hours. At the military desk, I was going to call up the MASH for a ride, but the MP said, "Look there are two us here, I'll give you a ride."

"Thank you very much!"

Fifteen minutes later I was knocking on Frau Belinda's door.

"Who is it?"

I said, "It's me, and I hate to interrupt your reading!"

Yes, she was reading, but that was Belinda. I was so tired, I went right to bed.

About the time of my head hitting the pillow, Belinda said, "Two of our neighbors work at the Kaserne, and will be glad to give you a ride."

Okay, great. "How are the boys?"

"Very good," she said.

Glad I knew these neighbors, from eating meals with them. This one was working for the Signal Corp, and I would be riding in with him until we left. Great! I made roll call just in time, and Jerry and the pharmacist and I made our way to the bay area. I asked Jerry if he was ready for his driving class. He said Yup! We proceeded to the motor pool chief, and off they went. I spent that time working with the pharmacist, and going over his inventory. Lots of pills and medicine. I asked him to open the drug containers and we checked out the whiskey bottles. Let me explain : All the way back to the Civil War times, all the Army field hospitals needed all the whiskey they could get, once they ran out of the anesthesia they were using. It seemed that all these years the inventory stayed with the Army, In my section, I had two bottles of old Matusalia whiskey, and four bottles of Old Crow that dated back to 1865. I also had several bottles of Jim Beam that was dated more recently. In those containers, there were some serious drugs for pain and surgery. So, I had to solve this problem before my departure, since my pharmacist was an E-5, and without being qualified with a 1911 .45 ACP, we had to get him trained quickly. I left him there in the bay, and walked over to our building to discuss the situation with the top sergeant. He said he would drive him over to the headquarters shooting range some time that week. Great, one less thing to worry about!

That day, I felt like eating at the NCO club, and I told my civilian friends who worked there that I would be leaving soon for the States, and so I said my goodbyes, knowing that I would be too busy for the next two weeks. I was sure going to miss their cooking. She said today was going to be the best schnitzel I ever had, and she was not kidding.

After lunch, I walked to the motor pool just in time to see Jerry backing the monster truck back into the bay with the motor pool sergeant guiding him. They said he did pretty good. Now he had to go to our training room and watch that long movie. Great, that meant by the end of that week, he would be qualified.

I called Belinda from the motor pool office to check on her. She was happy to know everything was going well with me, and as well for her. She told me that Nurse Sally called and had all the info about Letterman, so Belinda invited her for coffee and cake that evening. Good, I asked her if she got that letter off to her mom. Oh yeah! By the way, Belinda had been making these beautiful German cakes ever since one of the neighbors gave her the recipe when they made that NEO run to France. I guess I would write my mom that night and tell her that we would be stopping by on our way to San Francisco.

That night when I got home, Belinda said we got a post card from Harry saying that civilian life was good, and he was back working in home town hospital. We would write him when we got to the Presidio for sure. Then I got on the carpet and wrestled with the two boys, then we set up the train set, and Gregory kept knocking the locomotive off the tracks, so Phillip grabbed the locomotive and hit Gregory on the top of the head with it! (Boys will be boys.) Anyway, we had a great dinner, and I kept looking at the chocolate cake. Man, did I get a look from Belinda. I hoped Sally showed up quick!

Doorbell! Sally was happy to hear our news about going to Letterman.

She told us, "It's very hard to get housing, and it very expensive to live there." She told me that I would be coming home bone tired because of the workload.

I said, "Is there any good news?"

"Oh, Ray, it's such a beautiful city. All those exotic restaurants, the opera and baseball and that view of the Golden Gate Bridge."

I replied, "Yeah, if I will get the time and money!"

She said most of the military wives end up working to make it. I did not see a grin on Belinda's face at that moment. But now the good news: if the boys would stop fighting, we would have cake!

I finally had that talk with the major about Jerry's time at the hospital.

He asked me, "How much time does he need to complete?"

I told him, "Well, his school, OJT and eleven months at Valley Forge leaves him with about eight months or less."

"Tell him we can work that out."

"Very good, I am done here."

That was it. Belinda couldn't wait for her mom's cooking, and I couldn't wait to get to a Bob's Big Boy and a good seafood restaurant in San Francisco. (If my wife got a job…)

Well, we spent the remainder of our time getting ready for the packers and movers. It was hard saying all our goodbyes to our civilian friends, especially the Bicke family, including Frauline Lora. They asked Belinda who was going to take her place at the Randensacker Hofbrau? I asked a favor of Hans to drive me down to the Randensacker police station. We walked in, and there was the tall officer at the desk. He recognized me right off and greeted me with a good handshake.

"Guten Tag, Hern Gi_____, Vas das lost? Please sit down."

"I am glad we are back to English."

"Is everything okay?" he asked.

"Sir, please don't worry, everything is fine. I am leaving for the States very soon, and I just wanted to express to you one more time about my deepest gratitude in respect to how you treated my wife and me, plus our friends that sad night."

He quickly asked, "How are your friends doing now?" I brought him up to date on their status. "Ya good sir, may God bless you and your family, and please have a good trip to the States."

I said, "May God bless you, sir. Auf wiederhoren."

On the way back, Hans said, "Ray, my wife would cut off a finger to know this story."

"Well, Hans, let's just say that your old friend's wife had two different names and probably danced with Hitler!"

"Yaar, I think so. That's worse than dancing with the Devil."

Amen.

# CHAPTER 31

M y pharmacist told me that he had borrowed his friend's car and insisted on giving my family a ride to the Frankfurt Airport. I said that we were very grateful. I asked him how he was going to like being a section chief.

He said, "Nobody is going to give me a hard time, I got the loaded .45."

I said, "Please be careful with that responsibility."

He said, "I know, Sarge, I was just joking about that."

I said, "Good. Watch out, that bottle of old Metusalia is probably worth more than a year's paycheck."

It was not a pleasant ride home in the airplane, not just for us, but all the rest of the passengers, Even though the doctors gave the four of us a bill of good health on our exit physical, Gregory developed a severe earache from the cabin pressure, and I know we were above 35,000 feet. We tried warm towels and everything else. The flight attendants were just making every effort. He finally stopped when we hit the runway in New York. You should have seen the look we got from the other passengers. That was over eleven hours of "Why did you take this flight?"

Belinda asked me, "Why didn't you sleep like I did?" Can you believe my dear wife? You do remember that I already told you nothing stopped her from sleeping and reading!

I finally found a military info desk and found out that there would not be a bus to the port until tomorrow morning.

He suggested the taxi. I came back and told Belinda the news, and told her we might run low on travel funds for the trip west.

She said, "Honey, you are still taking us to Rhode Island to meet your family, right?"

I said, "Of course, Sweetie."

"Okay, if things look bad for us at that time, you can get help from all these famous Italian uncles you have been telling me about all these past three years! So let's grab a taxi. Give me your uncle's number, and I will call him and tell him we have arrived as planned."

We flew in the night hours, so if I got this car by noon, I could make it to Johnston, RI, before dark. Oh my God, I just started to think, "What if the car hasn't arrived yet?"

Besides, they said that ship was to arrive last week.

"Calm down, Raymond."

Maybe I was just excited to be back at my birthplace and seeing the family I grew up with. I guess it had been at least seven years or so since I'd seen them. The important thing was that they were going to meet my beautiful wife and children. That was why I was excited! We almost left without our luggage. That would have not been good.

The taxi ride was quiet. As you can guess, everybody except me was sleeping. *Raymond, just live with this, and try to learn from Belinda.* That was what she kept telling me!

Well, we were sitting in my Monza and driving to Rhode Island, hoping to get there by 2, barring any heavy traffic. I could probably arrive there before the late evening hours. Now Belinda opened her eyes for a second, and told me, "Honey, now you can say your prayer of thanks for a safe trip back to the USA, and be sure you tell your angel."

"Honey," I said, "this is scenery you have never seen before, and you're going to sleep?"

She said, "I probably won't wake up till we get to New Mexico."

"Well," I said, "try to say a few nice words to the family, okay?"

That was why I loved her. She was just plain honest about everything.

Well, I was heading northeast, just following the coastal route up to good ole Rhode Island. I told Belinda when we got to New Haven, Connecticut, we would stop for a grinder and a frappe.

She said, "You know this area, don't you?"

"Well, I did live here in my junior year. I told you all that before."

"Raymond, who can keep up with you? Okay, you got me, what is a frappe and a grinder?"

"You will see soon, go back to sleep."

Meanwhile the kinder were still asleep. We finally got to a roadside dinner in New Haven, and now it was time to get the little ones cleaned up and fed. Belinda had a strawberry frappe and an Italian grinder, and I had a coffee frappe and an Italian grinder. The kids wanted grilled cheese and fries, and they split a large chocolate frappe. They were happy. I called up Uncle Fred and told him around 8:30 or so.

He said, "Do you remember Grandpa's house, and how to get there off the highway?"

"I sure do."

"Okay, most of us are here waiting for you guys."

I was getting excited, and I was hoping Belinda would be awake enough. Well, she had another 100 miles before I got there.

So, a couple of hours later and I woke her up again, and said, "Hey girl, you got about ten or fifteen minutes to comb the sleep out of your hair, we are almost there!"

"Raymond! You should have got me up earlier!"

"You will be fine, dear," I told her. It wasn't completely dark outside when I pulled in the driveway, It sure was good to see Grandma's house again, God rest her soul.

I could see everybody rushing out of the house. It was exciting. Uncle Fred and Uncle Guy grabbed me with a hug, and then threw me aside to introduce themselves to Belinda. She was overwhelmed!

Then my Aunt Mary said, "Let these poor guys get in the house before everybody meets them." She was my favorite.

Aunt Mary picked up Gregory, and said, "Who's this good-looking guy?"

"That's Gregory," I said.

"And who is this other good-looking guy?"

I said, "That's Phillip."

She started to walk them into the house, telling them they had cake and ice cream waiting for them. When I got past the door, there was my grandfather standing there, crying.

He grabbed me, saying in his broken English, "Raymond, Lukka you, you stilla a skinny bones."

I grabbed Belinda and he said, "My Goda, shesa a beautiful woman," and he kept hugging her!

My two sons did not understand what kind of language they were hearing. So, Aunt Mary grabbed the boys and put them at the table to start eating, and said, "Raymond, everybody is going to sit together in the living room, and you can introduce Belinda properly. There's a few missing, but you will meet them soon."

Belinda was in shock with all this Italian excitement, I could tell.

So, I started off, "Okay, Belinda, you met Uncle Fred, and here is his wife, my Aunt Evelyn, You met Uncle Guy, and here is his wife, my Aunt Theresa, Here is Uncle Lebra, his wife, my Aunt Ann. Here is my Aunt Margaret, and her husband, my Uncle Neil."

Aunt Mary kicked in again and told Belinda that tomorrow, she would meet her husband Louie, and Aunt Grace and Uncle Barney. "Aunt Rose and Uncle Noah are down in Louisiana, so you will meet everybody except them. Tomorrow, the whole gang will be at my house, because we are having a party for you guys' homecoming."

Then everybody took turns and started to ask Belinda all kinds of questions. She was truly overwhelmed. I could tell they all fell in love with her. About one hour later, Aunt Theresa spoke up and asked Belinda and me if we would like to eat something, before we had the Italian pastry.

I quickly asked, "Aunt Theresa, is that pastry from Monda's Bakery?"

She said, "How did you know that, Raymond? You left here when you were just about twelve or so."

Oh, I remembered!

Well, she served us some of Grandpa's leftover pasta and calamari. Belinda said this was delicious.

When she bit into the calamari, "What is it?"

Uncle Guy spoke up and said, "Belinda, that's squid, basted in olive oil and herbs, then lightly fried."

Wow, she almost spit it out.

Uncle Guy said, "Belinda, you don't have that in New Mexico?"

"No, Uncle Guy, we don't, and I doubt that we ever will. But I do like it."

From then on, Belinda always ordered it, if it was available.

They all enjoyed talking to Belinda, then it got late, and everybody except Grandpa and Uncle Guy and Aunt Theresa (they lived there and took care of Grandpa) said good night, and Aunt Mary said that tomorrow she was making my favorite dinner (stuffed lobster).

Everybody said, "We won't be late!"

Uncle Guy said, "Boy, Raymond, my sister doesn't make me lobster."

Aunt Mary said, "You never ask me." You had to see the look on his face. Well, Aunt Theresa put the kids in a separate bedroom, and me and Belinda in another. Uncle Guy said good night, and gave Belinda a hug and a kiss. They hit it off great. Then Aunt Theresa did the same with Belinda.

I gave Grandpa a hug, and he said, "Hey youa missa your Grandma?"

"Oh Grandpa, I sure do very much."

He said, "Mea too!" he said to me, just like when I was a child. "Go a to beda, Ramon, and saya youra prayers."

"I always do, Grandpa, and good night." I gave a hug to Aunt Theresa and told her how good it was to see her again. She and Uncle Guy (the baby brother) were about eight or nine years older than me and my brother Angelo, and they were dating at the time they used to baby sit us. I told Aunt Theresa about the time we scared them on the couch when they were kissing one night.

"Oh, Raymond, you guys were such rascals."

We laughed!

# CHAPTER 32

That morning, we were all sitting around the table enjoying Aunt Theresa's cooking. (She learned from Grandma.) Oh, and of course, I had to have a mouthwatering Sfogliatelle (please Google that). I told Belinda, later we would take a ride, and show her all the different places where I had lived.

Aunt Theresa spoke up, and said I should go to Manda's Bakery and get more stuff to take to Aunt Mary's house that night. I told her I had already planned for that. She opened one of the kitchen drawers and pulled out a $50 bill.

"Whoa!" I said. "That's too much!"

"Raymond, do your auntie a favor, get twenty sfogliatelles and put some gas in your car, and don't say nothing to Uncle Guy (he's still sleeping) because he going to give you some travel money also."

I got out of my chair and gave her a kiss and said, "Thank you."

"That's okay, we know the Army don't pay that much, and you got a long drive to San Francisco, and you're going to stop in New Mexico, and then to your mom's. I wish we could give you more."

Well, we got all cleaned up, and Belinda and the kids were ready for their Rhode Island tour. Right about that time, Uncle Guy came in.

"Good morning, everybody." He gave Belinda and the little ones a kiss. He turned to me, and said, "You tall skinny soldier, come outside for a second."

We walked out the patio door, and he handed me a C-Note.

"Uncle Guy, I can't take this!"

"Hey, it's for your family and your trip, and shut up, before I punch ya!" Then, we did a hug.

"Thanks so much, Uncle."

"Let's see what my cheap older brothers do for you, huh!"

We chuckled.

The first place I drove her and the kids was to my birthplace, 11 Octavia St., Providence. I pointed up to the second floor, and said, "There it is."

She said, "Honey, you told me it had a yard with an old wooden fence."

I said, "Wow I guess this is it, right in the front here."

"Honey, it's about six by ten feet maybe."

Then, I told her that when we were small and growing up, everything appeared bigger, right? Ooh, Raymond. Then I took her to 22 Charter St., and then to 22 Beacon St.

"Honey, these houses are so tiny."

"Well, I said, my dad built them, and my Lord, I think our house trailer had more room."

"Honey, didn't you say your grandma's house was on 22 Alden Street?" I said yes. She said, "That's unbelievable, three twenty-twos. What does that mean to you?"

I said, "About sixty-six." I got a slap on the back of my head!

We drove to Narragansett Beach, and the kids sure loved it. I had to buy those little pails and those tiny shovels, so the kids could learn how to make sandcastles from the old pro. I went to the snack bar, and came back with Coney Island hot dogs. Man, did I miss these things. Belinda and the boys agreed. I told Belinda, as kids we would come here with Grandpa at low tide, and dig for clams. They were called little necks. Grandma would cook 'em up, and make a clam sauce for her spaghetti. I never could get Belinda in all our years to eat shell food, but did she love lobster, shrimp and calamari. (You do remember when I told you we were from two different worlds?)

She said one thing right there. "Raymond, I do like all the green scenery and the beaches here in Rhode Island."

"Do you want to move here when I get out of the Army?"

"Raymond, dear, are you serious? Get me back to my desert."

Ha, I told you.

"But Honey, I am enjoying your aunts and uncles, but they seem a lot different from your Mom."

I said, "Wait till you meet the older sister, Aunt Grace tonight."

Then I drove down Manton Ave. and walked in Monda's Bakery with my family, and guess who I saw? It was Mrs. Monda, looking just a little older, but just as beautiful as I remembered.

"Raymond, your Aunt Theresa called earlier. Give me a hug and introduce me."

Wow, after that, she wanted to know how my mom was doing. We sat and talked. By that time, her daughter recognized me. She had white powder all over her. Yes, we were the same age. She brought over a whole tray of goodies for us at the table. What a strange feeling I got just then. It seemed like I never left, but it had been about eleven years ago.

We got back to Grandpa's around 4 or so. Uncle Guy waved us into the yard. As soon as we got out, he gave Belinda a good hug and picked up the kids, and asked, "You guys going to be tall and skinny like your dad?"

If Uncle Guy could see me today, he would just say tall. He was asking me about the condition of my car. I filled him in on all the negatives.

He said, "Raymond, tomorrow morning, let's take it to Fred's car lot. (My Uncle Fred owned several car lots in Rhode Island) and have his chief mechanic look at it."

"Okay, Uncle. Let's get this pastry in the house."

"Yeah," he said, "I'll take that!"

He sure loved his pastry, and his Italian dishes. You can figure out why he called me skinny. Then we got into our room.

Belinda said, "Honey, I hope we are not eating early, because we had hot dogs and all that pastry. I am so full."

I said, "That's okay, honey, I'll eat your lobster tonight."

"Don't you dare, until I try it first."

"Honey, once you bite into her lobster dinner, you will fight to the death to guard it!"

"Oooh, can't wait," she said.

I walked out and asked Aunt Theresa what time would we be going to Aunt Mary's. She informed me Uncle Louie got home kind of late, because he had to make sure he got all three stores closed.

I said, "I thought he only owned one liquor store."

"Oh, Raymond, now he owns three."

I went into the kids' room, and they were out. Now, I was bringing Belinda up on all the news.

She said, "Raymond, if you and your brother stayed here, I can only imagine how much money you would have in your pockets."

I replied, "Yes, Honey, but I would have never met you."

"That's a good point, Raymond."

We both started to laugh.

We got to Aunt Mary's about 7:30, and Aunt Mary sat down Grandpa in the end chair (given his patriarchal position) of this long dining room table. The rest of us were still standing, when Uncle Louie walked up to Belinda and said, "Ah, you must be Belinda, I knew my nephew would marry a beauty!"

Belinda said to him that was very kind. She said, "It's so nice to meet all of Ray's family, because Ray is always saying nice things about you."

"He'd better," said Uncle Louie, and then he gave me a hug.

At that point, he walked over to the other table where the kids and my little cousins were sitting and talked to them. Okay, in walked Aunt Grace and Uncle Barney. Aunt Mary introduced Belinda to them. Uncle Barney said something nice to my wife, and right away, Aunt Grace yells out, "Belinda, don't pay any attention to him, he's Irish."

I bent over to Belinda and said, "See, that's Mom's older sister." So, here we were, Uncle Fred and Aunt Evelyn, Uncle Guy and Aunt Theresa, Aunt Margaret and Uncle Neil, Aunt Grace and Uncle Barney, Aunt Mary and Uncle Louie, Uncle Lebra and Aunt Ann. My Aunt Mary sat Uncle Louie at the other (patriarchal) end. She put me and Belinda close to her and Uncle Louie.

She was the only one standing when she said, "Belinda, let me tell you who is missing. Uncle John, and Mildred, and Aunt Rose and Noah, and my sister Pauline and Tony."

Then Uncle Guy said, "Okay, we got enough already, plus the Irish."

Uncle Barney spoke up and said, "Yeah, you got me, and Neil, and Evelyn!"

Uncle Guy said, "Just remember, you are outnumbered, so let's eat."

Aunt Mary said, "Raymond, do you want to say grace?"

I said, "Sure! Dear Lord, bless us, and this meal we are about to eat, and the hands that prepared it. Lord, we thank You for this family gathering. Amen!"

Aunt Mary said, "Okay, here we go!

My cousins Albert and Lucille helped serving. First came a bowl of pasta fazool (Google it). After that came a small bowl of lobster bisque (oh yummy), then baskets of Monda's fresh Italian bread, and a small salad, then the main event, Aunt Mary's famous stuffed lobster. (You can Google that, but Aunt Mary had her own style.)

Uncle Guy said, "Mary, do you have another one?"

Mary said, "I knew you would ask. Albert."

"Mom, I got it already."

Meanwhile, Aunt Grace was the only one at the table drilling Belinda for her whole life story, with questions like, "Are you sure you're not Italian? You look Italian to me."

Uncle Barney said, "Belinda, I got to live with her!"

There were some chuckles. Uncle Neil, who was a Navy jet pilot, asked me about my military life and so forth.

Uncle Fred made an announcement. "Let me know who can come to our house tomorrow night, because we are going to have — wait a minute. Belinda, do you like steak?"

"Uncle Fred, sure do!"

"Okay, it's settled. Raymond, your cousins will be there."

"Great Uncle, thank you. Well, Uncle Fred, I got a 3,000-plus mile trip ahead of me, not to mention our families to visit, and I got only twenty-eight days of leave left."

"You will be fine, Raymond. We will go to an early Mass Sunday, and you will be on your way."

"But tomorrow is Saturday."

"Bring your car to the Atwood lot about 8AM. Let Belinda and the kids sleep late. Just be there."

Belinda sure liked that sleep part, and I was sure Uncle Fred's mechanic would do a good job on the car. It took us a half hour for everybody to say good night.

"Aunt Mary, and Uncle Louie, it was a fantastic dinner and evening, and to you Aunt, for all that delicious cooking. We love ya a bunch and thanks."

"Don't worry, my dear, I'll relax at my brother Fred's. Tomorrow night. Raymond, you get the kids in the car, I am going to borrow your wife for a couple of minutes."

"Okay, kids, give Auntie and Uncle a kiss."

She finally came out, and I asked what all that was about.

"Your aunt told me to open my purse, and I was puzzled. She said that this envelope was from her and Uncle Louie for our wedding present long overdue."

So, off to Grandpa's house. It was very late. Uncle Guy said I ought to come and visit more often.

I said, "Why?"

"Hey, thanks to you and Belinda, I got lobster tonight and I get steak tomorrow."

"All right, Uncle."

We all said goodnight and I gave Grandpa a kiss. The kids fell asleep so fast.

I said to my honey, "Before I say good night, let's see what's in that envelope. Holy Cow, $300." That was a lot of money in 1965. I said to Belinda, "I know that money is yours, so you don't have to hide it."

"Good night, Raymond."

Aunt Mary was quite a woman. In the future years of my business travels, she was always the first one I would visit.

So, when I got up on this fine Saturday morning, Belinda, Phillip and Greg and everybody was still sleeping. There was Uncle Guy reading the paper.

He said, "It's almost 8, we will grab coffee and doughnuts at Fred's, let's go."

"Hey, I didn't know you would be coming with me. Glad to have your company."

"You are going to be more glad later."

"What?"

"Never mind, nephew, just drive."

We got there and I greeted Uncle Fred, and there was one of his partners, Mr. Brosco.

He said, "Ray, I have not seen you since you and your dad left for California. I remember he was in a rush to leave."

I said, "You ought to see how fast he drove us there!"

"Good to see you, Ray. I got to run. See ya, Fred!"

I looked over Uncle Fred's shoulder, and there was one of his workers taking all my stuff out of my car, and putting it in the trunk of this beautiful black Cadillac. and now he was taking paperwork out of my glove compartment. Uncle Guy was standing there giggling, and told me to just relax.

Uncle Fred said, "Let's go in the office and have some coffee and doughnuts, and I'll tell you all about it. My brother Guy didn't tell you anything?"

I said, "No, except that you were going to have your mechanic work it over."

He said, "Good. Grab your coffee and a doughnut, and I will be right back." He walked to his other lot right across the street. He came back with these papers in his hand, and he said, "What's Belinda 's middle initial?"

I said, "M."

"Okay, you sign here, and here, and can you afford $50 per month for thirty-six payments?"

"Yeah, Uncle Fred, but—"

"Nephew," he spoke right up "that little Monza was great for driving in Europe, but I can't see you, the wife and kids cramped up for 3,000 miles. How in the hell did you get those suitcases in there? Look I sold that car brand new to one of my friends for a decent price. He gives me cash, and now he's laid up sick and can't drive, and his wife had her son drive it back here last week. It is a 1964 near new Fleetwood with AC and everything else on it, and it's only got 1,000 miles on it. I only got about 2,500 tied up in it, and it's yours for thirty-six months at $50 per month."

"Wow, Uncle, I don't know what to say, except that I am in shock."

"Don't worry, your Uncle Guy is going to make up the difference."

Uncle Guy jumped up and said, "Blankety blank, hey, I am only an accountant."

Uncle Fred said, "Relax, you tightwad, just joking. But, you're buying the steaks tonight."

"Whaaat!" he screamed.

Uncle Fred said, "Raymond, drive him home."

"Yes, Uncle Fred, see you tonight." Yes, a big hug! "Let's go, Uncle, wipe your feet."

Wow, what a pleasant trip this was going to be.

Uncle Guy said, "I told you my brothers are cheap. He should have giving it to you!"

Oh, oh. "Uncle Guy, I was so nervous, I left my doughnuts and coffee untouched."

"Do not worry, Nephew, I stole some sfogliatelles from Mary's last night."

"Wow, and Aunt Theresa calls me a rascal." I looked up at the sun visor, and there was an envelope with my name on it. "Hey, Uncle, open this up."

Uncle Guy screams out, "That no good cheap brother of mine!"

"Oh my God, Uncle, that's $300."

He said, "I told you he was cheap."

"Wow, Uncle Guy, you are too much!" What a day, Lord, thank You, thank You!

As you can see about my Uncle Guy, he had a great sense of humor, and he was very proud of his older brothers. He served in the Navy during the Korean War. After the war, he enrolled at Brown University, and graduated as an accountant.

Belinda was really not a person who went crazy about cars, as you guys have guessed by now. Well, she walked around this one about three times, and kept trying all the seats out.

She said, "Honey, Phillip and Greg can sit up front with you, while I sleep back here."

I said, "Well, Honey, the trunk is a lot bigger."

"Raymond!" She said, "When we get to the desert, we just have to push this button?"

"Yup," I said. "That's your air conditioning."

She said, "Honey, from all the news you told me, we have more than enough money to cover our trip." Yes again. She then said, "Let me get the kids, and you will take us for a ride."

"Yes," again.

Phillip said, "Daddy, this is so big," and I said, "Yes. Now you and your brother can stop fighting for more space!"

Time would tell!

Well, off we went to Uncle Fred's and Aunt Evelyn. I told my children she was great, when my brother and I were growing up, she spent a lot of time with us, taking us to the swimming ponds, summer trips to the shoreline and all sorts of fun. The best remembrance I have of her was when she would get us dressed for Halloween, and walked us over to all the big estates or mansions, whatever. (She knew all these people, because of Uncle Fred's business.) She never wore a costume, because she wanted to be recognized. She would ring the doorbell.

"Oh! Hello Evelyn, who are these guys?"

"These are my nephews, and they are here to acquire funds for their college tuition."

"Trick or treat."

Sometimes, we would get a $1 bill, and a $5 bill, and every once in a while we got a $10. (She used to tell us, "Just stick with the Irish kids.")

Belinda was impressed with the size of the house. She thought Uncle Louie's was big, now this one! Well anyway, Uncle Fred said he got a lot of cancellation calls. So, the group would be smaller than late night.

There was Uncle Guy (of course) and Aunt Theresa, Uncle Louie and Aunt Mary, us and the children and my cousins. Everybody about that time heard about my new car, and I told them after church tomorrow, we would be on the highway. It was easy packing today with all that room in the trunk. My younger cousins were taking good care of Phillip and Gregory playing in the big game room they had.

Aunt Evelyn said to Belinda, "I heard last night that you love steak. But look what I made for appetizers." She handed Belinda her homemade crab cakes and her dipping sauce. Belinda bit into it, and her face lit up with a big smile. Aunt Evelyn was pleased when Belinda asked her for the recipe.

Then we all moved over to the big table. Uncle asked all of us how we wanted the steaks. He already started cooking them on his outside patio. Aunt Evelyn started to serve up a delicious salad. Everything was delicious.

After the main course was finished, Aunt Evelyn said to Belinda, "Are you ready for my homemade Irish desert, sweetie?"

"I sure am, what is it?"

"Well, we have two. We have my apple tart, and my lemon curd sponge cake."

Uncle Guy spoke up and said, "Belinda, tell my sister-in-law you don't eat desert, and I can get an extra portion."

We all had a laugh, and Belinda spoke up and said, "That is not going to work, Uncle Guy!"

What is worth noticing here is that my Aunt Evelyn and Aunt Mary both did a super job making her feel welcomed into the family, and I thought that was just great!

I walked over to the game room and checked on the boys and my cousins, and they were just starting on that fantastic desert. I knew my boys were getting spoiled here in Rhode Island. When I got back in the room, I asked Aunt Mary where Belinda was. She suggested we go catch up, because Belinda was getting a tour of Uncle Fred's new house. so, we found them in the master bedroom, and there was Aunt Evelyn showing Belinda all these fur coats and jewelry and other stuff.

She saw me coming in the room and said, "Raymond, I am trying to tell your wife here to pick out something for a gift, and she is fighting me."

"My dear Aunt Evelyn, you got to understand that she is more than grateful for your generosity, but she is a pants and sweatshirt girl from the get go!"

"Yeah, Ray, but look how she is dressed now and so pretty."

Then I said, "Of course we dress nice for social occasions and such. But when she gets home, it's right back to the sweatshirts."

"Okay, Raymond, make her pick out some earrings."

I looked at Belinda, and said, "Make Aunt Evelyn happy, Honey."

It took a while, but she finally picked out some beautiful earrings, and gave a big hug to Aunt Evelyn. Belinda was walking out of the bedroom when she told Aunt Evelyn how pretty the wall to wall drapes were. She informed Belinda that was a twenty-five-foot window. Then she pushed a button on the wall, and the drapes opened up to expose the beautiful view of all the hills with lights. Nice!

It was my guess that my family didn't go to Sunday Mass that early, so it was very nice that they joined us Sunday morning at St Ann's 8AM Mass. We were already packed, and I could not wait to get this Caddy on the road. However, my plans got changed when Aunt Mary spoke up and Invited us for breakfast, at a nearby restaurant.

# CHAPTER 33

Well, it sure was tough with all the goodbyes. We were all tired from waking up early, and I could see Belinda's eyes shutting down already. I didn't see any heads in the rearview, so the boys and Mom would wake up soon, and they would ask, "Are we there yet?" This was a good time for me to re-visit the prayers of thanks I said in church this morning. Here we were with a new car, and plenty of travel money. Just try to drive in a luxury sedan these days on $50/month payments.

Thank You, Lord, and now I ask for Your protection on this long journey.

I wanted to see if we could make it to the Pennsylvania Turnpike on this day. The summer weather was great and the skies were all clear. I was amazed, after driving that Monza for so long, I forgot what they call a smooth ride. Well, this was it.

Then Belinda said, "Happy birthday, Honey. Give Daddy your cards."

"Whoa, Belinda."

"Yes, Honey, you thought we forgot."

"No, no, Sweetheart, I forgot, with all this excitement going on."

"Honey, no one forgets their own birthday."

"Belinda, that's what I thought. Okay, everybody, please read the cards while I drive. Well, Sweetheart, what did you get me?"

She said, "Honey, you are driving it."

"Wow! Well, it's almost noon, everybody except me take a nap."

While they were snoozing away, I kept telling myself that nobody forgets their own birthday. Well, about two hours after, they were waking up, and Belinda did say, "Are we there yet?"

I said, "Belinda, almost. We will be at your mom and dad's in about 1,700 miles."

"Oh good," she said.

By day's end, I made it to Ohio, got a motel, and I too caught some good sleep.

Two-and-a-half days later, we were sitting in her mom's kitchen, thanking the Lord for a safe trip. Everybody was soaking up all our adventures. Her mom and dad just couldn't believe Belinda's story about our friend, Frau Brummer.

"Oh, my Belinda, were you scared?" Mom asked.

"No Mom, just very sad."

I noticed Jane had grown up, already fourteen and looking pretty like her sisters. Her bother, Firpo had already moved to California. He moved in with his uncle, and got a good job in the furniture business. Fina and Sal were doing good. Brother Guy was in the Marine Corps. We didn't see him, he was stationed at Barstow at that time. Jeepy was a senior, and Ricks was a freshman at the time. Ramona and her family were off visiting California. Her brother, Luper, and his wife came for a visit. Our boys were having fun with their cousins. It was a great homecoming. We stayed as long as time would allow (about four days).

We told everybody we would come home for a visit next summer for sure. It was tough for Belinda to say goodbye again to her mom and dad. It was even tough for me. They were such good people. I also would miss them very much.

Two days later, we pulled into my mom and dad's new house in Reseda, California. Yes, I made sure I called from Arizona to be sure I would not show up too early or too late. Well, let's put it this way. They just met my children for the first time, and Mom was extremely nervous while the kids were running around the house. Belinda and I were also getting nervous. They had all this plastic covering the furniture, but Dad was wiping the kids' fingerprints off the glass coffee table, while we were talking. I was surprised about seeing my baby brother, very tall and lanky for his age. I think he was about eight at the time. Guess what? Not one question about the past several years or whatever.

I said, "Okay, Mom and Dad, we will be back in the morning, I am going to check into a motel." I told Mom that we were all very tired from all this traveling, and we would call them in the morning.

When we got into the motel, I told Belinda that I really felt super tired, and I was going to bed.

She said, "You don't look normal. As a matter go fact, your skin has a little tint of yellow to it."

"Okay, Honey. See if you can get the kids to lay down, I know we are all tired."

Belinda later told me they slept for about three hours, and I slept about five, and it would be too late to call my mom. She said I was still a little on the jaundiced side. I said that I still felt very tired. We then we went out to dinner.

I called about 9AM, Mom told me we were all going to meet at Uncle Angelo's for a big get-together.at about noon. I told Belinda that I expected that, because of our kids. Her house was too small. Belinda surely agreed! Well, we had Angelo and Sally and their little ones, that was great to have some playmates for Phillip and Greg. That, of course, was the first time they met their cousins. My Aunt Fanny (Uncle Angelo's wife) cooked up a storm. It was all so delicious. Uncle Frank and Aunt Esther were there with my cousins also. So, all in all, we had a pretty good day, Naturally my car caught all kinds of attention, and Mom kept reminding me to make sure I didn't make any late payments to her brother Fred. Yeah, Mom, sure!

Did anyone want to hear about our time across the ocean? (Not really.) I think my sister-in-law, Sally, did show some enthusiasm (which was appreciated). I knew I was not feeling good, I just felt off kilter, so I told everybody that we would see them tomorrow some time.

On the way back to the motel, Belinda said, "Honey, no one made any plans for tomorrow."

I said, "They will figure it out over the phone tonight. We know Mom's little glass house is way too small, and they have a small yard, it will be Uncle Angelo's or Uncle Frank's."

I asked the kids if they wanted to go swimming at the motel pool, and the reply came back in the form of a scream, "Yes,

Daddy!" They loved the water. My sweet Belinda told me to go to bed, and she would swim with the guys, and I said, "Love you and thank you."

She replied, "I bet you say that to all your wives."

"Just the pretty ones."

Okay, this was the "Last Round-up" after today, visiting everybody, and whatever. Maybe a little bocci ball. Uncle Frank had a big back yard with nice grass. I finally got caught up with my brother Angelo and his family (he's the one they called Tony in high school). He had a good job working at Lockheed and a nice home in Canoga Park. After lunch, I noticed the bocci balls laying there on the grass, so, I picked up two and just then, I found out they felt pretty heavy. Belinda came over and asked me if I was okay, and I told her that there was something weird going on with me. She told that I was more jaundiced looking. My Aunt Esther looked at me (she was a practical nurse) and asked if I ever had this before, which I answered no! Well, by that time everybody was involved in my diagnosis. I informed Mom and Dad that I was due in San Francisco in a couple of days anyway, and there would be a whole bunch of doctors up there to take care of me. So, I told all the family that Belinda and my gang would be leaving tomorrow morning, and guess what my dad said?

"Gee, Raymond, we barely had time to talk."

So, once again, we all said the goodbyes. My brother Angelo said they had never seen San Francisco before, and would be coming up for a visit, before my discharge. So, I told him he had about twenty months to make it happen.

I asked Belinda to drive us back to the hotel. She did, by the way, share in the driving on this trip. The next morning we checked out, and we were headed for the Coastal Highway #1, a little slower, but a lot more scenery.

I told my sweetie I was not up to driving. I did not have any energy at all. But I said if she thought she would go fast, I would wake up if I was asleep.

"Sure, Raymond, you know I never speed."

I said, "That's like St. Patrick being Italian."

We made a pit stop in Santa Barbara. Cute little coastal town. Had a nice little lunch, and back on the highway, Looking out the corner of my eye, I could see that Belinda was worried about me. She extended her hand out to me and just shook my hand up and down and said, "You better be okay Raymond. I am not used to seeing you so quiet and docile!"

I said, "I love you, and put both hands back on the wheel! When we get to Letterman, I am sure they will get involved in my diagnosis."

Belinda at that time told the children, "Let's all be quiet, so Daddy can sleep."

I woke up in a rested mood, and I told Belinda that I should drive. She sure looked tired! I told everybody that it was only another hour or so that we would be in Monterey, and could they wait until then for food and restroom breaks? Everybody was good to go.

I said to my wife, "Of all the roads I've been on, this is the most beautiful!" and she quickly agreed. I started to tell Belinda, that when I was in boot camp, and got our first weekend pass, all the rich guys went to Monterey, and us poor folk went towards Salinas.

She asked, "Which way are we going?"

I said, "I put you in charge of our travel funds, how are we holding up?"

"Honey, we are okay,"

"Then here is my plan. We will play around Monterey and take in the sights, then we will have late dinner, and then we will go to Salinas and get a not-so-expensive motel, and then to the Presidio."

The kids screamed out, "Yea!"

Right about that time, we were in awe of the scenery passing Big Sur. I told the gang that some time the future we would be coming back to this beautiful area. (In my head I was praying to the good Lord that this jaundice was not going to be a big deal.)

Belinda and the boys had fun walking up and down at the beach. It was a beautiful August day, and Monterey was certainly beautiful. I was too tired, and I stayed in the car watching my wife and children with such delight, and thinking, "All this by the grace of God!"

Well, we pulled into Salinas kind of late. Belinda told me that tomorrow was a big day, and she put me to bed. I was lying there, looking at my fingers. They were so yellow.

Belinda caught me, and said, "Raymond, did you forget that your assigned angel will get us through all this?" And we all prayed together for a better tomorrow.

I was thinking when I awoke the next morning, what would happen if this thing really was coming from a bad liver? From all my training, I learned such things, but I didn't want to discuss this with my Belinda, because I knew if she had this problem, she would keep a positive attitude, until all the facts were in! So, I got dressed in my uniform, get breakfast for everybody, and made the short trip to the Letterman Hospital.

# CHAPTER 34

San Francisco

We arrived at the Presidio gates around noon, only to find a large crowd of hippies screaming and chanting their protest against the Vietnam War. Yes, one guy threw a rock, and busted my left mirror. That could have been my face! All this idiot cared about was that I was in uniform. We all talk about prejudice, and this idiot who threw the rock had not a clue as to why my family and I were driving in the gate. On top of all that, I knew he was not going to pay for the damages on my car. (Don't get me started on this subject.)

At the second gate, the MPs read my orders and directed me to the medical company building, and I found myself standing in front of a colonel (MD) with my orders and pointing at the chair. I gladly sat down. I was still shaken up about the incident. He asked me if my family traveled with me, and I said yes, and they were sitting in the vehicle. He then said that I appeared to be pretty nervous, and asked what was wrong.

I explained what happened at the gate, and that I was not feeling good. He asked me to stand up and lean toward him. He looked into my eyes, and then pinched my fingers.

He said, "Soldier, as bad as I need you in Radiology, you're not going there until we get this figured out."

I said, "Sir, what about my family?"

He called in the secretary and told her to contact the Presidio guest quarters and see if they could fit a family of four. "You are going straight to the ward as soon as we get through all this paper-work." He sent out the sergeant to get my family in the building. He then told the sergeant when he returned to get a Polaroid camera and take a picture of my damages and give it to the MPs for record. (Go back to the early chapter where I mentioned how many good officers I would meet. Well, here was another one!)

My family and I were sitting in this big room, and the kids wanted to know why Mommy and I were crying. We told them that everything was going to be all right, and make sure to say their prayers. Belinda said she was all confused, because she was going to need to get her ID cards and such, and she knew that the children couldn't visit the wards in the hospital. She asked the secretary where were the pay phones.

She said, "You just sit at this desk," and asked Belinda for the phone number. She put in her code and dialed the number and passed the phone over to my wife.

I heard her say the name, "Firpo." When she came back to the couch, she said, "Honey, don't worry about us, because my brother is on his way. He is leaving Norwalk right now, and I told him to just come straight to the hospital."

"Belinda," I said, 'your brother is just going to drop everything, and drive 400 miles? Wow, Belinda, that is such good news. I won't have to worry about you and the kids."

(Do you remember in that chapter where I told you about what kind of family this was!)

Belinda said, "Knowing him, he will drive straight through."

The secretary said, "If that's the case, he might be here by midnight."

I asked my angel to jump in the car with him. (If he had time.)

The Colonel came over and told Belinda to follow him into his office. I told the kids that we would play a game of "Who's who." She was gone a good half hour. She sat down and told me that I was in good hands. The doctor said that because of my age, and the fact that it just sprang up, the odds were my side. He told her that they found some temporary quarters for her (the guest quarters were all filled) and it just might end up being our permanent living quarters. It seemed that during World War II, this building was used as a communications center, and after the war was over, it was converted into a house. He came over to me, and requested to get out of the car any items that I would need for my hospital stay

He sat down again, and informed us that he called military housing, and they were on their way to this house with furniture, and they would turn on all the utilities. He told Belinda that we would not need air conditioning, because this was the Bay area, but at night we would be glad to have a heater. "And by the way," he said, "I found out there is a washer and dryer there."

I told him, "This is totally past any expectations of what it would be like at my new assignment here, and you are so kind to get involved in this. I have been in the Army long enough to know that full bird colonels don't get involved in these situations."

He replied that he was a doctor first, and he was happy to be involved.

I said, "Sir, I can imagine how busy you must be with all of your medical staff in receiving all of the American casualties from Vietnam."

He looked straight at Belinda, and said, "When we get this x-ray tech on his feet, he is going to wish he was born with an extra set of legs, What we need is a bigger hospital!"

Belinda said she would go to the car and get my stuff. The Colonel said that he saw us pull up earlier, and wanted to know how an E-5 (P-1) could afford a car like that.

I said, "Sir, you are right about that, My uncle in Rhode Island is in the car business, and made me an affordable deal."

He said, "I have some friends that reside in Rhode Island. If I go back there, I would like to meet your uncle."

"Sir, that can be arranged for sure!"

He said, "I hope you got good insurance on that car, because that mirror is all electric."

"I think I am good, sir."

"Specialist, let's get you to the ward before the shift changes. And Belinda, my family and I live about fifty yards from your old comm center, so you are going to follow me in your car, and you will see how easy it is to come right down from the hill, and park your car right where it is now, and just walk across the street into the hospital. When you get all done getting settled, you can visit Ray in the ward, and wait for your brother there. I will call the ward nurse later this evening, and we will have the children probably take a nap in the ward visiting room if it's empty. Now, let's get up to the house. I know where they put the keys."

I turned around to see this corpsman standing next to me with a wheelchair. I called Phillip and Gregory over, and I said, "I know you two are confused. Everything is going to be all right, Please take good care of Mommy while Daddy is in the hospital, and tonight pray hard to Jesus for me to get better, okay? It's hug time. Belinda, remember there is a broken mirror on the driver's side, and I'll see you this evening. Please don't rush yourself. I will be in the ward. They will tell you at the front desk, and just think, you are going to have your brother to watch over you and the boys. Sir," I said, "will I be seeing you soon?"

"Of course. I am a doctor, and I do make patient calls with the staff."

Belinda and I could not let go of each other.

The Colonel said, "Break it up, newlyweds, you are going to see him tonight."

We waved, and off I went for a ride to the hospital I was supposed to work in. Oh, Lord, I prayed! I knew what Belinda would say to me: "Raymond, no negative thoughts, and pray!"

By 5PM they gave me a very light dinner (It was so light, I wouldn't have to brush my teeth). The night nurse told me the assigned physician would give me a work-up tomorrow morning. Okay.

Poor Belinda. I thought about her walking into a cold house and doing all that stuff to get settled. I wish I was there with her! Well, the nurse was right, it was time for some sleep.

I woke up knowing somebody was holding my hand. I was very groggy. Then, I knew it was Belinda.

I heard another voice saying to me, "My sister said that you are supposed to be working at this hospital, not sleeping in it!"

Yes, that was Firpo, and I told him how glad I was to see him, and how grateful I was for his support and love. His reply: "Hey, Bro, that's what family is all about. I am going to take them up to this castle, as Belinda calls it, and see if we can somewhat get settled, and I'll see you back here in the morning."

That was when Belinda said, "Only you, Raymond!"

I said, "What do you mean, Honey?"

She replied, "Raymond, this place has twenty-foot ceilings, and some of the rooms are big enough to park your Cadillac in, and here is the best part, we are right across the street from the entrance of the Golden Gate Bridge. How come nothing is ever normal with you, Honey," she said as she squeezed my hand.

I told her, "I thought it was normal to fall in love with you."

"Oooh, Raymond!"

*NOTE: The last time I was there was twenty years ago, and that old comm center was still there. The old hospital and all the 19th century buildings are marked with historical markers. When you go up that Presidio Road looking to get on the bridge, look to the last building on your left, just before you turn on the bridge.*

The following morning (early), there were two medics standing next to my bed. I said good morning, they replied in same. They happened to be the chief, and the assistant chief of radiology (Sergeant 1st class, E-7, and Staff Sergeant, E-6). They began by telling me that they were informed that their new tech they were waiting for was taking a nap in one of the wards. Well, I started the story, and they said they were looking forward to my recovery, and they would check on me every day. I wished at that point I would know what it was that I would be recovering from!

Then came another very light breakfast meal.

The nurse said, "Sorry, we have to get your diagnosis before we figure out what to feed you."

Just about that time, there was a captain looking at me. "Hello, I am Dr. Anderson. Let's get to work here." He did all the usual touching and probing. He stuck two fingers into my liver and asked me if that was painful, or just uncomfortable. I replied with the latter. So, now he was writing all kinds of stuff in my medical records and telling the nurse about all kinds of blood tests, urine, and all. He then said that he preferred a specialist to look at me this afternoon, after all that lab work.

I said, "You mean an endocrinologist?"

"Oh yes, and are you a medical person?"

Then I explained.

"Okay, then, I will see after all the test results."

Here came a wheelchair, and off to the lab. I couldn't believe all the blood they wanted, not to mention other things you readers don't want to hear about! On the way back, I asked the Red Cross lady who was pushing my wheelchair if she would be nice enough to show me Radiology. Okay, she said. We made a few turns and there we were.

I said, "Look at all the beds and stretchers in the waiting area!"

She said most of the patients they got there were in stretchers or Stryker frame beds. I started to think about what the Colonel told Belinda yesterday.

When I got back, my nurse asked me how it was that I happened to be admitted by the hospital's chief medical officer, so I explained.

She then said, "Oh good, you are not a VIP then!"

I said, "You mean no special privileges now?"

"Lay back and get some sleep, soldier!"

Never in my whole life could I fall asleep this fast. When I awoke, there were Belinda and Firpo standing aside my bed. I told Belinda not to worry about me, I wanted to hear all the details on this so-called cement fortress.

Right away, Firpo spoke up and said, "You know, your kids can fly model airplanes in there."

"Wow, it's that big?" I said.

Belinda told me she was glad it had a big heater, because the walls were cement. Then she proceeded to tell me about the fog horns sounding off from the bay. Then I found out about the fog, and how spooky she thought it was. I asked my brother-in-law how long he could stay, and he told me whatever it took. I asked about his job, and his family, how could they spare him?

He said, "Please don't worry about that, I am covered."

I could not have married into a better family! Thanks, Lord.

The nurse came by and informed me that I was going to get a chance to visit radiology. It seemed that they ordered a gall bladder study for tomorrow. That meant tonight, specials pills that I would take and special diet. Belinda said that was my problem, which was caused by all that Italian pastry I ate in Rhode Island. (I wondered.)

Well, according to what I heard from Firpo, everything was being taking care of. They even got the MP report and the Polaroid picture of my mirror sent off to the insurance company.

I asked Belinda, "How and where are you guys eating?"

She informed me they could get discount meals tickets at the hospital front desk if they were related to a patient.

"What about the furniture and sheets and all that stuff?" I asked.

She told me that she signed for the furniture and linen and all the other stuff, and they were going to the Commissary to shop for groceries this afternoon, and today, the kids were at the base nursery.

Belinda said, "Honey, hope you don't get spooked at night in that big house with those polished cement floors, everything echoes, and the all-night ship's fog horns. I told her to go to Sears and get a bunch of throw rugs for the floor.

"Belinda, I just won't care about anything once I get out of here." (I hope).

The nurse said, "Here comes your specialist."

This was a major, MD. He introduced himself to Belinda and her brother. He told Belinda that he knew there were a lot of questions, but please let him do a lot more testing.

Then she said, "Well, Doctor, I can tell you right now that he is not normal, but I love him! Bye, you guys, see ya later."

Then the doctor started probing and asking questions and telling me that once he saw all the lab results and the gall bladder report tomorrow, we would see what was next.

*Okay!* I thought, and said, "Let's see where this road is taking me. What would I do if Firpo didn't show up?"

Then the nurse said something to me. "Can I call you Ray?"

I said sure.

"Okay, Ray, grab this mirror, and tell me what you see."

I told her, "I think I see a lot less yellow, and this is only my second day of bed rest."

Then she said, "The doctor wants another blood test this evening. He's going to keep checking your bilirubin count each day."

She told me that I was going to eat a fatty meal before I took those pills this evening. "Now, take a nap!"

"Yes, ma'am."

Again, I woke up feeling a warm and loving hand grabbing mine. Belinda and Firpo both thought I was looking a little better, and then I told her that I thought my nurse agreed. I told her I would meet my colleagues tomorrow in radiology. That would be an abnormal introduction to my new assignment.

Belinda said, "There never has been any 'normal' in your life, Raymond, except for the day you married me!"

Everybody, including my nurse, had a good chuckle! Well, I told them to go home and put the groceries away and please tell the kids I loved them, and I should be back from x-ray around noon. "So Firpo, make sure everyone sleeps late. and you Belinda give me a hug."

She leaned into my ear, and whispered, "I know what you are thinking, Raymond, but I don't date guys that are Jaundiced."

Ooooh, Belinda!

Now the pills after that delicious meal.

They put me in a wheelchair, and off we went to x-ray. I was dying to see what type of equipment I hoped to be working with.

The civilian at the front window said, "So, you are the guy that went AWOL on us, huh?" She said her name was Grace, and they would take good care of me.

I said, "I am sure of that!"

A few moments later, two good-looking female techs came up to me and said, "Hi, Ray, my name is Polly, and this is Jackie. We didn't think we'd meet like this." Polly was E-5 Army, and Jackie was civilian.

I said, "This was not in my plan either."

"Well, they got you down for the gall bladder, abdomen series, and a chest."

I said, "Oh, I thought it was just the gall bladder."

Polly said, "The orders were called in this morning. Let's get to it."

Before I could whistle *Dixie*, these two techs worked as a team. While one did the body positions, the other was behind the lead glass window setting up technics.

I had to say it: "Do all the techs normally work in pairs.?".

Jackie quickly said, "Once you see our workload, you will understand."

Before I knew it, I was being pushed back to the ward. I was telling my nurse the story.

"Ray, we get casualties around the clock. Tripler Hospital is overloaded in Hawaii, and we are just as bad. Believe me, I've been to x-ray with my patients, and I can tell you, they want you now! So, let's get you back to bed."

I told her I wanted to ask a bunch of questions about the department, but I wouldn't dare ask seeing how busy they were.

"Good decision, Ray," she said. "Look, here comes your doctor and your wife."

"Hi, Honey, where is Firpo?"

"Oh, he's home with the kids. He's doing a lot of work around the place, putting up shower curtains, lining drawers and all kinds of things."

"Wow, I am blessed to have a brother-in-law like that."

The doctor said good morning and told me my bilirubin came down a few points, but still was around 1.9 or so. So he said we would do another test this evening. All of the blood panels and urine and other specimens were negative. "While you guys visit, I will walk down to Radiology and get your x-ray results."

So, Belinda and I got caught up on both sides of our current events.

She said, "Honey, you look better each day."

"Well," I said, "my energy is coming back a little each day. Belinda, I sure do miss you."

She held my hand and told me she was praying all day long, and she knew the good Lord was going to get me out of there!

Okay, the good doctor was back, and he had good news, and bad news. The good: all of x-ray reports were negative. The bad: He said it would be like breaking a medical commandment if he didn't do a liver biopsy.

Too bad that I knew what that was. So, he explained to Belinda the details. There was a minor percentage of serious bleeding, and some other complications if the patient did not follow instructions. So, he asked me if he could call me Ray. (This was getting contagious.)

Of course, doctor!

"Ray, I think this will be done tomorrow morning about 9AM."

Belinda spoke up quickly, and asked for more details.

Of course he said, "We will do this procedure right here in the ward. We will move him to a flat stretcher, on his back, then sterilize his right lower chest and upper abdomen area, then after giving Ray some breathing instructions, we will insert a long needle into the liver, and take out a tiny specimen of tissue and send it off to the lab for a report. Before the procedure, Ray will be given medication to relax, and we will be numbing the area where the needle goes."

I said to Belinda, "A piece of cake."

"No," she said, "a piece of your liver!"

Right then, the doctor and the nurse burst out laughing! That's my Belinda!

# CHAPTER 35

O kay! It was a piece of liver, and the procedure went well. The only problem was that I had to remain on my back, without movement for about sixteen hours. I looked up today's procedure, and because of new technologies it's only about four hours of no movement.

Well, let's look and see where this road took us. I was counting on getting out of this bed, and going home to my family. I was dying to see this historic building that we were living in. Firpo and Belinda said the kids were in the nursery having fun, so they would stay with me and see if the report came back today. The nurse heard us talking, and she said that it would take a lot longer than we thought. It could even take a couple of weeks. She told me that if my bilirubin report was better by that afternoon, the doctor just might send me home for the weekend on bedrest. Meanwhile, today they started me on some vitamins, and told me to abstain from any alcohol drinks for three months. I said that would be no problem.

Belinda turned to me and said, "I bet you your companion angel knows the results of your biopsy."

I said, "Yeah, but how do we communicate?"

"Raymond, through prayer!"

I looked to Firpo, and asked how was he holding up, and said he must be exhausted with all the chores of the past five days.

He replied "Hey Bro, whatever it takes, and I am sure you would be there for me under the same circumstances."

I said, "You can be sure of that!"

The nurse said, "Here comes your doctor."

"Okay folks," he began, "here is the way it plays out. We think we are safe letting you go home tomorrow morning, to make sure you are not bleeding from the biopsy, and my peers and I figure once we see a negative report on your specimen test, we will be almost positive this will be Gilbert's Syndrome. Your jaundice is just about gone, and the nurse tells me you have a lot more energy, is that right?"

"Yes, sir," I said.

"Okay, then tomorrow you go home, and it is either the couch or the bed. Do I make it clear?"

"Yes, sir," I said.

"Be at my office Monday at 11AM. I am going to order more bedside lab tests for today. I will see you Monday."

I shook his hand, and said, "Thanks for everything."

"Your nurse here has a personal story for you to hear this afternoon, and since you will be flat on your back until tomorrow morning."

Belinda finally spoke up and said, "Okay, if nobody else is going to ask, I will! What the heck is Gilbert's Syndrome?"

I said to myself, *Why did I not ask?*

"Okay, nurse, tell these guys your story. Bye!"

She told me she would be right back so she could see if the other nurses could spare her for twenty minutes. When she came back, she told Firpo and Belinda to take a chair. Then she spoke. "Mrs. G, I could not say anything to Ray until the docs confirmed it up, but your husband has the same thing as my cousin, who just finished law school. Only 5 percent or less of the population has this, and mostly prominent in males. It's not anything to worry about, and there is no treatment for it. So, please don't worry about your husband."

Belinda looked over to her brother and said, "You see, Firpo, didn't I tell you, there is nothing normal about Raymond? Now he's probably going to tell me how fortunate I was to marry in the rare 5 percent category."

Our nurse said she was going to tell her cousin what Belinda said.

Belinda stood up and walked over to my stretcher and said, "Raymond, you did tell me a few years ago that you were a rare find, but I didn't think you were referring to your liver! When you write your book years from now, don't forget this part. I love you, you odd one!"

*NOTE: Okay, you nice people, please Google Gilbert's Syndrome. They can explain it better than me.*

Wow, the boys were all over me with excitement when I finally went home, and their voices were bouncing off the high ceilings and cement walls. It did finally return to normal. This place was unbelievable. There was no doubt that this place would have lasted through an invasion. Looking straight down the road that went into the hospital, I could see all the officers' houses. Our house was above them and closer to the bridge. The difference was that our place didn't quite look like a house, it looked like a building. But I am not complaining, it did get all fogged up at night.

Ask my children how big was the area that we called the living room. It turned out that Belinda and Firpo bought them tricycles, and as they raced across the room and turned toward their bedroom, they would be completely out of sight. Our backyard wasn't actually a backyard, it was basically a forest. The trees went on forever. Once I felt better, I would take the family hiking and see where it all went. There was a big negative: No garage for my limo. Belinda told me how wet the car was in the morning. Oh boy!

Tomorrow being Sunday, Belinda and I said to Firpo that his job and his family would rather see him back right about now. He told me that he was convinced of my recovery, and he was very glad to have helped us out. I told him once again that I was deeply indebted to him, and we would never forget how he helped us. I dare not think how bad it would have been on Belinda and the children without him!

I thought I would sleep longer, but the smell of bacon and whatever else was cooking was drawing me to the kitchen. Belinda said for me to hit the chair and stay there. Firpo was already at it, and the boys, still sleeping. Then she brought me breakfast with a TV tray. I asked her where did she get it. Firpo spoke up and said that they were in the large closet. Belinda remarked that it was not a closet, it was a huge supply room!

"Well, Belinda, can you remember our apartment in Las Cruces, and the house in White Sands, and most of all, the Randersacker apartment?"

She said, "We could fit them all in here!"

"Honey," I said, "look at all the roads we traveled so far, and we have only been married a little over four years."

She said, "Wow!"

My brother-in-law, and I said our goodbyes to each other, and we did try to wake up the guys, but to no avail.

I watched Belinda and Firpo through the window outside, hugging and all. When she came back in, she was crying, and that was when I asked her to sit next to me.

She said, "Honey, what would I have done if he didn't show up?"

"Belinda, that's what love and family are all about. He did it for us, because he knows we would have done the same for him."

Yes, I was at my doctor's on time, and he said the last bilirubin was almost normal, and yes I could show up for work tomorrow! Thank You, Lord! He said that by next Monday that biopsy report should be back, and he would have his nurse call me at radiology. I went back to the waiting area where Belinda and the boys were, and told them the good news.

Belinda said, "I know what you are thinking, Raymond. Go ahead and visit x-ray, then come to the cafeteria, and we will have lunch."

I met Grace at the front, and she said, "You sure look different since the last time I saw you. You looked like an orange."

"Well, thank you," I said. We both laughed. She took me down to Sergeant Ramstead's office, and there were both of the sergeants sitting at the desk. They were happy to hear the news, and right away we were on our way for a complete tour. As we went into each exposure room, he made all the introductions. I could not believe that they had six x-ray rooms, one special procedure room, three portable machines, and an adjoining cast room, plus a special skull room. First time I had ever seen one of those. (It was designed for foreign body localization, bullets or grenade fragments and bamboo punctures.

"Welcome to the war!"

The sergeant said they would train me on that tomorrow.

He told me that I was the ranking E-5, so that meant I would be in charge of the students who graduated from San Antonio. Okay. Then came the biggest surprise of all. There were two Eastman Kodak film processors sticking out of the dark room wall.

I said, "No dark room duty."

He said, "Nope, we have two full-time civilians in there. However, we all have to learn about the operating and cleaning procedures, because you will be on night duty periodically!"

Then they took me into the reading room to meet the radiologists. There were six in all, and they all seemed very nice. Yes, I met the two golf partners of my doctor. (By the way, there were five Army, and one civilian.)

I joined my family for lunch, and then I told them the good news about Daddy being just fine, and guess who is going to ride over the Golden Gate Bridge today. Oh yeah, they screamed out. Wow, what a sight that was for the first time, and in the future months ahead, I told Belinda we would go up to Sonoma and check it all out.

I came back to the Presidio and drove past our house and went straight to Fisherman's Wharf. We all agreed that this was going to be an expensive place to live, because we walked around all the restaurants and saw their prices that were posted outside.

Belinda said, "I've gotta get me a job!" I agreed. Then she said, "You are going home to rest. Tomorrow is your big day!"

That first week was a killer. Way too many causalities. Chuck (the NCOIC) didn't let me work past eight hours, as some of the military staff had to that week. (Doctor's orders.)

Monday morning (second week), Grace said, "I got a message for you."

"Great, who from?"

"Your doctor's nurse called, and said, tell Ray his little chunk of liver was oh so negative. Did you get your phone in yet?"

"Not for a few more days," I replied, "but I will tell Belinda tonight, first thing."

Once again, my assigned angel was there, and I said my prayers of thanks very quietly while I was working with my patient.

I had six students, so every day I would rotate them in different rooms. The students were just as shocked as I was when we witnessed the condition and anatomical shortages and the trauma of these American soldiers who had given the ultimate sacrifice to their country, whether they were drafted or joined. How dare those people stand outside that gate every day with their stupid signs? I would like to go and get one of them each day, and bring them here to witness this horror!

Every time I finished with the procedure, I always asked the patient, "Is there anything else I can do for you?" Believe me, not all the requests we're doable.

Belinda was very happy with my news, and she said she would send Firpo a post card. I also had more news for Belinda. One of my fellow techs (Roy) was talking today at lunch as to the cost of living here in this city. I found out Roy was married to one of the hospital's Army nurses and her nurse girlfriend worked in Dietary in the main cafeteria, and they happened to be interviewing for a secretary transcriber.

I told Belinda, "Too bad I couldn't call you once I find out more info tomorrow."

She said, "I don't see why not," as she was pointing to our new phone.

All right! It looked like we were getting settled, and it was a good feeling. She said that she would call the insurance company and find out the status of our claim. That prompted me to go look at my poor dirty car. I think I had enough energy by this weekend to give it some attention.

The next morning, I stopped by the snack bar for a cup of coffee, and there was Roy waving me to his table. He then introduced his wife Dee to me. She seemed very nice. She was a 1st lieutenant. When we got to the question about the possible job opening, Dee said that she would call her friend that morning and get the number Belinda needed to call. Great!

Another day of patient pile-up, but that was okay, that was what we were here for. I would like to describe some of the patients we got from the Neuropsychology Ward. In today's terminologies, it's referred to as PTSD, but back in the other century, we called it shell-shock.

Chuck called me into his office and handed me a request with a colonel's name on it, and explained that his doctor had written *Extreme Caution* on a request that for a routine chest x-ray.

"Ray, just simply ask him, rather than tell him anything, and speak very softly, and whatever you do, don't rush him. Give him all the time he needs."

(All new to me, but I thought I understood.)

"Hello, sir, my name is Ray. Are you doing okay? Your doctor would like for you to have a chest x-ray, is that okay with you, sir?"

"Well, I guess so," he said.

"Good, sir. Is it okay if I push your wheelchair into the x-ray room?"

When I asked him to take off his robe and pajama top, he slowly took off the robe, and proceeded to fold it up so neatly, you could have put it in your glove compartment!

Then the pajama top, again, fold after fold, so slowly. This process took him about twenty minutes. Well, right about that time, here came Polly and Roy walking into my room (Chuck probably said to go see if Ray was okay or something). The colonel turned in their direction and let out a scream louder than my drill sergeant in boot camp. I waved my hand in a "get out" gesture, and they left.

The patient grabbed me around my shoulder, and said, "Soldier, good job, you shot both of them. Let's take cover and get ready for another raid!"

I sat him down in the wheelchair, and dressed him the best I could. He was crying, and started to shake. When I pushed him out of the room, there was Chuck.

I said, "Let me push him back to the ward and explain to the nurse, and we can try this again tomorrow." Chuck gave me a big "yes" nod.

At the ward I was talking to the nurse, and she said, "Wait here a second." Then she returned with a copy of the *Stars and Stripes* newspaper, and handed it to me. She had circled in red the article. I certainly can't recall exactly what it said this many years later, but it referred to a Korean War Army lieutenant who saved an entire platoon of men. I can't remember his exact heroic act, but he was awarded a Bronze Star, and other medals. I realize that story was lengthy, but I thought you should know that not all our war veterans who come home are just physically wounded.

The next morning, Chuck walked up and handed me a request for a portable chest x-ray to be done on the ward. He said to me, "I know you E-5s don't do portables, but I thought you might want this one." Yup, it was my colonel, and I was proud to do it! Yes, it took about a half hour, but who cares!

When I told Belinda about this colonel, she told me that it must feel good inside, knowing I was helping these veterans. I told her that I had been in this man's Army for almost six years, and all I was missing was a small piece of liver!

She said, "Honey, it's getting late. Let's go pray for these soldiers."

I still do every night.

# CHAPTER 36

Things were moving along in a routine manner. Everybody was healthy. I was only pulling weekend call about every four or five weeks, so we sure got around to learning this city on the weekends. It became more affordable, because my wife did get that job at the hospital Dietary office. Not only that, last month I took the P-2 test, and I was a happy camper. I scored 89 percent. My boss (Chuck) was an E-7, and he couldn't draw Pro pay.

The assistant in charge was Staff Sergeant Ramsted, E-6, he was drawing P-1 pay. The other two E-5s were Polly and Joanie. Both had less than a year to go in their three-year enlistment, so they couldn't take the test either, unless they enlisted again, and that would have defeated the reason why they got their x-ray school via the Army, because their families could not afford a two-year tuition fee. That might give you an idea why the Army was overloaded with E-5 pay grades.

Jackie was our civilian tech, and she was great to work with. Polly, Joanie and Jackie became very good friends of ours in that period of time. We lost contact with Joanie about ten years ago. We still stay in touch with Polly and her husband to this day. (Would you believe I ran into Jackie in Hawaii in the late '70s? She was working at Tripler Army Hospital.) Belinda and I had quite a few dinners at our comm center in those days. All three girls gave Belinda all the help she needed. Her famous soft taco dinners won everybody over.

The boys were doing good. They attended day nursery, which included early education.

By the way, we finally got the mirror replaced on the Cadillac, and of course my group of friends thought Belinda and I had money, because of that car. Wrong.

We ended the year of '65 with a nice little cold and foggy Christmas Day, staying home. I wish I could tell you that the war was slowing down, but not! It seemed there was talk going around that we might hire two more civilian techs to work the weekends. What was amazing was if we went around the local area, we would never hear people talking about this war. Life for them was totally normal. Things are a little better today, because of the vast amount of cable news, but here again, we still have lots of citizens who do not support our veterans, or even our Flag, and this 9-11 war has already lasted nineteen years!

I personally think they should extend high school an additional six weeks, for boot camp, to spend that time in military training. That would help them to gain more knowledge of what type of sacrifice it takes to maintain this country's freedom. (But hey, that's just my opinion.)

Wow, time was marching on rather quickly, and it seemed that this coming Easter vacation, my brother Angelo and wife were coming up for a visit. That would be very nice, and afford an opportunity for us to get to know more about each other, considering it had been eight years since we had spent quality time together.

Belinda and I sometimes had our moments of disagreement and anxiety due to living a military life, especially for her, because of her relationship with her family. I knew she missed her style of living as compared to this town of San Francisco. I knew she really did not want to get a job, knowing she could spend her time with the children, but we couldn't make it otherwise. So of course, like in other marriages, we had some spats and tantrums. What saved us, as usual, was the love we had for each other. I prayed all the time to the Lord to give me more patience and wisdom, and to stop wanting things I couldn't afford. When I look back to see that my parents kept buying all those toys that my brother and I had, they surely spoiled us. I was married to a very practical women, and I prayed I could learn from her about waiting and planning. For sure, that was my downfall. I never could figure out how Belinda could read into the early morning hours without moving or twitching. I only read when it comes to my studies, and it was hard for me to sit for a long time. Belinda said a few years back that I was like Elvis. I couldn't keep still, always had to be moving around. Well, guess what, at the time of this writing, that is no longer my problem. (Since I already told you what year I was born.)

Well, here we were celebrating Easter, and Angelo and Sally had arrived. My kids were kind of sad, because I told them they would be seeing their cousins, but it turned out they stayed with their grandmother (Sally's mom). Well, we took them all around the sights and even took in some famous seafood restaurants and took a boat ride out to Alcatraz. That was very interesting. Well, they only planned three days, so I think we did a lot in the short period of time.

You heard me mention our friend Polly, so here is a cute story to tell you about meeting her husband. It was a typical busy morning and the good sergeant was handing out to us all the x-ray requests as he did every morning. Polly and I sometimes traded with each other to make sure we got a variety of studies. We were standing there in the hallway, getting ourselves ready, when the aide pushed a stretcher up against the wall and yelled out, "Stat ankle, patient going to surgery," as he handed the paperwork to Grace for processing. I walked up to Grace and told her I could take it right now. Then I asked Polly to help me with the stretcher.

She then said really quick, "Let's trade, I'll take him."

"Why?" I said.

"Ray, did you look at him? He is wow, so handsome!"

"Take him, Polly."

They were married the following spring. We've been good friends all these years.

By the way, do you remember the nice colonel who greeted us at the beginning of Chapter 34? His name was Colonel Joseph Sterling, US Army, MD. I told you that he lived down about four houses below us. Well, a few months later, I was out in the street, washing my car, and here came the colonel, decked out in his golf clothes, walking his dog.

He said, "Ray, how are you and the family doing?"

I said, "Just great. Are you enjoying this beautiful day?"

"Ray, I will be honest with you, I was hoping to catch you outside, because I am dying to see the house, and how they fixed it up in the inside."

"Doctor, please come in, you can bring your dog in also, it looks very friendly."

"Oh, yes," he said.

Belinda greeted him like he was an old friend, and the kids had the electric train set running In the living room. She told him to watch his step. Then, he sat his dog down in the corner and told the dog to stay, and the dog did not move. I told Belinda that the doctor would like a tour of our comm center.

When they came back, he said, "Wow, if we ever get another earthquake, I am taking my family here."

I said he was more than welcome. He told the wife that someday this would become a historic place in the Presidio, and sure enough, it did! Then, I asked him if he played golf with my two radiologists, and yes, he did as a matter of fact. He also told me and Belinda that both of the radiologists were retiring after twenty years of service next spring, and they were opening their own radiology center in Sausalito. I said that was a very beautiful place to live, if one could afford it. He agreed.

Here's something interesting: I got a call from Uncle Fred. He got my number from Mom. He told me that Grandpa had a yearning, so to speak, that before he got any older he would like to see the Pacific Ocean. I said that would be great. What were the details? He said that he was going to fly him to his sister's (my mom) place in LA, then Mom and Grandpa would fly to San Francisco together for a couple of days.

"Well, Uncle, I'll make sure he has a good time, and make sure he and Mom will be here for a weekend."

"Raymond, I am sending my sister the money, so make sure he gets to eat in all the seafood places in Frisco."

"Uncle Fred, call me in the evening hours when you get the flight schedules."

Then he asked, "Raymond, how is the car?"

I then told him what the hippies did to the mirror, and believe me, I can't type what he said!

Later, I found out that they would be arriving in San Francisco on a Friday at 1PM. I managed to get the time off, so my family and I got to the airport and picked both of them up. My mom looked really good that day, and she was happy to be with her father once again. My children were excited, because they loved to hear Grandpa talk with his broken accent. So, once we got them settled in the car, I screamed out to Grandpa, and asked him if he was hungry.

"Oh yeah, Ray-mon, thosa people onna thata plane.justa give me those stupid peanuts!"

"Okay, Papa, we will go to the Wharf right now and get you fed.

As I told you earlier, this man was from Trieste, and he only ate seafood. So we were driving down the beautiful Embarcadero Road heading toward the Wharf, and I told Grandpa and Mom to look at all those beautiful homes. He must have noticed that they were all built with no space between them, and sure enough, he said, "Raymon, whya thosa houses all stucka together lika that?"

I said, "Well, Pa, I think that's because they would stand up better in case they have another huge earthquake."

He says, "Hey, you kidda me, Raymond, if ona them gosa down, they alla gonna falla down!"

We all burst out laughing, then the kids joined in.

I took them to Alioto's #1 on the Wharf, and Grandpa ordered a shell food plate with some spaghetti served with his favorite clam sauce. He was in heaven, and my mother also joined him. We all ate like royalty. Then I reminded Mom about the funds that Uncle Fred mentioned.

"Oh yeah, Raymond, I almost forgot." Hmmm.

Papa was amazed when he saw the Presidio. He said it reminded him of the fortresses on the coastline of Italy. He and my mom could not get over our comm center. On Saturday, Mom told Belinda that she would make Grandpa his breakfast, because he was very fussy about his eggs. (If you saw the movie, *Moonstruck*, you may have noticed how Cher's mother put the eggs in the cut-out of the toast. Okay.)

That afternoon, we all got in the car and drove over the Golden Gate, and Papa was so happy about the scenery. I thought he was going to cry.

Belinda said to me, "I don't think Grandpa is going to want to go home!"

It was a great weekend for the kids. They liked to move around like me when they got the chance. Polly told me to make sure I took Grandpa to Zack in Sausalito, and I got to tell her, we all enjoyed that. I just looked it up, and now it is called Salito's Crab House.

Then on Sunday morning, we all got dressed up and went to St. Mary's downtown for the late Mass. Papa said that he would like to go back to Alioto's #1 again, if we all didn't mind. We all said, "Let's go!"

On the way home, my dear Belinda said that she was sure glad we got this car with all this space. It made the weekend much more enjoyable.

# CHAPTER 37

W e had fond memories of that visit with Mom and Grandpa, but now we were back to normal, having the knowledge that we wouldn't be eating like that for a while. I did call up Uncle Fred and expressed our many thanks.

Well, back to work for me and Belinda. That Sunday night after coming home from the airport, Belinda and I stayed up late talking about all our blessings, and how grateful to God we were, knowing that there were so many people out there who would gladly trade places with us.

Sure enough, time again moved forward into Thanksgiving, and into Christmas. Our Chief Medical Officer (my neighbor) sent out a directive to pool our efforts and talent together and see what we could do for our wounded warriors that Christmas. Everything from cards, decorations, small gifts, homemade Christmas pies and other goodies, pending dietary restrictions. We were to check with all the nurses for written orders and advise. Buses and drivers were made available for city light displays or major Christmas decorations, for patients who were eligible.

Belinda and I had a Christmas Eve party for some of the single staff members. That was nice. The kids were excited because they got a few gifts in the bargain. After the guests left, I asked Phillip to stand on the kitchen chair and hold a piece of lettuce really high, then I grabbed my sweet wife and said that was my version of mistletoe, and gave her a special Christmas kiss, and presented to her a $100 coupon for her Book of the Month Club.

She said, "Hey you, where do you get a whole hundred dollars in this man's Army?"

I said, "I sold our thirteen silver dimes, since we never use them."

You never heard the word "What?" screamed so loud. She sure scared me and the kids.

"Tell me you're joking, Raymond!"

"Of course, Honey, I am joking!"

"Wow, thank you," she said. "Then where did you get this money on our budget?"

I simply replied, "I sold twelve of your old books!"

"I am going to get you, Raymond!"

I said, "I hope so!"

Belinda looked a little sad or tired. I could not figure it. So, I said to her that we should sit down on the couch.

I told her that it must be tough working every day, and trying to balance that with being a mother and a wife. "So, Belinda, you okay?"

She told me that it was that time of year, and she missed her family, and her job was kind of tough and all.

"Well, Honey, can you wait just five more months, and I will take you home for a visit?"

She said, "What do you mean, in five months?"

"Belinda, I know you are tired and all, but did you forget that my Army days are over May 21 of 1967? That's one week and five months away."

"Honey, I don't believe it. I am glad you are looking at the calendar."

Belinda, in a couple of months, I will be sending out my resume, looking for a civilian job."

"Wow," she said.

"Okay, kids, guess what? Tomorrow is Christmas, so we better be getting to bed."

"Daddy, is Santa Claus coming tomorrow?" Gregory said.

"Only if you guys get to bed now! No, no Belinda, we will clean up this mess tomorrow, you too are going to bed."

January 1967

There is a saying in the military, that when one gets down to the last few months of service, he is called a Short Timer. Well, that was me. Belinda said to me one night, "Boy, the civilians won't be ready for you, that's for sure." Amen!

My two (soon-to-be-civilian) radiologists offered me and Roy positions at their new radiology office. I told them that I was certainly going to discuss that with my wife. Oh, by the way, they also offered it to Polly, but she and her husband were on their way to Oregon to take over his dad's printing plant. Nice. One of the students that were on staff here told me that when he got discharged in a couple of years, he was going to UCLA Hospital for work. I asked how could he be so sure.

He said, "My cousin is the administrator of radiology there."

I told him I would look him up about that time. Our good friend Harry already told us that he thought we should move to his state of Michigan. I told Belinda to write him back and ask him the average daily temperature in the middle of winter.

I asked Belinda if she was going to miss her job when we left, and she told me the job was very demanding, due to the fact that the US Government insisted on the very best dietary supplements for our troops (That's the way it should be.) Belinda said her boss was a dedicated professional, and expected the same from her staff. Belinda said she liked all of them, and she would miss them.

Then I changed the subject.

"Okay, Belinda about six-and-a-half years ago, everybody came at me from every direction, and told me that they were concerned about the stability of your future, as well as mine, and the Colonel arranged a re-enlistment contract so I could attend x-ray school, and then to Europe to serve out my two-year program, Now, I address you, my lady, to inquire about my performance in the last (almost) six years. What do you think? Did I do good?"

My lady replied, "I guess so."

"Well, since you guess so, I should tell you I and some of the gang have been offered employment in the new clinic in Sausalito, my Ladyship. What say you, my Lady?"

She said, "Nah, we could never afford to stay in this city, never mind Sausalito. Besides, you really can't take the girl out of the desert."

"Well, my lady, all the people I work with, including our civilian Jackie, agree that the best starting wage is in the LA area. There isn't any place in this country that is not hiring techs because the technology is changing so rapidly. You have your brother and aunts and uncles in that area. I have a brother and a little brother, and your favorite in-laws."

She said, "Thank you, my lordship."

We just kept laughing!

Meanwhile, the patient load was getting worse every day. I was told we couldn't fit any more beds, and so some of the causalities were going to other military and VA hospitals all the way across the States.

Everyday I would get a copy of the "Stars and Stripes" newspaper, and they would quote the number of deaths and wounded, and the numbers were high... *The only Americans that know this are the ones that keep up with the news, and back in the '60s, watching the news wasn't that popular. I myself was shocked to learn all this started in 1955!*

What I had found out so far in my young life was that it took an overwhelming amount of staff, who (do not) have patient contact, to run an operation of this size. Inventory, restocking supplies, paperwork, logistics, food, clothing, linen medicine, narcotics, and the list goes on and on. I have always said, if you know young people who are looking for steady employment, send them into the medical world!

Well, the whole military staff had been asked to stay on duty every day until 1800 hours (6PM) rather than our usual 5PM to give the night shift a jump start with the increased patient load. So, I told Belinda to drive to the day care and get home. I could catch a ride from Chuck or Jeff. I felt bad, because she still had to cook dinner for us, Yes, I did the dishes in that old sink every night. and at 9:30 or so, I was in La La land, and there was my gal with her little flashlight reading in bed. (So cute!)

Okay, this holiday schedule was busy, not just because of our workload, but trying to help out all the wounded by cheering them up. I did not mention this before, but they did bring in entertainers here every once in a while. There was a small auditorium right next to the cafeteria. One particular afternoon was a young singer just starting his career: Mr. Wayne Newton. I think he was around twenty years old at the time, but I could be wrong. Jackie, Roy and I were in the cafeteria sitting next to some of the patients we knew, and I could hear this very high voice of Wayne's, penetrating the wall next to us.

One of the patients asked Jackie, "Who is this chick? Is she as pretty as her voice?"

Jackie said, "Ooh that's not a chick, that's a guy!"

He started to back out his wheelchair, and said, "I am going to see for myself!"

I had sent out at least six resumes, after talking on the phone with several hospitals. We were going to drive down once I could button up these interviews down to a two-day window. I had lots of leave time coming from this past eighteen months of really not using but a few days. The good news was my replacement already had arrived. The poor guy was drafted right after his graduation from x-ray school in Denver, Colorado. He was a RT, so he only spent eight weeks in boot camp, then they shipped him here for the remainder of his two years. I told him he most likely would never see anything but his whites every day, and most likely never see anything that resembled military life other than living in his barracks. He said he could live with that. Ramsted would take charge for a while, Chuck was being transferred to Tripler in Hawaii with a promotion to E-8, then he would retire after that. Ramsted of course was forced to ask me to re-up for his position. I knew that was coming. Even though I would be promoted to staff sergeant, I would still be drawing P-2 pay as an E-7, so the deal was good, except for the fact Belinda and I had already decided that San Francisco was not our kind of town. The Presidio base recruitment officer tried really hard to change my mind. It would not be easy leaving because I knew so many patients who had been there for a while, due to their rehabilitation process. Back in the '60s, the prosthetic devices were not nearly as advanced as they are today. So, the whole process took longer. We are not talking just arms and legs, but false ears and noses and more. I often think that these roads that led me to Belinda also led me here to lend a helping hand to these American warriors. Hearing about this is certainly not the same as seeing and living it!

We made the trip to the San Fernando Valley and met all the doctors I had sent the resumes to. It turned out that these guys were all part of the same private radiology group that contracted their services to different hospitals in the San Fernando Valley. So, it was decided that I would be interviewed by the senior partner of the group. (He happened to be a RT before he became an MD.) Oh boy! I hoped my angel was with me that day!

"So, Ray, my name is Dr. _____. It is nice to meet you. Your resume seems to lack any civilian training or experience, is that true?"

I said, "Yes, it is true, but what has that got to do with anything?"

He went on and on that he had never been in the military, and he really did not know what would be the difference. So, I said to myself, *This doctor is playing a mind game with me, or he is waiting to see what I might do.* So, here it comes, doctor!

"Well, sir, if you can convince me that you civilians have not the same number of bones and organs that I do, or that your equipment is not manufactured by the same people, or your human diseases are different from mine, or you civilians use different calculations for tissue mass, and bone density, or you don't have the same electrons running through a high-voltage transformer, or you use a different three-phase voltage system, or — .should I go on, doctor? Because I certainly have more interviews."

He said, "Ray, relax please, I was just kidding around to test your character. We knew we were going to hire you when we confirmed your resume. That's if you want the job."

"Okay if I start the beginning of June?"

All this time, Belinda and the children were in the main waiting room of the hospital, and when I walked up to her she was all frazzled, because the boys spent all that time fighting with each other. There would be some serious discussions that night. I called

Mom and told her what was going on. She did invite us over for dinner, but made no mention of sleeping over. I told Belinda that after supper, we would get a motel, and then get back up north tomorrow morning.

She said, "Thanks, I will sleep better!"

As usual, we were all eating dinner, and no questions were asked of us as to the current events. I had to remind my children of their grandparents' glass house, and please behave while there. I got a few questions from my little brother, and that was about it. There was no denying that Mom's cooking was always great. Her mother taught her well. Belinda got up to help Mom in the kitchen, and what she got back was, "Belinda, you just sit down, I will take care of it myself!"

Okay, time for us to say our goodbyes

When we checked into the motel, I had my little discussion with my two little lightweight contenders.

Belinda was dying to hear all about my interview and all, so I told the kids to suit up and jump in the pool. That gave her and me time to talk.

She said, "Honey, you don't seem happy about this. Look, Sweetheart, I know your mom and dad did not invite us over, but it is a small house they have, so put it out of your mind."

"Okay, I love you, my little bookworm."

She said, "See, I am glad you said that. That is exactly how I can leave this world, and walk in another planet of fantasy and adventure, and drop my worries. This is what you gotta do once in a while. Read, Raymond.

"Now, let's hear about your interview. Wait," she said. "You're tired, I'll get the kids out of the pool and you go to bed, and we will talk about your future tomorrow! Give me a kiss, you almost a civilian! Wait, wait, Sweetheart, that's why you're in a slump, isn't it? My God, Raymond, I didn't realize that this is the first time in over eight years that you won't be wearing dog tags and keeping your gear ready to leave at a moment's notice, and not to mention all the rest of the military obligations. You weren't even eighteen when you joined, and now in a little over thirty days it is going to be over, and you probably will miss all your comrades, and the memories, off all the roads you have traveled at such a young age."

"Honey," I said, "it was all meant to be, because that's how I found you, and that's why I believe in angels. Anyway, Belinda, I start my new civilian job the first week of June."

"Well, Honey, I am staying for the ride!"

"Sweetheart, I am sure it will not be boring."

# CHAPTER 38

The civilian roads.

Yes, it was tough saying goodbye to some of our patients and the radiology staff. Our friend the Colonel was a super nice doctor and medical leader. He told Belinda to tell me that I had thirty days if I changed my mind. I told Belinda I was ready to make the jump!

Okay, we bought our first house on my GI Bill in Van Nuys. That's right, only about three miles from where I joined the Army over eight years ago. Who would have guessed!

There were quite a few old actors I met on my new job. I think I told you earlier that most actors lived here in the Valley. To mention a few of them, there was Rory Calhoun, Phil Ahn, Shelly Winters and Red Buttons. My problem with this radiology group was how they kept changing the game rules, and they certainly lacked professional ethics, in my opinion. It became obvious to me, when I would tell the doctors that the patient had questions or they were uncomfortable or whatever, the response was, "Hey, Ray, time is money, let's get the next patient in quickly." (Do you get my point?)

One day, my brother Angelo (he was working at Grumman Aircraft at that time) called me and said to get my butt over to Rocketdyne in Canoga Park. I asked my brother what in the world I would have in common with a huge company that built rocket engines for spacecraft. He then told me they were looking for a RT and the pay and benefits were great.

I made the call just out of curiosity. What the heck. They convinced me that we should meet, so I managed to take off a Friday
afternoon, and we met. I was really impressed with the medical
clinic there. I found a completely up-to-date radiology room and
a Kodak film processor, plus a very nice desk and sofa. The two
doctors who worked there were certainly past retirement age, but I
figured that was why they were there. They told me that this facility
only existed because of industrial accidents, or executive physicals that included a complete patient examination, chest x-ray and
lab work. I said to them that was not much for a person trained to
do a whole lot more. They agreed. They were hoping I would be
a little older, but they said that the salary and benefits that would
be available to my family would be the game changer! I said they
could look at the possibility of hiring a limited licensed technician,
like the ones that worked for chiropractors.

They quickly said they had to adhere to the laws of the
California Health Bureau due to all the government contracts that
were involved, so they could only hire a ARRT. So, I asked the big
question: What does the job pay?

The doctor said to me, "First of all, can you show me that you
are qualified?" At that point, I took out my wallet and removed the
registry and the American Society cards. He then said, "Excellent.
If you would take these cards back, just walk out of this door, and
walk in the next building right there, make a left, and report to Mr.
Wilson at Personnel, he will gladly release the salary amount to you.
I will telephone right now, and he will be expecting you."

Well, at that point I was hooked. I had to know that info, to
make a decision!

"Are you kidding me? Take it!" That was the voice of my angel.

The manager said, "When can you start?"

I asked, "Who is your tech now?" I told him that I did not see
anybody there when I was talking to the docs.

He then told me her name. She was moving to Colorado, and
would be back Monday, and that would be her last week.

"Great," I said. "That would allow me to give at least one week's
notice to my present employers."

So, he presented me with a whole packet of Info, and a bunch of federal forms I would need to fill out. I quickly walked back into the clinic and told the two old docs. Wow, they were happy.

I drove up to my house, and gave the woman a serious kiss, and she pushed me back and said, "Well, what happened on your interview today?"

"So, we just forget about the kiss."

"Oh, Honey, come on and start talking."

"Okay! Do you think we should get a bigger house? Do you think we can move to a better school district? Do you think we could be living near shopping centers? Most of all, do you think your husband is tired of getting called out of bed in the wee hours of the morning? And Belinda, do you think I am happy to see how these contract doctors treat their patients?"

"Okay, Ray, stop right there. Is that four yeses, and one no?"

"Yes, you are correct, my ladyship!"

"Great. Then, how much? Wow! That's a lot more than you're making now, and not to mention the benefits."

"But, Belinda, I will not be that busy, and it might get boring."

She said, "Great. Did you forget about using your GI Bill, and getting back to school Raymond?"

"Well, I can go see Pierce City College about their evening classes, and start working for an associate's degree in communications and marketing."

Belinda said I should take my time, and don't worry if I missed a few classes once in a while.

I said, "Honey, I think I will have time for my studies at Rocketdyne."

That weekend, we went house hunting in Canoga Park. We could walk to the shopping and the movies, plus the newer restaurants. All good, and the elementary school looked real nice.

1969

It did take a while for us to sell one, and buy another, but we finally got settled on 7815 Vicky Street. Just in time for the young ones starting a new school year. I will tell you, that these two old doctors were the nicest you would ever meet. Their life stories were very interesting, they loved to travel, and I met the two wives. They had an equal amount of energy as their husbands had. However, here is the good news: After about six months into the program, I got to meet most of the supervisors. So when time was available, I would go out and put on my hard hat and googles and I got to learn almost all of the non-Secret areas. Very, very interesting, and of course, Belinda would always say, "Raymond, you get involved in everything, don't you? Why can't you just read books?"

What was fun for me was when the vendor that took care of our Kodak processor and our x-ray supplies made his monthly maintenance call to clean and service the unit, and check our inventory, He would always say to me, "Come on, Ray, this has to stop, I am going to get in trouble if you keep cleaning this processor yourself, not to mention replacing parts when needed."

I said, "Hey, Paul, I have the time and knowledge and I always enjoy listening to you about all the different hospitals and clinics you go to, and all of the people you know in the business, and I find that all interesting, so it's a good trade."

Then he had to ask, "Where did you get to learn about these Kodak film processors?"

I said, "From my uncle."

He said, "Wait a minute, I know everybody who is in this business. Who is he?"

I said, "Uncle Sam, U.S.Army."

"Whoa, How long were you in for?"

"Over eight years. What about you, Paul, were you a draft dodger?"

He said, "Oh No, I was 4F. I got real flat feet."

I giggled when I said, "Yes, I kind of thought you walked funny!"

He said, "Hey watch that." Right before he left, he told me that his boss, the owner of the company, wanted to meet me. I asked why. "Well, he is looking for a salesperson who has a degree in x-ray technology, and I saw yours on the wall in your office, so I kinda told him a little about you."

"Oh, I see," I said. "Well, bring him with you on your next trip if he wants to."

"Okay, Ray, that might happen, and I will call you if he does."

When I got home that evening, Belinda made the mistake of asking, "What's new, Raymond?" She said, "I keep telling you, are you writing all these events of yours down, because when you are old and retired, I want to see that book."

I said, "I told you the last time you brought that up, what do I know about writing a book?"

"Okay, Raymond. What do you think this guy wants?"

"I really don't know, Honey, but we will find out if and when he comes out to meet me. Honey," I said, "I am always going to listen, if it means a chance for advancement.

She then told me she went with the kids to their new school and met the teaching staff, and was impressed.

"What do you say, guys, if we give Mom a break tonight, and get in our limo, and grab a large pizza from Larry's Place and go to the drive-in and see *Planet of the Apes*?"

"Yeah!"

My wife said, "This better be a good movie!"

"Honey, it can't be bad if Charlton Heston is in it!"

I thought the movie was great, and my wife said, "Well, I hope they don't do a sequel!" Oh really? "Well, Raymond, I have a surprise for you."

"Oh good, you bought me a new shotgun."

She made it clear, that wasn't the surprise. "Guess who is coming for a visit next weekend? Here is a clue. He said he never had the privilege of meeting a civilian named Mr. G_____."

"Wow, I give up."

"Harry is coming to see us," she said. "And you should have guessed, because he always called you Sarge."

"Well, that is great, I can't wait. Hey kids, go pack up your sleeping bags and your pajamas."

"Where we going, Daddy?"

"We are going to Norwalk to visit Uncle Firpo and family."

Belinda was happy to hear the news. She said, "Raymond, why are you packing your shotgun?"

I said, "Because it's long overdue that I do something nice for Firpo. From our previous talks about skeet shooting, I think he's going to love it!"

"Raymond, you are such a nice guy." She patted my head.

"Stop that!"

Well, we had a great time seeing Firpo's family. The kids had fun with their cousins and all, and I always enjoyed talking with Firpo. We surely made plans to see each other soon.

The first thing Harry said when he pulled in the driveway with his little rental was, "Hey, Sarge, where is your Monza? Or did it grow up to this?"

It was just great with us here and both being civilians. It sure was going to take a while before it sank in.

Saturday noon, Belinda said, "Hey Harry, I don't suppose you were thinking about soft tacos and all the trimmings, were you?"

"Oh, Belinda, I was praying that you would bring up that subject!"

So, it seemed that in the last five or six years, Harry had formed a company that sold and taught lab supplies to a whole bunch of countries around the globe. I always knew Harry loved to travel, but not this much. He told me he couldn't get enough of it. Belinda told him that with all that international traveling, he was bound to find a wife. He said that he had to make sure she could cook as good as Belinda, first.

It was a great visit. We went to the Santa Monica beach area, drove through the canyons and swung right through Beverly Hills, and stopped in one of those sidewalk coffee shops, and mixed right in with the high society folks. We would see Harry often, because most of his trips were to the Orient, and that meant stopping in LA.

The following week, Belinda started something new. She said that she was interested in taking art lessons, and would like to see if we could get a screened-in patio room built on our outside patio deck. Then she would have room to put in an easel and stuff. I told her that the husband of our lab tech at work, Imogene, was a contractor, and he would give us some advice. I will check with her Monday.

I had a rather weird experience one morning. I forgot to pin my security badge to my smock. I always wore a blue zipper smock with shirt and tie, Kind of fit in with the space and science scene. Anyway, the first gate security guard said, "Good morning and put his hand on my chest, to stop then asked, "Where is your badge?"

I said, "Charles, I guess I forgot it, and I am almost late."

There was no way, even though he had known me for quite a while, that I was going to get past that gate. So, I turned around and got in the car and drove back home.

Okay, I was pulling in the lot again, and who did I see? It appeared that Paul had brought out the owner for a visit.

He introduced this well-dressed gentleman, and I told Paul it might take a while to get his boss processed through security. Paul knew where to take him.

I said, "See ya in the office when you're done."

My two docs said, "Good morning," and "Wow, you're never late, what happened?"

When I explained, they agreed that this plant was the most highly guarded in the country. It looked quiet, so I went next door to the lab, and found Imogene and Delores (our staff RN) drinking coffee and eating doughnuts.

They offered me a doughnut, and said, "We better give him two, look how skinny he is."

I said, "I beg your pardon, I am weighing at 160 pounds, I should be on a diet."

They had a giggle over that. So, I did give them my history about my weight when I was young, So, while I was chatting with my associates, I could see through the glass that Paul was walking in with Howard, whom I had just met in the parking lot.

We started the conversation by Howard asking me why I left the radiology group that I worked for. I decided not to hash over the personal reasons I had, so I explained about all the call time, losing sleep, and the mere fact that I came here for financial gain, and family benefits, plus still keep my professional standing in the ARRT.

He then stated, "That makes sense to me. So, Ray, are you going stay here at Rocketdyne until you retire?"

He was trying to be coy.

My answer, "Howard, I happen to think that my call in life is radiology. As long as I can stay in radiology, I will always be looking for advancement for me and my family."

"Paul tells me that you had intense training in the military."

I said, "The best."

"Ray, here it is, plain and simple. I need someone like you, who can go into radiology and actually talk their language, and see what products and services may be valuable to their department. Does this interest you at all?"

"Yes, I believe it does!"

"Ray, Paul is going to drive me back to the office, and that's where I will put a complete package proposal to you, and it will include our entire catalog. Tomorrow morning I will have Paul, since he has his vendor card, drop off the package. And by the way it will be sealed! After you look it over, and discuss it with your wife, please call me (he handed me his card) at this number, and we will see where we go from there."

We then shook hands, and said, "Adios."

I went back to my desk. Nothing in the request slot. Well, back to Imogene to talk about my wife's wishes.

So, the day was done, time to go home and see what kind of day Belinda had.

"Hi, honey, I'm home."

She came out of the kitchen to greet me. "What's new, Honey?" she said.

I just kind of gave a look of over-confidence, and sat down on the couch, and patted the spot next to me, and said, "Please Sit."

She slapped her forehead and said, "Oh my God, Ray, here we go again. Am I right? Okay," she said, "I gotta check the oven, you go and see if the boys are doing their homework, and if they are fighting, tell them no dinner! Then at dinner you can give me the news."

Our house wasn't very big, and I knew the kids heard her, because when I walked in their bedroom, they looked like two young scholars figuring out the weight of the world!

Well, at dinner I told her every detail of what transpired between me and Howard, so I told her, "Let's see what he offers for salary and benefits."

"Honey, tell me we're not moving!"

"No, no, there is no need to worry about that."

She replied. "Oh, thank You, Lord."

"Okay, this coming Saturday morning we're going to meet a contractor to bid our patio. He is supposed to be a good friend of Imogene's husband." Then we spent time talking to the boys about school and everything.

Belinda told me she would be saying prayers for good news tomorrow. I said me too. I told her I was a little surprised about this oil painting thing, but I would certainly support her on that.

Of course, I woke up with a few butterflies in my stomach. Belinda and I had some coffee, and the kids were getting ready for school. I told my lady that it was my turn to buy the doughnuts at work, so I would skip breakfast.

She said, "Okay, the kids and I will have your favorite French toast. Hugs and kisses all around. See Ya!"

I drove over to the doughnut shop, and picked up a dozen, then pulled in our parking lot, and said good morning to Charles.

He said that he was sorry, he couldn't let me in unless he could see inside the box.

"Yes, Charles, I know." I opened the box and I said, "The one with the white frosting, right?"

And he said, "Yup!" and off I went with eleven doughnuts.

The morning routine was to turn on the main voltage, and check all the readings, then turn on the processor, and run a test film through. Then, the ladies and our docs and I met in the break room.

Imogene got in a little early and made the coffee. She opened the box, and said, "Did Charlie get his white frosting?"

I said, "How do you think I got in?"

Well, Paul showed up kind of early. He must have smelled the doughnuts. I walked over to the office with him, and he handed me the large envelope, and said, "Good luck, Ray, I gotta get going."

And I said, "Thanks and I'll see ya!"

The package was sealed with some kind of weird tape. It looked like aluminum. So I cut the paper open. I started to read, and, "Wow," I said, "I gotta call Belinda." I told her that I would pick her up for a quick lunch. We went to our favorite drive up joint, Bullet Burger. It was a regular beef patty shaped oval, and served in a torpedo bun. Delicious. So, I drove her home quick and told her to read all of it, and we would discuss it tonight. I didn't want to be late. Now, I had even more butterflies in my stomach.

Well, that evening, there we were, the young ones in bed, and me and the missus were still going *wow, ah, really,* and so on.

Belinda said to me that no way could we turn this down, and I sure agreed. I told her I would call up Howard in the morning and make an appointment, so I could drive down there and looked this place over. Back in the day, we only had the good old *Yellow Pages*, and all I could find out was that there were only two large medical chemical service companies in the LA area. I knew which one was his, and the other one more or less said the same thing.

The Breakdown: A new company car, fully insured by Howard, all fuel and maintenance paid by Howard, which could also be used for personal use. A beautiful health plan, fully paid for, An annual salary 50 percent better than Rocketdyne; sales commission paid on all equipment sold @ 5 percent. The only downside was that the territory included the entire southern California territory. That was a total of ten counties, over 56,000 square miles. Belinda always agreed that if anything went wrong, I could always fall back to x-ray.

# CHAPTER 39

1970

S tarting a new career in marketing and sales. My gal Belinda
took me out shopping for some beautiful three-piece suits and
some wingtip dress shoes. I decided that it was going to be business all the way.

My visit to Howard's company went very well indeed. Very
impressed with the staff and his operation.

It was kind of tough saying goodbye to the Rocketdyne folks.
They had treated me very good there. The two docs were such char-
acters. Lots of personality. Imogene and Delores said that I was
doing the right thing, because I was much younger, and that was
a great job for them at their age group. They already retired once,
before coming here.

We now had another son born. Steven Anthony. It was a very
difficult time for Belinda, a long nine months of discomfort, and
some pain. When the time came, I rushed her to the hospital. Our
doctor was waiting, and he rushed her in really quick. He came
back into the waiting room about a half hour later.

I jumped up real quick and said, "Boy that was a fast delivery!"

He said, "Please sit down, Ray, we have a problem. The cord is
wrapped around the baby's neck, and the positioning is not good. I
need to tell you I may be able to save just one. And —"

"No, Doctor, don't finish that sentence. You are going back in
there to do your best, while I go to the chapel and pray my best."

I prayed and talked with the Lord, and I told Him how much his daughter Belinda meant to me, and how much she helped me in this world, and much more that I wanted to be with her.

So, "Thy will be done."

There was this nurse standing by the chapel door. "Sir, are you ready to come and see your wife and baby boy?"

I felt my angel jumping in my pocket.

During the next several years, I had the pleasure of watching my beautiful wife become a wonderful oil paint artist. About a year after her classes, we took her paintings to a local fair, where they encouraged new artists to display their work. Well, the manager of the fair said that it would not be fair to have Belinda display her paintings, because they were not amateur rated in his opinion, and they would be forced to give her the blue ribbon. Right then, I told Belinda, "Let's get our paintings back in the trailer, and leave these amateurs alone!"

The elementary school our kids went to was only a block from our house. The staff knew Belinda pretty well by this time, and they offered her a teacher's aide position. She really loved it. Once they found out about her art talent, they put her in charge of painting a mural on the entire side of the building. The scene depicted the early Spanish history of Los Angeles. The name of the school was Capistrano. She had several teachers involved in the project, and later, some of them became Belinda's students. Throughout the following years, she made paintings for everyone in her family, and as of today, they are proudly hanging in their houses. Yes, my mother's and brother's house also.

Back in those days, I was involved in two hobbies, skeet shooting and motorcycles. My sister-in-law Sally's brother lived near me in Chatsworth, and called one weekend and invited me to go shoot with him at the Chatsworth Gun Club. Of course yes!

When we pulled in the main parking lot, Dennis said, "Wow, where are all these cars coming from? There is no free barbecue today." It didn't take long to find out that there was a shoot-off from a prior match that involved Robert Stack and Roy Rogers. It seemed that they both tied in the previous match. Dennis told me all about Mr. Stack's background. Prior to World War II, Stack was

America's top Olympic shooter. By the way, all Americans can be very proud of Robert Stack's service during World War II.

"Very interesting," I said. "What about Rogers?"

He said that Rogers was very well-known for his ability at shooting a .410 gauge (very small pellet pattern compared to Mr. Stack's .20 gauge). Then I informed Dennis about my brother and I years ago meeting Roy Rogers.

He then said, "Yeah, Angelo did mention that!"

Even though the other skeet fields were open to shooters, we decided to just sit there and see how this played out. We found out later in the day that Mr. Stack offered to Mr. Rogers one off his .20 gauge guns. Mr. Stack told him he didn't want to take advantage of the fact that Mr. Rogers was going to shoot the smaller gauge.

Well, before we got there, it was already decided that the King of Cowboys would use his very own .410 gauge shotgun. Dennis and I found out that it would be a three-game shoot-off. Each game had twenty-five clay birds that flew out. So, the best score would be seventy-five! At the end of the second game, they were both sitting on fifty. Wow, I had never seen that done before, with a .410 gauge. So, it was decided they would take a refreshment break before the last game. Mr. Rogers and Mr. Stack had a bunch of people around them at the table, so I thought it best to wait before I tested his memory.

Okay, folks here was the last game, and Mr. Stack won the coin toss, so he started off. It was unbelievable, almost at the end. On Station #7, Robert Stack missed one of his doubles. (Down one.) Mr. Rogers cleaned all four. The final Station #8, Robert Stack missed his high house. (Down two.) Okay, Mr. Rogers would have to miss the two last shots to go into another tie, But, perfect score, seventy-five out of seventy-five. Mr. Stack, seventy-three out of seventy-five. Unbelievable shooting. I was so glad to have witnessed this.

I kept watching them talking and shaking hands. It seemed to go on forever. Finally, Roy Rogers was walking into the parking lot, ready to load his gun case into a beautiful station wagon. I was ready to go for broke.

"Excuse me, Mr. Rogers, may I ask for just a minute your time?"

He turned around and said, "No sir, I am not selling the gun!"
"Oh no, sir, I am sure you won't. My name is Ray, and I met
you back in the middle '50s, when I was raking out the stalls at
Glen Randall Stables."
"Oh," he said, "I sure miss that place. A lot of fond memories
of Glenn working with my horses. Best trainer in the world." He
then said, "I am trying to recall meeting you." Then, I quickly
reminded him how hard he laughed when he heard my accent. "Oh
yeah, weren't there two of you?" I said yup. He said, "Yes, now I
remember, I am sure glad you are talking much better now!"

We both laughed, and I said, "Sir, thank you so much for your
time, Congratulations on your wonderful shooting today."

He said, "Okay, gotta go, maybe we can shoot a game together
soon." He got behind the wheel.

I walked back, and found people still standing in line for Mr.
Stack's autograph.

*I just now Googled, and found out that Robert Stack still holds
the record for 350 consecutive .20 gauge skeet hits.*

Dennis and I shot a couple of games. No, they were not twen-
ty-fives, but it was a great day. Dennis asked me if Roy Rogers
didn't mind being interrupted.

I said, "He is the same kind gentleman that my brother and I
met back in the day!"

When I walked in the house, Belinda said, "I know that grin,
Raymond. What happened today?"

I told her of every detail about Rogers and Stack. She said
Robert Stack was her sister Fina's favorite actor.

She said, "Raymond, I will say it over and over. Life is never
boring living with you, and are you keeping notes for your book?"

"Yeah, I sure am!"

By the way, I have to tell you. As soon as I got my job working
at Howard's company, we did put up that enclosed patio room, and
what the heck, a swimming pool and built-in Jacuzzi. Belinda and
I and the kids loved it.

I finally got an appointment with Cedars Sinai in LA, to meet
Mike, the radiology manager. The meeting went great, because he
put me to a test. He asked if I would like to give a quality assurance

seminar to his staff. It seemed that he had heard about the one I gave at St Joseph's in Burbank. I said of course, so we arranged to do it on Wednesday afternoon at 4PM. He said that way it would not interfere with his patient load. I stood up to shake his hand to say goodbye, and guess who walked in the office, and screamed out, "Ray!"

Yup, it was Vincent, one of my students from Letterman. This could have not happened at a better time. Vincent started to tell his boss about me.

Mike interrupted, and said, "Ray I am looking forward to Wednesday."

I pulled out another business card, and wrote my home number, and handed it to Vincent on the way out.

Yes, he called that evening. Sure enough, Mike did ask him about my training and experience. I asked Vince if Mike was happy doing business with my competitor, and Vince told me I would not have gotten the appointment if he was.

I told Belinda the good news about my day. She of course, as usual, was happy for me.

Well, maybe this is a good time for me to pause here, and tell you that this was what made me so happy that I was married to Belinda, because I don't ever forget about that young boy who tripped over that Army sign that day, and started on another road that finally led me to my wife. That time of my life, I did not know where I was headed, but, you know what I wrote in previous chapters about how Belinda gave me direction and self-confidence and pride in myself to stay on the road, and stayed focused. So, I told Belinda often, "I loved you then, I love you now, and I always will." She always said that I probably said that to my other wives.

I invited Vince and his young bride up to our house for dinner. We still keep in touch with each other.

Mike at Cedars Hospital and I kept a very nice business relationship over the next few years. He said to me, "There ought to be a law that all sales reps should be RTs." He said most of the reps came in the office and started talking football or basketball scores, and they always said, "Hey, have you heard this one?"

I said to Mike that I met most of them when I worked with the radiology group. He then informed me that Vincent was one of the best RT's he could have hired, and Vincent told him he learned a lot at Letterman, and he certainly enjoyed being my student. I said that I was very proud to hear that!

I told Belinda that I showed Mike her art portfolio, and she had better find the time to do her big floral in those nice gold and brown colors, because Mike fell in love with it. So, I handed her $150, and said that was the retainer, and she would get the other $150 on delivery.

She said, "Wow, I am an artist!" and I said, "Yes, and a real pretty one too."

About three weeks later, I put Mike's oil painting in the car. At that point, I already had made a date for lunch. So, I parked in the vendors lot and locked it up and went to the radiology reception window and announced my appointment with Mike. She said to take a seat for a few minutes. I looked around and there was only one seat vacant next to someone in a wheelchair, so I grabbed it. I could not see who this was, because he had his head buried into the newspaper. A few seconds later, the paper on his lap fell to the floor. I quickly picked it up and handed it to him. He put his paper down and said thanks.

I was looking directly at him, then I said, "My pleasure, Mr. Holden."

He said with a grin, "I see you enjoy the movies."

I said, "Only the good ones that have good actors."

"Wow, thank you," he said.

Then I asked him about the *The Bridge on the River Kwai* movie. He said, "It wasn't easy, but I am sure glad I got the part."

Right about that time, someone grabbed his wheelchair and said, "Ready to go, Mr. Holden?" He reached out and shook my hand, and said, "See ya."

During lunch, I asked Mike what did he know about his condition. Mike said that he co-owned this big African ranch where he devoted his time to animal preservation or such, and he seemed to have contracted some weird virus that stemmed from that area.

Mike was all thrilled about his painting, and said he would like to meet the artist in person. That was all arranged later.

Belinda said, when I walked up to her with my big silly grin, "Okay, Ray, is it a who, or is it a what, that happened to you today? Don't you dare tell me something happened to the painting!" I gave her $150, and said Mike was elated with her talent. "Okay, Raymond, there is something else, spill it!"

"Oh, I had an interesting chat today about movie production with my buddy, William Holden."

She said, "Well, that's my Raymond. Did you invite him out for dinner?"

"No, you know I am too busy for that."

That weekend we invited up Firpo and his family. By that time, I had two bikes in my garage. I told Firpo to make sure he brought his shotgun, because I was going to take him skeet shooting on Saturday, and besides swimming, we might also go for a motor-cycle ride on Sunday. Belinda called him back and told him to throw the kids' bicycles in the back of his truck. Good, I forgot!

Well, I gave Firpo all the things he needed to know about skeet shooting, and then I let him go solo, He did his first game at eleven, and his second game at fourteen. I had to make sure he knew that it was way above average for a first time shooter. So he kind of shook his shoulders and said, "Okay, Bro, I'm in!"

Firpo asked me if I shot every weekend, and I said about twice a month for sure. I just had been so busy these past few years. I shot two games: 1st = 23. 2nd = 23.

He said, "Okay, let's shoot another game."

Had a nice barbecue dinner around the pool that evening. The cousins all swam together, and when I looked over to Belinda, she seemed happy and content, because when her brother was around, it reminded her of the family she grew up in.

And that reminded me!

"Belinda, aren't we overdue for our trip to New Mexico?"

She said, "Yeah, let's leave tomorrow!"

I asked her when did school start. She said in two weeks.

"Okay, we will plan to leave here this coming Friday morning. I need some time off, Belinda, and so do you. We will take the camper."

I had just recently bought a truck and cab-over camper.

Last week, Howard turned in my car, and leased me an English made Ford, called a Capri. Nice car!

# CHAPTER 40

We had about a week and a half to get down to Las Cruces and back before school started. I could hear the noise in the camper above the cab. I suggested that we bring down the younger one down in front with us. It would be a professional guess that he was getting picked on upstairs. I couldn't believe he was already three.

It was always a sight to see Belinda embrace her family upon our arrival. Believe it or not, she got so excited talking to everybody, she actually didn't know I was there. Please don't think I just said something negative, because by the end of the next day she started to come down from her cloud of excitement and she would walk up to me and say, "Where have you been, Honey, I have not seen you close by."

"I am right here, Honey. Are you enjoying your time with your family?"

"Oooh yes, Honey, thanks for bringing us down."

The good news was that everybody in the family knew we were sleeping at Fina and Sal's house, so they came to see us, and got together and started cooking on the barbecue. Her daddy was super-talented, and man, could he play that guitar and sing so beautifully. The summer weather was always very hot there, but we had too much fun to notice. I did put the small motorcycle and the kids' bikes in my trailer. Down there, every child in the family inherited property from their dad's farmland, so most of them built their houses about every four acres apart. They had plenty of space, and no city lights to worry about. When Belinda and her sister and brothers were growing up, their daddy was farming cotton and chile.

Belinda was proud and happy to see that the whole family was doing well, raising their children, and working at their jobs, and most of them living close by to Mom and Dad.

Well, it was a great trip, but it was sad for Belinda to say goodbye. I always told her we would be back next year.

So, on the road, heading back to Canoga Park. The kids were all worn out from playing with their cousins, so they should sleep most of the way. I usually found a KOA campground just above Phoenix for our sleepover. Boy, back in that time of my life, I loved to drive, and now I had two other people in the car with me all the time.

Arthur and his cousin Itis, (That's a quote from Belinda's mom).

Well, the kids were back in school, and Belinda took some time off to stay with Steven, until he got ready for preschool. Meanwhile, I had a lot of territory to cover. I was called by the radiology manager at St. Joseph's and asked if I could do another quality assurance seminar for their new class of students. I would be happy to do that, because it got me off the road. I kept telling Belinda that going to City College two or three nights a week was taking its toll. I could see that it was good that I was not home some of the evenings during the week, because I saw a few more completed oil paintings in the patio room.

Christmas

Yes, this was the time of the year when things slowed down a little. A little less stress, because the business slowed down, but we picked up another type of stress trying to figure out how to please everybody for Christmas! Anyway, I called my brother and told him we were going to take a few vacation days and hit the desert with our dirt bikes, and our dune buggy, and let the kids have some fun. He said that sounded like fun, and they joined us. Belinda never liked camping at all. As a matter of fact, the only way she survived it was to bring her books for sure. We got back to the Valley two days before Christmas

Every month meant a trip down to the office in LA to meet with Howard and give him a territory report, and talk about service or chemical problems or whatever. This was the month I was going to tell him that this territory was way too large to cover, because he promised me about a year ago when the profits were at an all-time high, he would bring on some more help.

Well, I could forget about all that, because when I pulled in to park, there were all kinds of vehicles that I didn't recognize. Once upstairs, I found all the secretaries waving me over to their area.

"Ray, have you heard, did anyone call you?"

"What is going on?" I said.

"Ray, Howard sold the company!"

Yes, Howard sold the entire operation to some national conglomerate that was buying a lot of chemical and service companies across the country. Well, at this point, I got nothing to lose by telling Gloria to ring his phone, and tell him I was there for the meeting that he set up for this day and this time!

She did, and she said, "Ray, they want you in there."

*Ha! Here I go!*

You have probably never seen anybody spit out so many excuses so fast when I confronted Howard. His face was red as a candy apple.

When he finally stopped, I said, "Howard, you still have not told me why I did not know of any of this."

Then came more verbiage. Then, this Mister Bill Broe stepped in and told me that he would like to keep me in his company, because of my talents and my ARRT. However, he was bringing in his own sales manager. (Yup, his son.)

Howard spoke up very quickly, and said, "Ray, I anticipated your move, I have already set up with Mr. Broe here your severance pay, which equals out to one year's salary. Ray, I hope you know how sorry I am, but my age and all other things considered, this was a good move for me and my family."

"Okay, Howard. What about the car?"

Then Mr. Broe spoke up again and said, "Ray, by all means you drive that car home, and we will make arrangements to pick it up sometime next week. And please make sure that whatever company products or equipment you have can go in the trunk. Thank you, and please reconsider my offer."

"Sure thing. Okay, Howard, let's keep in touch."

"Yes, of course Ray!"

I could hear my angel saying about Howard, "Goodbye, and remember, don't take it personally, it's only business!"

I said to the ladies, "I have always appreciated how you guys supported me, and always did a great job with my contracts and proposals and letters and such, and I will miss all of you!"

Then Gloria spoke up and explained that all the secretaries who worked for Howard, with the exception of just two, were also leaving!

Belinda greeted me at the door, and said, "Hey, how did your monthly meeting go?"

I said, "Call the boys in here." They came running. "Well, family, what do you all say if I told you that I am in the mood for Benihana's Restaurant and Mommy is buying."

"You're kidding. I don't have that kind of money in my purse!"

"Trust me, Honey, the check is in the mail."

On the way to the restaurant, I asked Belinda if she had any-thing in the car that belonged to her. She told me just her makeup kit in the glove compartment.

"Why are you asking?"

"I will tell you tonight. It's all good."

Had a wonderful meal. The two older sons of mine knew I was in a good mood. Of course they ordered crab and lobster meals. Just this once, I was in a good mood!

Driving home, I said, "Hey, Honey, do you remember meeting Charlie from GAF at the mid-winter convention I took you to?"

She said, "I certainly do, because he kept making job proposals to you almost the whole evening."

I said, "Well, guess what? I called him earlier today to see if he was in his office, and he invited me to come to La Habra, and chat. And chat we did."

My bride said, "This is going to be a new chapter in your book, isn't it Raymond?"

"Yes, I will tell you when we get home. It's all good!"

# CHAPTER 41

By the time we got home, Steven was ready for the Sandman, and we said our prayers together, and I kissed him goodnight. The two older ones said they would like to go for a quick swim before saying goodnight. I said okay, and I invited Belinda for a nice relaxing Jacuzzi and I would tell her what kind of day this was!

So, as soon as she came in, I started from the moment I got to the office, then driving all the way to La Habra. As I was going through the facts, Belinda said at different intervals, "What?" "You're kidding." "No way." "I thought he was a friend!" "That much?" "When do you start?" "We're not moving, are we?"

Ya gotta love her!

"So, Honey, what do we do with that check? Honey, ever since we got married, you have always been in charge of the money, whatever you think is best. You could buy me a new motorcycle."

She then said, "Raymond, I'll say it again!"

"You ready, Honey? I said yes!"

"If wishes were horses, beggars would ride."

That was when I told the boys to get all dry, and time for bed. She did like the part about not moving!

When I first arrived at the Valley upon my discharge, and went to work for the Valley radiology group," I met Charles Byrne. We called him Charlie. I gave him a chance to demonstrate his product, and to submit a price quote. I was impressed with his presentation and his technical skills. Every few months or so he would drop by, and we would chat while having lunch in the hospital cafeteria. We kept bumping into each other while I was working for Howard, and that was when he insisted that I go to work for his company.

Soon I was driving another new company car with good company benefits. Now that Charlie was the regional manager for GAF Film, I insisted that he join me for my first product demonstration, to be done at St. Joseph's in Burbank. Over the past several years the rad manager and the chief radiologist had always trusted my judgement. The reason why I picked this hospital for the test was that this used to be Howard's biggest account, and I was dying to see how Mr. Broe's company was doing since the buy-out. Happy to report that when Charlie and I sat with the doctor, and Ben, they quickly told me that they cancelled the contract after only one week into the program. It seems that they could not produce the same services that I was performing with the student program, and the new sales manager displayed his lack of technical skills when questioned by the chief radiologist. I was happy the rest of the day for sure!

Well, at 4PM, Charlie and I were driving back to the office, congratulating each other on the fact that we now had St. Joseph's hospital running on GAF film (the big Kodak boys must have been having a fit) and the chemical service contract was handed over to Picker X-Ray Corporation. Get ready, Mr. Broe, because the only one happy right then was Howard, who was home counting his money!

*Note: Finally received my AA degree from Pierce College in 1976 in marketing and communications.*

Right along about 1979, the GAF company went into a down period in quality control. I had to make the call to my major account at St. Joseph's in Burbank and informed the chief radiologist that the news was not good, and at that time I advised him to switch back to his previous vendor. He thanked me for my honesty, and our relationship stayed intact.

He then informed me that Picker X-Ray Company was looking for a support manager and that he would be happy to call them and recommend my name as a candidate. He said it would be nice to keep me around, since Picker had their service contract.

My resume pulled me through, and I started employment with them in 1980. It was a good feeling to stay with St. Joseph's.

# CHAPTER 42

In 1982, Picker was ready to announce their silver reclamation unit to the hospital radiology market, and I was asked, as a manager, what thoughts I may have to announce it at the big radiology convention that was to be held in Salt Lake City that year. As all of you know by now, I always discussed every subject with Belinda. So, that night at dinner I explained the project that I was assigned to.

She got up from the table to fetch something, and turned around and said, "Why not a silver bullet? Have your company call the Lone Ranger's agent, and see what they come up with. Maybe he can come to the convention in his TV duds and present the silver bullet as a door prize or something like that."

Holy cow, Belinda. Look at you. I did not know I was married to a marketing entrepreneur!"

"Don't credit me, you're the Quad A that I married, you still watch his re-runs on TV every week."

"Oooh Belinda, I loved you then, I love you now, and I will love you forever."

"Good, Raymond, put that in your book, but don't you dare tell your company that this was my idea. I don't need any job offers at this time of my life!"

We laughed, hugged and kissed. My angel would have said, "I told you that you would find a good woman."

The company heard my story, they did call Clayton Moore's "The lone Ranger" agent, (it took time) and they asked me to be the guy who would take care of the details of his flights, his hotel reservation, and pick him up at the airport. They gave me his agent's number.

When I arrived in Salt Lake that week, I already had some butterflies in my stomach, and all my co-workers all said that once I
picked him up at airport, please bring him to the pool area so they
could meet him.

Well, I was at the gate when he got off the plane. When he got
to the gate, I raised up my sign that said: **Ray — Picker.** He walked
over to me and shook my hand, and said, "Yes, my agent said you
would be here!" We then went to the baggage area and picked up
his bags, and off to the car we went.

Now, we were in the car when he said his thanks to me for
meeting him at the airport. He then said, "Ray it's a pleasure
meeting you, tell me more about Picker X-Ray Company."

I said, "Before I do, I must tell you that we met way back in
about 1954 or '55 at the Glenn Randall Stables when I was a very
young teen, raking out the stalls and such.

He said, "Wait a minute, I do remember something that Jay
(Tonto) said at dinner once, he said he met you at the celebrity
picnic some time way back, and you told him your story that we
met before. Well, I remember what Jay said, and that's all I need
to know. The rest of my memory is not that good, but it's nice to
see you again!"

Then I reminded him how nice he was to me and my brother at
that time. He said thanks for that. I gave him a quick breakdown
on the history of Picker, not charging the government any fees for
all the portable x-ray equipment they provided during the Big War.
He was impressed with that.

Then Clayton asked me what was going to happen next, so
I informed him that the whole gang wants to meet him at the
pool area.

"Well, Ray, let me ask you. Will there be drinking and smoking
and telling jokes and such?"

I replied that yes, these were boys and girls who were away
from home, and tended to have a little fun like that. He said to me
that he was really not into such practices, so would it be okay if I
just checked him in and escorted him to his room, and then tonight,
pick him up and bring him to the big party. I said that would be
no problem.

He then said, "Please Ray, call me Clay. After all, you and I go way back." We both chuckled.

It was kind of tough telling the gang that they wouldn't see the "Lone Ranger" tonight, but I just told them that he was very tired.

That night was perfect. He said his line very well standing on the stage in his grey outfit with his two silver guns, and said, "Well folks, very nice to be here with all of you, and I am holding in my hand a pure silver bullet that has been minted from Picker's new Silver Reclamation unit, and I will pull out the winning number now."

Then, when he announced the winning door prize number, we could hear this lady scream out, "Oh my Gosh, that's me, and I love you Lone Ranger." The whole crowd busted out as she walked up to the stairs to the stage, where Clayton already had his hand extended out to help her up. She was like me, and probably grew up watching her TV hero saving people.

On the ride back to the airport the next day, he asked me where I lived, and I said Canoga Park.

He said, "Wow, I don't live far from you, I live in Calabasas." Then, he knocked me over and said, "Here is my phone number, and please don't show that to anybody. Maybe we can get together and chat again."

I said to him not to worry about anybody getting his number. When I dropped him off at his gate, I shook his hand and told him that I was so grateful for the pleasure of his company once again in my life. To this day, I don't have any reason that I could come up with and figure out why I never did call him. I seriously regret that very much!

I had fun telling Belinda and the kids all about him, and how nice a man he truly was.

My dear sweet wife said, "Yeah, Honey, he is the Lone Ranger!" And of course she said, "Make notes for your book."

About a year later, the Picker X-Ray Company started to make big changes, such as merging with other X-ray companies in order to get ready for the new "Era of digital Technology." We all knew it was coming from what we had learned at the annual Equipment conventions that we attended. Naturally, it called for a lot of new manager's and job changes. I was not sure I wanted to fit in with all these new people and their marketing concept. It was right about the time of all these changes, I was offered a position with the Pyne Corporation, (exclusive Dealer for Fuji Film Corporation ) in the summer of 1984. This new job was to be positioned in Albuquerque, New Mexico, (only 230 miles from Belinda's birthplace)…she was so happy , and so was I to see her excitement!

We had been living in Albuquerque ever since Pyne sent me here in 1984. I told you a while back that I never enjoyed flying. Well, in 1970 I started going all over this great country of ours, and it finally stopped in 2000. I care not to remember all of the incidents that took place. Every time that plane landed, I could see the blood coming back to my knuckles, and I would thank the Lord for a safe trip as always. But all the above that I just mentioned was done because of business, not because I wanted to go and leave my family behind. The years flew by quickly as we started to get older. I remember telling Belinda how we noticed our parents were slowing down and just getting older. Belinda always was saddened when we made our trips to Las Cruces just to see that her dad was not working around the property like he used to, and her mom was no longer sewing and making clothes for all the grandchildren. I told her back then, nobody escapes their fate in life. God has a plan for each of us, and if we were all the same, we would all have the same fingerprints and so on.

Belinda asked me once, "Raymond, when your time is up, will you be ready to meet your Creator?"

I said, "Sweetheart, yes, I certainly will be ready to meet Him. Question is, will He be excited to meet me?"

"Raymond, I think He just might keep you here, because you're good for the economy, the way you spend your money."

"Ouch, Belinda!"

1991

This was the year that my dad died because of black lung disease. All those years of welding, and in those times they didn't use any masks to protect themselves from the fumes. He was only seventy-one. When I got the call from my brother Angelo, I called my dad in the hospital that very night, and asked him if there was anything in this world that I could do for him, please tell me, and I would do it right now!

He said, " No son, there is nothing to be done."

I said, "Dad, I know that you never said the word *love* to us when we were growing up, but I do know we were the finest dressed, and had all the things any boy could have ever want. Is it okay if I tell you that I love you?"

He said, "That's very nice."

"Dad, is there anything that you want to tell me?"

He said, "No, son, you take good care of yourself."

Click!

My Belinda heard that conversation, and there I was crying, and I kept telling Belinda while she was holding me in her arms, "Honey he just couldn't say he loved me.

She said, "Oh Ray, he loved you, but he was raised during some rough times by his parents just coming here from Italy and all. In those days men only used the word *love* to a woman. It was a different world back then, Raymond, but in his heart, he loved you!"

Thank you, Belinda.

# CHAPTER 43

1999

This was a difficult time for my dear Belinda. Her daddy passed away. This was so hard for the entire family, especially Belinda's mom, and all her brothers and sister. It was a beautiful funeral, and of course, just like weddings, it brought in all the rest of the family from the surrounding states. As I told you in earlier chapters, he was a wonderful man who was proud of his family, and was always to me a role model as the patriarch of the family. (May his soul rest in peace)

This was a time in our lives when jobs and careers were no longer as important to us as before. We became acutely aware of God's plan. The reality of becoming a senior citizen started to set in, and we realized we better see a doctor as to our health status.

Well, I got a call from my brother Angelo, and he told me that our mother was giving everybody a hard time in California. She was losing her temper with the whole family, and they didn't know what to do. I explained that based on what we knew about how many years she fought with Dad, and suffering with those terrible migraine headaches, now she might have Alzheimer's or dementia setting in. I told him to take her to a doctor, and then call me back.

We finally got the call from Angelo that Mom certainly had a problem, the diagnosis involved Alzheimer's and early stages of dementia. It was decided that she and my baby brother were to move to Albuquerque and get an apartment not too far from us, so we could oversee her conditions and medications and such. We also took her to our medical system, and the outcome of her exam did confirm the same diagnosis. They prescribed a series of medication for her condition, and it was obvious that as long as my brother Tony was close to her, she was in a calmer condition. The doctors told me that in this state, most of the people who suffered with this seemed to pick out one or two people they favored. In Mom's case, it was my baby brother Tony, and her younger sister Mary, who lived in Rhode Island. I could count on Aunt Mary's love as always, so she came to visit Mom several times over the years and made lots of phone calls to my Mom.

When I first got hired into the Fuji world, They were the exclusive dealer for the entire United States. I joined them because over the years, I had been evaluating and testing film systems that would ensure the doctors had the best product in their hands to make a better diagnosis. Well, hands down, I can tell you that their product beat all the competitors, including Kodak. Well, anyway I was automatically invested in their profit-sharing program. So, it was obvious to me if I could spend the next few years in Albuquerque and surrounding areas converting hospitals, I could build a nest egg of retirement security for me and Belinda.

So, one day the big managers I had known for years called me and said they had good news and bad news. What it boiled down to: since Fuji world bought out Mr. Pyne's company back in '86, there were about eight or nine of us still vested in profit-sharing. I asked them if that was bad, and they said indeed it was now, because the buy-out conditions had expired. As it turned out, here remained the last of the old employees making higher salaries, and still owning their profit share amounts that had accumulated over the years. He added one more thing that boosted my ego. He told me that since I came to Albuquerque, the annual sales for my territory were up to $7.5 million per year, and when we started in '84, they were at $650,000. So, he said that the company in Tokyo would like to congratulate me, and they would be glad to release my profit-sharing check to me as soon as they could get me and the others to accept retirement.

So, I asked them, "Where is the bad news?"

He said that they were worried I might not want to retire at the age of fifty-nine, and I would need to acquire medical benefits for my family.

"Ray, do you remember when you played golf with Mr. Yakura at the Riviera Country Club in LA at the annual meeting?"

"I sure do."

"Well, he asked me if your game has improved any since then?"

What!

When I came to Albuquerque in '84, it became obvious that all the major hospitals in the area liked to play golf. At that time, I informed my boss that I did not play golf, and I didn't even like the game. I was into the shooting sports, horses and motorcycles. Well, they quickly told me that they were going to apply for a membership at the nearby country club, and I would be starting my lessons ASAP!

Belinda said, "Ooh Honey, you are going to look so cute in your colorful golf attire."

You guessed it, I played for the next sixteen years, and had to fake my so-called enthusiasm. Well, after a while, I did get to like it a little. As a matter of fact, since my wife made fun of my colorful attire, I insisted that she take lessons along with my younger son. He was already in high school at the time we moved. Steven took to golf like a duck to water, but my Belinda needed some extra lessons.

About the second year of living there, I finally bought a nice Quarter horse. His name was Regal Rascal, and had a few ribbons racked up for barrel racing. I met his owner the first year there. She had more trophies than she could display. She was indeed a rodeo queen.

On a lot of Saturdays, Steven and I would go play golf, and of course we always invited Mom.

She would say, "Nah, you guys go ahead and play. Someone in this family will have to feed and exercise Rascal down at the stables!"

I said to Steven, "I think we better take Mom out to dinner tonight for sure!"

So, after several chats with the boys at Fuji Medical, it was decided that they would like to draw up legal paperwork that would explain my so-called Golden Parachute, and for legal reasons, it wouldn't hurt to have legal representation. Well, that was easy because my friend and neighbor next door, Dave, said he would gladly help. After a few rounds of negotiations, we finally settled on:

1. Purchase my company car for $10.
2. My entire profit sharing.
3. Keep mobile phone and pagers.
4. Receive one complete year's salary.
5. Receive one year of full medical coverage.

Belinda and I felt really good about all this, so it was decided that we would take about a year or so off, and as soon as the medical coverage expired, I would seek employment as an x-ray technologist at one of my friendly customer sites, and then officially retire on my sixty-fifth birthday, and go on Medicare and all that other good stuff. Since my salary was always in the high bracket, I knew I could also rely on my SS check. Belinda and I both agreed that the profit-sharing check would be deposited into our investment account, where we already had some stocks and bonds put away, and that money would be for our living expenses. Sally, our rep at Edward Jones, said she would figure out, when she sat down with Belinda, a monthly check that would cover our expenses.

I found out that Mr. Yakura was coming to Fuji USA for a meeting in Stamford, Connecticut, and he was going to make a stopover in Albuquerque. For sure my district manager, and the regional manager would make themselves available to probably give me a gold watch or something.

Belinda hit it right on the nail when she said, "Honey, this is just another good reason to play golf for Mr. Yakura. He knows the weather here is pretty nice, compared to Connecticut at this time of year."

"Belinda, guess what? This will be the last time that I will pick up my clubs. My shoulders and my knees are killing me."

"Honey," she said, "I am still in shock, after all the years working in hospitals, either as a soldier, consultant or a technologist, the road stops here."

"I want you to know for sure that the road does stop here, and we are not going to buy a new house, we will visit your family every month. We might even be able to persuade my mom to visit Las Cruces, and would you mind if we just spend time doing really nothing?"

She said, "Honey, what are you going to do for the next year anyway?"

I said, "Maybe I will build some furniture, or see if I can beat Robert Stack's 350 straight hits!"

"Really Raymond, I think you should stick to your first promise, and just try for a straight seventy-five!"

"Belinda, these last forty years of being with you have been great. Do you wanna go for thirty more?"

"Why not? Raymond, you will see to it that I won't ever be bored."

"Honey, I know that you will always have your books and your artwork to enjoy."

She told me she was going to start giving the grandchildren art lessons, and I knew she would be good at that for sure.

I was officially released on my brother Angelo's birthday on February 2, 2000 (Groundhog Day). I did have a hard time for the first few months. I kept thinking I was supposed to be somewhere doing something important. Belinda as usual was always coming up with things, like, "Okay. we can paint the house, dig up that dying tree in the back yard, we could give the dog a bath, clean those windows, go shopping for groceries, or Raymond, we can go down to Cruces and visit Mom."

"Okay, honey, let's go get packed."

"We are already packed, Honey."

"What? How do you know I wasn't gonna dig up that old tree?"

"Yeah, sure Sweetie!"

Her mom was diagnosed with Type 2 diabetes, and all the sons and daughters were taking good care of her. At this age of her mom, Belinda was concerned. What still gives me a tickle is when Belinda always said to me when we pulled in Mom's driveway, "Boy, Honey, that was a fast trip!" As soon as we hit the I-25 Freeway heading south for 235 miles, she was out for the count. (Every time.)

Back in 1971, when we lived in our first house in Van Nuys, we had that earthquake in the very early morning hours. I was so scared. The house was going up and down, the baby's crib rolled out of the bedroom heading down the hallway, the kids were screaming. We finally got out in the street, and all the neighbors were out there, realizing they didn't have enough clothes on. Then our neighbor asked where was Belinda. Oh my God, I thought she was with me. I turned and ran back in the house, and right then came an aftershock. The house started dancing again.

I ran into the bedroom and screamed, "Belinda, are you all right?"

She replied, "There is nothing you can do about this, get the kids back in the house, and I will make some hot chocolate."

Are you kidding me? I did not sleep in that house unless I had my boots and pants on for at least a month.

# CHAPTER 44

The time was up. We already got to 2001, and our medical insurance was almost up, so I ended up making a few phone calls to the hospitals.

One of the managers I knew very well said, "Ray, I had no idea you were going to retire at this age. I am sure going to miss playing in your Fuji golf tournament every year. Do you suppose that they will continue with the program?"

I told him that I surely would not know!

"Okay, Ray, here's what's going to happen. You are to report tomorrow to our employment center, and they will process you into the system. You will get your ID badge, and Monday morning, you will start your orientation at the Pain and Spine Center. We figure that a guy your age can handle a job like that. What do you think?"

I said that suited me fine, and thanks so much for caring about senior citizens. Ha!

Belinda was so glad for me, and the first question she asked was about the medical insurance. I told her the monthly deduction was very fair, and we were covered very nicely. That certainly put Belinda at ease. She now was doing some fancy and very intense needlepoint work. I could hardly see those little tiny holes on the canvas, where she put the needle through. I once told Belinda she was the only person I knew who constantly uses her eyes so much.

One day we were in the local book store here in our neighborhood. By this time, everybody who worked there knew Belinda well. She found the manager and asked him a whole bunch of questions that dealt with some very old books. He asked Belinda how she gained so much knowledge.

He said to her, "If you ever decide you would like to work here, I sure would like to have you."

Here is what Belinda said: "Okay, shall I start on Monday?" (And she did!)

I said, "Wow! Belinda, I bet right now you are floating high, knowing you will be living in your world for eight hours a day, and getting paid for it."

She said, "Honey, I also have an angel."

I said, "Maybe so, or that could be mine putting in some overtime!"

I was so happy for her. After all those years of supporting me, she deserved this. Thank You, Lord! Back in that period, I can remember stopping by in the evening and always seeing people standing in line to ask Belinda a question. Things were rolling along pretty normal at home and at work. It always felt good when main radiology would call and ask for some assistance with their quality assurance. It was kind of like getting back in the game. It had been in my blood since San Antonio.

We took a lot of Rides around the country to visit our children and friends, and of course visiting Belinda's mom and family. We made a few trips up to Paso Robles where my brother and family lived. Did some bass fishing every once in a while, and still tried for my seventy-five in skeet shooting. To be honest, the best skeet score I ever got was when I was shooting two or three nights a week at Chatsworth Gun Club back in the 1970: seventy-two straight hits. At my present age of seventy-eight, I think I will stay with trap shooting now.

Ooh, poor Belinda, how dare the owner pull a "Howard" and sell his book store out to a national chain! She was so sad, she kept saying, "Best job I ever had." I told her that she still had her library at home, and her art studio I built for her in the back yard, her grandkids coming for art lessons, her needlepoint, and she had me to support her.

She said, "All that's good, Raymond, but I want that job back!"

In late December, both our moms were not doing too well. Belinda's mom was starting to get more advanced in her diabetes, My mom had to be admitted to a nursing home. That was the very last place I wanted to see her in. (I will not discuss the details here.) We prayed for Mom twice a day, every day. I called up her sister Mary, and she agreed with me that she and her daughter would return soon, even though they were here recently.

## 2003

Belinda's mom passed away, there were no words that could describe the pain one suffers at the loss of such a beautiful woman. She had so much love for everybody. She simply loved people, and always wore a smile every day. Very devoted to her Christian faith, and such a deep love for her entire family. All her grand-children at one time or another went to school wearing something she had sewn. Back in the '80s when we lived nearby, she made me some beautiful Western shirts, which I was proud to wear. The entire family was there by her bedside at her last moments, and as expected when she said goodbye, she was wearing her daily smile.

We all love you, and may your soul rest in peace.

Belinda needed time and space for a while. As we drove back to Albuquerque, for the first time she did not sleep. She was saying her prayers, I'm sure.

That spring, Belinda told me we should get her annual eye check-up, because she wasn't seeing too clearly.

I told her that I usually ate at the hospital cafeteria, and a few months ago I met a very nice ophthalmologist, and based on my chats with him, I thought it best we make an appointment with him. As it turned out, we were probably about a year too late! The doctor told Belinda that her left eye was already showing signs of leakage posteriorly. Thank God we were not two years late. Yes, she had contracted macular degeneration. I am sure a lot of you know about the shot these patients need on a monthly basis. The injection is right in the center of the eyeball. Before the injection, the RN spends about fifteen minutes or so inserting drops off anes-thesia to numb the eyeball before inserting the medicine.

Well, my sweetheart told the good doctor, "I knew you did everything right, but before next month, sir, you better find some-thing better than what the nurse used today!" She held my hand walking out of the office, and said, "Honey, that hurt so bad, and you know how I can tolerate pain!" Believe me, I knew she could take just about anything.

"Okay, Sweetheart, that's over, what can I do or get for you right now?"

"Take me to the Owl Cafe and get me a chocolate milk shake." Yes, ma'am!

About a week later when the bill showed up, I almost dropped to the floor. I called up and spoke to the office manager, and said, "What is this?"

She told me that our insurance didn't cover the shot, but come back to the office, and they would help us apply for special needs. Okay, but the co-payment was still $500.

We got the billing squared away. Now the doctor told us that the scan showed the leakage, but his hopes were that the medicine would keep it from getting worse. He said after our conversation, based on what Belinda did for her hobbies, he could try to make a special lens for her left eye. However, it would be very expensive.

I jumped and said, "When can you start making it?"

"Come back in three days, and we will try it out!

We were driving home, and she started telling me she was falling apart.

I said, "Honey, we live in modern times. If any of your parts, as you say, start to fall off, we will just go buy new ones!"

My dear Aunt Mary and my cousin Lorna came out to make another visit to Mom. It was wonderful to see she still recognized her favorite sister Mary. I couldn't believe how calm she was. I was happy to witness that.

My aunt liked New Mexico, she loved the clear blue sky. She and my cousin really enjoyed Belinda's company. They fell in love with her artwork. We took them up to Santa Fe. They couldn't believe how small the city was, considering how much they heard about it in their lifetime. Aunt Mary told me how many times my mother called her up and said, "Mary, you better come out quick, Raymond is beating me up." Aunt Mary told me she cried and cried thinking about me and Belinda going through all this with my mother. Then I told how hard this was on Belinda, even though she was the one who suggested Mom coming to Albuquerque ten years ago. I told my aunt this was a terrible disease. The longer it went on, the more brain cells died off.

Christmas Eve

Belinda and I thought we should go and check on Mom that afternoon. If we caught her in a cognitive state of mind, we could talk about what she would like for us to bring her to eat for Christmas.

You hear in your lifetime (or not) the saying, "God works in mysterious ways." What we found on that Christmas Eve was my mom seeing me walk into the room, and quickly saying, "Raymond, I was wondering when you were coming, is Belinda with you?"

I was completely not ready for that, but I said to the Lord, "Thank You so much."

"Okay Mom, what would you like for us to bring in tomorrow? You do know it's Christmas, don't you?"

Her reply, "Oh, Raymond, I won't be here to eat, I will be going to see Jesus for His birthday tomorrow!" Her voice was so clear and full of conviction, the hair on my neck tingled.

"Okay, Mom, Belinda and I will go to midnight Mass, and check on you early."

We kissed her goodbye, and she waved us off with a smile on her face that I could not recognize. It had been so long since I had seen her smile.

Christmas Morning

I woke to the sound of the phone, and I knew the voice of that nurse.

"Raymond, I am so sorry, your mother passed away a few minutes ago."

I jumped out of bed and dressed quickly. Belinda was sleeping so soundly. I drove to the hospital, only two blocks away, and they had her lying on the stretcher. I pulled the sheet back, and kissed her, and told her, "Mom you are finally at peace, and I know you are going to enjoy the party, and I love you."

It was a very quiet Christmas for me and Belinda, who spent the rest of the day at my side holding me.

# CHAPTER 45

I t was a cold winter, one of the worst we have ever seen here in Albuquerque. Belinda was doing fairly well with her new lens. So, of course she was into the books as much as possible. I told her that I could put a portable heater in her art shack, if she wanted to paint. She finally told me she was starting see angles in her vision, some kind of weird distortion, Especially when she had to focus on something. The doctor explained to her that the leakage behind the eye caused that, so maybe she should slow down on her artwork and her reading for a little while, "give those eyes some rest, Belinda."

At our age, we seem to find ourselves making too many visits to the doctors. My wife and I had our annual physicals, and Belinda was diagnosed with Type 2 diabetes. That was a tough blow to Belinda, knowing her mother just passed away from the same disease. The doctor told us that we would start off with pills, and see what happened in the next six months. I did not walk out of there good either. It seemed that my PSA jumped up a whole bunch since last year. Yes, more tests.

Well, we made a trip out to California again, to visit my brother and family. We took our oldest grandchild to Disneyland, and as usual, it was hard to get Belinda out of the park. She once told me that this was like her books; the results were the same. You forget reality, and drift off to happy land. When we got home from that trip, she was very tired, and I asked her about that. She would just tell me she was okay! Mmmmm!

The PSA keep going higher, so they decided to do a biopsy. That was a horrible day with that procedure, but they let Belinda stand at the head of the table. I was surprised I didn't break her hands from squeezing them so hard during that procedure. (She was my gal.)

One week later they called me at work and told me that the news was not good. So they told me that the first thing to do was to get an abdominal CT scan, to make sure it didn't spread. If that would be good news, then they would give me several options to study up on, as to what type of procedure I would pursue. Belinda and I always prayed daily, but now, we would ask the good Lord to get us through this. Belinda said to take my angel companion with me for my scan.

"Raymond, listen to me, you're going to be fine, your scan will be negative." (Yes, a big hug, and a few tears.)

The scan was negative. Belinda and I bowed our heads and prayed with sincere gratitude, and then headed out to the parking lot, and I said, "Where to?"

She said, "Chinese. Let's go!"

We talked about the next step. Belinda said we would get on the computer and go to all the major hospitals in the country and ask all the questions. And after that we would sit down and weigh the facts. We did that for about two weeks. Every day at work, I discussed this with the staff at our Pain and Spine Center. It turned out that one of the hospital physicians went through all this. When I approached him personally, I quickly made it very clear that I did not want to probe into his personal life, just please give me your doctor's name and phone number. He did say, "Good, because I don't want to talk about that!'

It turned out that Dr. Anthony, the radiation oncologist's specialty was the one procedure we picked out.

The procedure was radiation implant of the prostate gland. You certainly will not get the facts from me, way too much detail. (If you have a reason as to need to know, I suggest you look this up.) My surgery was February 22, 2005, and I had seventy-two radioactive seeds implanted into my gland. I owe a bunch of thanks to Dr. Anthony. Here it is almost twenty years, and my PSA is very normal!

I was back to work in just three days. Then, I said to Belinda, "Which one?"

She said, "The India House."

Let's go!

This year, the eye specialist told Belinda that her left eye was beyond help, and when he did a scan on the right, he then informed her that the macular degeneration was just barely starting in that good eye. Monthly injections would stop in the bad eye, and start in the good eye every month. He once again charged us a fortune to make Belinda a special lens for her to keep reading and painting, and he strongly suggested no more needlepoint. Belinda said to me that she was becoming very expensive to keep around.

I told her, "Did you forget what our co-payment was for my implant surgery?"

She said, "Okay Honey, but this thing with my eyes is really scaring me."

I said, "Let's wait for your new glasses."

"Well, okay," she said.

One of her old friends from the old book store called Belinda and told her that her sister, an RN, said they were looking for a bi-lingual medical clerk at the VA Center, and if she was interested in applying, here was the number.

My sweet little wife said, "Honey, I think I will apply for it. I don't think I will get it at my age, but Sweetheart, I need a change in my life right now, I am tired of all these doctor visits. You know me, Raymond, I am just going to put all this crap in the wastebasket."

I then said to her that with her medical resume, they would have to hire her.

I was right, her new glasses were working fine, and she was gainfully employed on Ward 4-D. I just realized that I would officially be retired on my upcoming sixty-fifth birthday on July 30. Once again I become a short-timer. I asked Belinda if that was going to bother her, me being home, and her working. She said she was just like me, and she loved working with her vets, and she also mentioned she had our World War II Navajo code talkers on her ward.

Right around her birthday, her doctor said her blood panel showed some areas of concern, and she ordered some tests. It turned out her blood pressure was a little too high, her thyroid gland was too low, and her A1-C tests indicated she had to increase her insulin. Belinda was not happy at all, and off we went to the pharmacist. Now Belinda was taking pills for high blood pressure, thyroid, diabetes, and a large super vitamin for her eyes. I knew what this was doing to Belinda. Here she was a tough little farm girl and she was healthy most of her life, and now her medicine cabinet is full from top to bottom. I was somewhat glad that she was working at the VA, because it helped take her mind away from this new lifestyle change.

Meanwhile, I was going back and forth with follow-up exams related to my surgery. We had no idea that we would be involved with so many co-payments. That sure put a big dent in our budget. The doctors told Belinda she was now pretty squared away with her meds and all, so it would be very beneficial to her to go on a low carb diet, and please try to refrain from the sweets. I told her we would do it together, and we both would profit from it medi-cally speaking.

For the next several months, things ran on a smooth level, and Belinda was enjoying her job a lot. We would get in the camper on the weekends, and spend time at the lake, and I did some fishing, she did her reading, and we would walk every day, and of course, we took in Las Cruces for family visits. One day driving back to Albuquerque, she started to laugh.

I said, "What's up with you, Honey?"

She said, "Oh boy, Raymond, back in the day, when me and my brothers and sisters got together, we would talk about the good old days on the farm, growing up and getting caught swimming in the ditches, and do a little gossiping and all, and we would laugh and trade off some jokes and now, all we do is compare our pre-scriptions, and our latest diagnosis, and ask, 'are your pills the same color as mine?' and what parts of our bodies, are not com-plying with our wishes. Boy, Raymond my dear, growing older is not for wimps."

And then, we started to laugh.

Then came July. Time was running on the Concord, whatever! So, pretty soon we both would be on Social Security and Medicare. I gave ample warning to my boss, so they could start getting a replacement.

Belinda said, "You won't have to pay your annual fees anymore to the ARRT, and ASRT, after paying them for the last forty years. How's that feel?"

I said, "Where did that forty years go?"

## 2005

Well, it was time to wake up and get to my last day of work! I rolled over to wake Belinda, and oh my God, the left side of her face had collapsed, and she was trying to speak, but could barely get the words out. I threw her robe on, put her slippers on and got her into the car, and drove straight to the Emergency Room. They got her on a stretcher. I knew all of the doctors who worked there, and they told me to sit and try to relax while they sent her down for a CT of her skull. The doc told me that they would like to rule out that it was a stroke. I asked what would it be if it wasn't a stroke.

"Ray, calm down and go sit in the corner, and don't move!"

Well, one hour later, I was holding her hand, and they were telling her she got hit with Bell's Palsy.

I asked the doc what brought that on. He informed me that in some people it could be their diabetes or a type of virus, like herpes simplex.

"Calm down, Ray, this is going to go away, and Belinda will slowly get her speech back."

Oh, my poor Belinda, she lay there in the stretcher, still holding my hand, and just kept shaking her head, no, no, no!

She had to take time off work because her speech was impaired. The left side of her face was still paralyzed.

This was not going to be easy for Belinda. Her mood was not good. She grabbed the pad and pencil and wrote, "See Raymond, more pills, just what I need, on top of all the other stuff, more Pills!"

She finally went to sleep, and I just prayed.

The following week, I thought it best to get her down to the brothers and sisters for a visit. She was still slurring her words, but it was getting better. I also told her that the dog and I would talk to each other while she slept as we went down the highway. I did get a little grin out of her. There was no doubt that she started looking and feeling better once the family all got together. That weekend really put Belinda back in the saddle.

Belinda went back to work at the VA. I told you earlier, she still had a few of our country's Navajo code talkers on her ward, and they had built up quite a friendship with each other. Belinda would get their snacks and whatever else they needed, and when they needed an interpreter, they would always call on her. One day, she came home with this jackknife that was pretty much worn out, and she said that one of her code talkers asked if her husband would like to have it. He said to tell me that both blades in the knife were completely worn down to half their size. He told her that he used that knife throughout the entire Pacific war every day.

He said to her, "You told me that your husband was a veteran, and I want him to put this away and not let it get lost, and tell him he can hand it down to another veteran." He passed away in 2014 at ninety-three years old. according to my wife's notes. His name was Chester Nez, born in Northern, New Mexico. My son Steven was a Panama War veteran, so as of this writing, I will inform him that he will be the new keeper of the knife.

There is a movie that shows the bravery of these Navajo code talkers, and the great sacrifice they made for this great nation of ours, and I am proud to be the present day keeper of this soldier's jackknife!

# CHAPTER 46

Our good friend Harry came for another visit to Albuquerque. Belinda told him this time, "Harry, don't you think it is time for you to show up with a wife, after all these years!"

He said, "The Sarge here took the last good women on the planet. I am still looking!"

She said, "Yes, Harry, we are having soft tacos tomorrow night, with all the trimmings."

Now we were talking! Harry did say to me, maybe his next trip might make Belinda happy. Well, every time we got together, the stories of our German escapades came out. I actually forgot about the time that we joined up with the rifle and pistol team. We actually went from town to town competing with different Army divisions. We even racked up a first place medal with the M1 Garand, my favorite rifle. Harry still made us laugh, when we got back to our infamous soccer game we played with Hans and his teammates. He said we never got the ball over the center field line. That was when Han's actually lay flat on his back in his goal net, pretending to take a nap. Harry said he would never forget that day! However, Belinda sure did put him in place playing twenty-one. I wonder if her name is still on the wall at the restaurant?

Harry said to me, "Ray, I've been meaning to ask you something, because I know we are both movie buffs. Back in January '86, I remember you telling me on the phone that Fuji was booking your national sales meeting at the Riviera Country Club, and you were going to participate in a celebrity/guest golf day. How did that turn out?"

Belinda spoke up and said, "You know my Raymond always gets involved!"

So, I told him I was very impressed with the entire place, the grounds and the golf course and the beautiful 19th century Spanish-style buildings nestled in the Santa Monica Canyon. It was like looking at the movie *Pat and Mike*, starring Katherine Hepburn and Spencer Tracey, all over again. Anyway we were told the next morning the golf carts would all be lined up outside with the assigned names in each cart. One Fuji guest and one celebrity. Not only that, the first night there, they had a Sonoma vineyard giving away free wine all evening. Needless to say, myself and several others, including, Mr. Yakura, moved to the bar and took a seat. All my guys were sitting to my left, and we were all just jabbering away.

The person sitting next to me on the right tapped me on my arm, and politely said, "Excuse me, sir, would you mind letting me bum a cigarette from you?"

At that time, I turned toward him and slid the pack right up close to him, and I said, "Please, my pleasure, and I was looking right at Mr. Vincent Minnelli. He appeared to be friendly, and he said to me, "I hope you are planning to quit these things (cigarettes) soon." I told him that my wife and I were already talking about it.

I said, "Sir, I have a book at home that tells all about the great work you have done, and I am glad to have the pleasure of meeting you!"

He said, "Call me Vincent. What is your name?"

I said, "Vincent, my name is Ray."

He then asked me if I was a Fuji guy, and I said Yes. He proceeded to tell me how much he liked and used our movie film. Then of course I had to tell him I represented the medical market. Anyway, I told him it would be great if I was to pair up with him in the morning.

"Are you kidding me? Look how old I am. I don't play that game, and if my doctor saw me with this cigarette, he would cuss me out something awful." He then asked, "Ray, what is your last name?" I told him. He said, "I knew you had to be an Italian." Then as he was sliding off the bar stool, he put his finger on the pack of cigarettes, and said, "Remember what you told me about these."

I shook his hand and we said good night. I can recall hearing on the news about six months later he had passed away from emphysema and pneumonia. I quit smoking that October of '86. Belinda also quit, but she never really had the habit, thank God.

Harry said, "But Ray, you didn't ask him enough questions about his profession and all his great works."

"Hey, Harry, I sure could tell you he appeared to be very tired, and he was ready for Bed."

"Okay, what about the next morning?"

"What about it?" I said.

"Ray, who was in your golf cart?"

"Oh that, yeah, I paired up with Donald O'Connor, and he had all of us laughing all day!"

The next morning, we drove Harry to Santa Fe, and shopped around a little. Then Harry told me he would love to stop at some of the old arroyos and look for old arrowheads. Well, we came up dry as the sand in the arroyo.

Belinda said, "Let's get back on the road if you want your dinner tonight."

Harry said, "Indeed Belinda."

My wife and Harry always had a great time talking about the books that they had read, and I always enjoy looking at Belinda's face lighting up on those occasions.

The next several months, we put in a lot of miles driving out to several states visiting our children and our grandchildren. Every time we travelled, I had to make sure she brought all her meds. Believe me, she would rather have forgotten them, because she really hated the idea of living on pharmaceutical support. The best thing that happened for Belinda was that she became friends with the pharmacist where she worked. She always checked Belinda's inventory of meds to make sure they complied with her diagnosis.

Belinda and I always supported each when life threw some hard punches in our direction, especially when we lost our loved ones through the years, It was so hard for Belinda when her mom passed, and I couldn't help but wonder what was going through her mind of late. I knew how much we hated going to the doctors. Every visit we made, Belinda said to me, "Well, Honey, what are they going to throw at me today?"

"Honey, I am here with you!"

We were moving through time rather smoothly, and I began to realize my wife wasn't hearing so well. I asked her why she had not told me anything.

She said, "Raymond, has it not dawned on you that I am going downhill here? Honey, right about five months after my Bell's Palsy, I started going deaf in my left ear. I didn't choose to tell you because you would get all worried and start dragging me back to the doctors, and they would give me more pills, and you would have to build me a bigger medicine cabinet. Where does it stop, Raymond? Leave me alone!"

I simply touched her on the shoulder, and called the dog, and we drove around for a while. It was getting dark, so I headed home. I stayed in the garage and started to clean up my messy tool bench. She walked into the garage holding a cup of coffee in her hand and put it down on the bench.

She told me, "Raymond, I can remember when you used to keep your garage nice and neat. What happened to you?"

I said, "Oh, I guess I just got old and lazy."

"Well, Raymond, do you mind if I tell you a few things?"

"Please do," I said.

"Okay Honey. First thing is that I love you very much. The second is that when you talk to me, make sure you are on my right side. The third is to try to remember that you can't ask me to look at the sunset, or look at that house, or Lin, look at that beautiful bird! The fourth, hey Honey, come and watch this movie with me. Or hey, do you want to go to the movies this weekend? Honey, everything that went wrong with you, including your cancer, they fixed it, and thank God they did, but Sweetheart, they can't fix anything on me, so I want you to stop trying so hard to make believe everything is fine! Please understand what I just told you, and that way, I won't have to pretend I can see the stupid bird!

"Raymond, please know that I am handicapped, and that's reality. I know you are trying so hard to avoid the facts, and I know you love me, and I know you feel bad, when I tell you to go to see a movie without me, but please go, and don't feel guilty about it. And down the road, I might ask for your help about getting a seeing eye dog!"

"Well, Belinda, how many seeing eye dogs can drive you around to the market, or to the dentist, or wash and vacuum and dust, fix your electric toothbrush, and tell you if your makeup looks good, and most of important of all. find your lost earrings? Woof, woof, I am your seeing eye dog, and I don't make messes on the floor. Woof, woof."

Yes, she laughed pretty good, and I had better pay attention to what she just told me!

# CHAPTER 47

**B**elinda resigned her position with the VA hospital due to the fact that her sight was getting to the point she read her books with this super thick eight by ten-inch magnifying glass, and her hearing certainly never came back in her left ear. For the next several years, we continued our traveling. I called my brother Angelo and told him we were going to take Belinda to visit our friends in northern Florida, and then continue our drive to Fort Lauderdale, before Uncle Fred got any older. At the time of that phone call, Aunt Mary and Uncle Louie told me to tell Belinda that they would make us one of those great lobster dinners. Angelo said that he and Sally would fly down to Lauderdale, and we would be their private taxi, and we all would visit Uncle Fred, who was now widowed. (Do you remember how much fun we had with Aunt Evelyn? I always thought of her.)

At the time of this visit, we found my Aunt Mary in the hospital with leukemia. The last time I talked to her on the phone, I thought she was doing better. It was going to be hard, knowing my Aunt Mary was not going to get better. We held hands at her bedside and talked about everything and the good times we had together. Uncle Louie was having a hard time with this. So, we said goodbye to my Aunt Mary with hugs and kisses, and that was the last time I saw her in person. We did stay in touch until she died in 2011. Uncle Fred was enjoying our visit with him, and he was getting old. He told Belinda, "I bet I take more meds than you do!"

Belinda laughed. So, while there, the four of us with Uncle Fred went to some nice places. He had his favorite restaurants. He was no doubt my grandfather's son, when it came to seafood. Uncle

Fred made his final trip home to join his wife and family in May 2013. All my aunts and uncle left me with good memories.

The next several years we slowed down for Belinda. She told me it was time we stopped traveling and became homebodies, and of course I agreed with her. Well, my Belinda and I just took it nice and slow, and here we were already finishing 2018. We would talk every day about our children growing up, and not to mention our grandchildren already grown up, and yes, we also had three great-grandchildren, a total of ten.

On New Year's Eve 2018, Belinda told me she would be turning eighty this year, and she was content knowing all her children had grown up.

She said, "Raymond, you do know, all the roads we traveled together were not always without bumps and potholes, but I can't think of anybody who would made the travels more exciting than you."

I said, "We are not done yet, my dear co-pilot."

She said, "Honey, do you notice how much sleep I get these days, and there is something else that bothers me lately, and that is I am having a hard time remembering what I did during the day, and I certainly don't know what I did yesterday."

I told her that everybody at this age sleeps more, and they only remember the important things, and don't worry about it. "Let's you and I get to bed early, and I will take you out for breakfast."

"Honey," she said, "that will be nice."

The next morning, I was lying on my back, and extended my right arm out to touch her. At that moment, her head rolled over into my hand. I felt this huge bump, and decided to wake her up. She told me to go back to sleep. I thought she might have been bitten by a spider. It took a while to get her convinced that I wanted to make sure I got it looked at, because there could be some poison involved. The doctor said it wasn't a bite, and to be safe, get her a CT of the skull.

Belinda had a large tumor on the lateral left side of her skull. My dear God in Heaven, I cannot type this without difficulty, so I am going to tell you I will leave out all the hospital details that took place on Valentine's Day, February 14, 2019. My family was told, and they would be there after the surgery Then I told her family not to drive up during the surgery, it would be better that they visit the next day. During that long four-hour period, I was fortunate enough to have my friend Ed with me. Ed and I used to work together. I met him in the '80s. We sat and prayed, we walked up and down the hallways, and I made into the chapel.

I told the good Lord, "Do You remember, Lord, back in 1970 when Belinda was giving birth to our son, and the doctor told me that he may not be able to save both, due to some serious complications, and I told the doctor, that he should get back in there and just do his best, while I would go in the chapel and say my prayers? And Lord, as You know it all was fine. Now today, I am back in the chapel of this hospital praying to You, to just bring back the one that I love."

Finally, the surgeon came out and told us that the tumor was gone and the surgery went well. Ed and I hugged each other. He had to run back to his family, and I ran back to the chapel with tears of joy, and thanked the Lord Jesus, from the bottom of my heart. I made my phone calls to everyone.

That evening, everything went wrong. I will give no details here. Belinda passed to her final home at 9:33AM, on March 20, 2019 at the Presbyterian Hospice center. The nurse left me in the room alone with my Belinda, and I had my finger on her wrist and felt her last pulse. At that very moment, her face just glowed with her natural beauty, I bent down and kissed her and said, "Honey, you just entered Heaven."

There are no words I can conjure up to tell anybody what I feel since that day, and the loneliness that is with me every day, but I make to the next day because I have fifty-eight years of memories that carry me through. Every time I am in church, I still can feel my hand holding hers. It was my birthday July 30, and I was sitting down and holding up our wedding picture, and here came her words:

"Raymond, now it's time to write your book that I asked you to do, and I will be the first one to read it."

I should mention that in the past three years, Belinda also lost her two brothers, Firpo and Luper, and her sister Ramona (Monchie).

My family and I want to say to all of the following names below, our heartfelt thanks, and may God bless you all.

Firpo's daughter, my niece Tricia made me the most beautiful patch blanket made from Belinda's clothes, all hand-stitched with the dates of my children, and the date of our wedding and more.

Thank you, Tricia, all my love

And during the entire time of the thirty-five days that my wife spent in the hospital, my nephew Joseph was with me the entire time. I would spend all the day hours, and Joseph would come in the evening right after work to relieve me, and he produced a beautiful video of Belinda's life. Thank you so much, Joseph, all my love

Since I live in Albuquerque, and the funeral and burial and the buffet lunch all took place in Mesilla, that was all accomplished by Fina and Jane and nieces and nephews. My love and gratitude to all of you.

And for helping me with personal issues during my hours of need, Jeepy, Ricks, Sal, Robert, Danny, Charles and Sal Jr. Thanks so much for your personal time. To Belinda's cousin Pauline, who has been on the phone with me every week till this very day, with her love and support. Thank you, cousin, all my love.

And a shout out to my new friend from Austin. Thank you, Jerry for your kind words and support.

And my friends who live next door, watching over my dog all those days and weeks during my absence. So thank you, Dave, Beverly, and Carol.

My friend Sandra in California. Thank you so much for crossing the T's, and dotting the I's and giving me Googles instead of goggles. Love to you and Bill.

And to my neighbor and friend across the street who keeps me busy, by taking me to baseball games, and hot rod shows, so I don't get lonely. Thank you, Tommy

Yes, Vince, thank you and your loving family for taking me into your home for Easter dinner, and continuing to call and check up and doing lunch with me. Thank you.

My lifetime friend Harry, and Belinda's book companion and friend, thank you for all your visits to me and Belinda over the years. I am glad Belinda finally saw you walk in our door with your lovely wife. Thank you for a lifetime friendship.

And Uncle Louie, and my cousins, Lucille and Lorna and Louis back in Rhode Island. Uncle, thank you so much for all your calls and your kind words about Belinda, and we get to share our loss, when we talk about Aunt Mary. Happy ninety-fifth birthday. All my love.

My heartfelt thanks to the wonderful nurses and staff at the Presbyterian Kaseman Hospice center. I thank you all from my heart.

Father Charles, the hospice nurse told me they already called for a priest for Belinda's last rites. It was such a comfort to me, to find out it was you. Thank you so much.

My friend Ed, thank you for your support. And Ed, it meant a lot to me having you there with me in the hospital.

My friend John in California. Now I know how much it hurt when you lost Diane, and thank you for your calls about Belinda. Thank you so much.

And Al G., thanks for the weekly phone calls to pick up my spirit. Much appreciated.

And to my brother Angelo and Sally for your calls and your support throughout Angelo's Cardiac rehabilitation. Much love.

And yes, GO ARMY!

And to my sons and their wives, and the grandchildren: Your mom and grandmother loved you all very much. And I ask the Lord to watch over all of you, as I also love you very much!

# FINAL CHAPTER

B elinda was buried at St Albino's Church Cemetery, and her
funeral was given at St. Albino's church. Her ashes were
placed on the same altar where we got married fifty-eight years
earlier. Belinda, I loved you before you ever spoke a word to me,
and I love you now, and I will love you forever. . .